Composing with Finale®

Mark Johnson

Course Technology PTR
A part of Cengage Learning

COURSE TECHNOLOGY
CENGAGE Learning™

Australia • Brazil • Japan • Korea • Mexico • Singapore • Spain • United Kingdom • United States

COURSE TECHNOLOGY
CENGAGE Learning™

Composing with Finale®
Mark Johnson

Publisher and General Manager, Course Technology PTR: Stacy L. Hiquet

Associate Director of Marketing: Sarah Panella

Manager of Editorial Services: Heather Talbot

Marketing Manager: Mark Hughes

Executive Editor: Mark Garvey

Project Editor: Kate Shoup

Technical Reviewer: Kami Johnson

PTR Editorial Services Coordinator: Erin Johnson

Copy Editor: Tonya Cupp

Interior Layout Tech: ICC Macmillan Inc.

Cover Designer: Mike Tanamachi

Indexer: Sharon Shock

Proofreader: Kate Shoup

For product information and technology assistance, contact us at **Cengage Learning Customer & Sales Support, 1-800-354-9706**

For permission to use material from this text or product, submit all requests online at **www.cengage.com/permissions**
Further permissions questions can be emailed to **permissionrequest@cengage.com**

Finale is a registered trademark of MakeMusic, Inc. All other trademarks are the property of their respective owners.

Library of Congress Control Number: 2008902417

ISBN-13: 978-1-59863-573-7

ISBN-10: 1-59863-573-5

Course Technology
25 Thomson Place
Boston, MA 02210
USA

Cengage Learning is a leading provider of customized learning solutions with office locations around the globe, including Singapore, the United Kingdom, Australia, Mexico, Brazil, and Japan. Locate your local office at: **international.cengage.com/region**

Cengage Learning products are represented in Canada by Nelson Education, Ltd.

For your lifelong learning solutions, visit **courseptr.com**

Visit our corporate website at **cengage.com**

Printed in Canada
1 2 3 4 5 6 7 11 10 09

For Katie.

Acknowledgments

This book could not have been written without the loving encouragement of my wonderful wife Kami, who also took no prisoners in her technical review of it. I would also like to thank the folks at MakeMusic for their continued support, expertise, vision, and entertainment value. And thanks to the communication and organizational skills of Kate Shoup and her crew at Cengage Learning, who made the writing process smooth and delightful.

About the Author

Mark Johnson has been an employee of MakeMusic for more than eight years, where he has worked as a technical-support representative, quality-assurance technician, and technical writer. He has a Bachelor of Arts in Music Theory and Composition from St. Olaf College, and composing and engraving experience with Finale. He has authored several Finale guides, including *Finale Power!* and *Finale 2008: A Trailblazer Guide,* and continues to work with Finale on a daily basis.

Contents

Chapter 3
Moving Stuff Around   43

Chapter 4
Listen   59

Chapter 5
Managing Your Instrumentalists   73

Chapter 6
Arranging and Rearranging   101

Chapter 7
The Composer's Wild Kingdom   121

Chapter 8
Lead Sheets   149

Chapter 9
Piano Scores   181

Chapter 10
Choral Scores   203

Chapter 11
Guitar Scores   231

Chapter 12
Percussion   245

Chapter 13
Instrumental Ensembles   257

Chapter 14
Jazz Band   271

Chapter 15
Wrapping Up   281

Chapter 16
Unleashing Your Masterpiece   295

Introduction

Finale: A Composer's Treasure Chest

This book is all about releasing creative energy. It is dedicated to understanding the properties and capabilities of a set of tools, and then using them in the least horrendous way possible to achieve something of beauty, mystery, tragedy, or whatever the seeds of inspiration demand. Finale is a unique instrument from a composer's perspective and must be approached differently when used to invent rather than interpret. This book is for the individual with an idea and the drive and inclination to bring it to life: It's about using Finale as a creative tool.

You might approach Finale like a painter. You have situated your easel, palette, paints, and brushes around you and have focused on your subject. Now, you must commit it to canvas. You draw upon your understanding of each brush, color, and technique, which all help you remove limitations and open doors to your most inspired whims. You might say any creative action is a conscious decision against a vast pool of possibilities in favor of the one chosen. Expanding the size of this pool liberates your imagination to pick from options you might never have considered before. By making the most of your blending, splattering, or 3,000-psi industrial paint sprayer, you can achieve things that may have even been inconceivable otherwise.

Of course, some methods are superior to others. For greatest precision, the brush must not be handled between the toes. At the same time, it is virtually impossible to achieve authentic toe-painting results any other way. Above all, composition itself depends on the artist adapting the environment to meet his or her unique demands, and sacrificing as little as possible to the tools' limitations. My challenge is one of economy: to describe the most practical and universal solutions to extend a composer's existing methods and imagination, remove rote and frustration from the creative process, introduce new possibilities, and inspire new ideas—and do this with enough consideration for those required to conduct and perform it.

My expectation is that, once learned, some of these methods will be routinely and consciously eliminated from the pool of possibilities in almost every creative decision. Others may become second nature to you as they are to me.

A Minimalist Rhapsody and Variations

Some general rules of Finale usage will be bent in this book, others broken. I trust my audience is a breed seldom afraid to remind us that innovation sometimes requires impudence. So, I have not been afraid of stepping beyond the conventions when required. And along those lines, I'd like to share with you a few words on the origins of this utility, its nature, and the spirit of its continued development. Finale is a powerful machine and it can be a relatively rough road out there. After all, the tools available to the painter are created specifically, and unquestionably, for painting.

Fertile Soil

When the programmers of Coda Music Software ventured to develop what became Finale 1.0 in the late 1980s, they were responding to a desperate need for a reliable computer program that could efficiently notate and print professional-grade sheet music. At that time, the production of a large musical score was only delivered after a significant investment of time, skill, and expense; a music publisher's options were limited. They could hire copyists who would, as quickly and neatly as possible, draw notation from a composer's sketches by hand using ink and vellum, often painstakingly transcribing each instrumental part from a conductor's score. Alternatively, a publishing house could hire one of the few remaining plate engravers to labor over a sheet of zinc meticulously carving a mirror image of the score. These arduous and time-intensive methods continued to exist well after word processors had replaced typewriters, even after early scorewriters appeared.

Programmers came to the rescue in the early '80s, but found the exhaustive variety of characters, shapes, and ways to arrange them a formidable challenge. The first practical solution, SCORE (although still used by some today), depended on a command-line interface, precise coordinate definitions for every element, and page-by-page editing. (No simply moving a measure across a page; both pages would need to be reworked entirely.)

This was fine for the pros, but the learning curve was too steep and the rewards too limited to be practical for students and (most) composers; engravers still reigned over sheet-music production.

Ta Da!

If you owned a Macintosh in 1988 and could spare $1,000, you could purchase Finale 1.0 and finally use a point-and-click pseudo-WYSIWYG (what you see is what you get) interface to notate and print legible, professional-quality sheet music. Computer-literate composers could conceivably self-publish their handwritten work. The battle was finally won! Finale's advertising materials even read, "The last word in music notation software."

Winston Churchill, on the other hand, said, "This is not the end. It is not even the beginning of the end. But it is, perhaps, the end of the beginning." I think this quote applies here. This is where the clarity of hindsight really kicks in. Whether they fully realized it or not, the Finale developers were changing far more than just sheet-music creation. They were re-stitching the very canvas of music creation itself. Professional music makers of all sorts began putting computer monitors on top of pianos (also shown on Finale 3.0 advertising). Suddenly, amateur composers, arrangers, educators, and a notorious population of hacks (myself included) had access to the entire music-publishing process, from conception to printout.

The Universal Compromise

With the help of easy piracy, the pieces had finally been assembled to usher in a creative revolution. Fundamentals of music notation themselves, such as transposition, were now completely automatic. You could transfer music directly from the keys of a piano to a grand staff. An inexhaustible supply of lousy, thoughtless garbage began landing on music stands throughout the globe. At the same time, small miracles of musical genius could be trapped behind a wall of misspaced, incomprehensible excuses for notation.

But, of particular concern to music creators everywhere, Coda now had a mission: to satisfy the score-writing needs of every engraver, copyist, composer, arranger, student, educator, church musician, metal head, preschooler, marching percussion coordinator, and mountain dulcimer specialist... more specifically, anyone with a checkbook who could keep the Finale development steam tractor chugging (and fund the company's rising star, Vivace, now referred to as SmartMusic).

And, as I understand it, this has been the balancing act ever since: Provide the pros the tools they need to efficiently engrave for the publishers and Hollywood, and simultaneously ensure profitability (and continued improvement) by expanding the features attractive to the mass market (audio, scanning, and the like). As a soldier in the trenches for eight years now, I have always admired MakeMusic's dedication to musicians and educators (who are really educating future musicians), and believe they are responding remarkably well for a product that does so much considering the wildly diverse needs. It is a worthy goal, a dedicated and passionate group, and we are all the beneficiaries. How exactly has all this ended up benefiting composers the most?

Notate Free or Die

From the beginning, Finale designers delighted in any opportunity to open a door and rejected the many factors that tempted them to deliberately close one. Rumor has it the original notation engine at Finale's core was built to sell to several competing interface designers, and perhaps (one could speculate) each resulting product would be designed and marketed to a specific audience. To demonstrate some of its capabilities, developer Phil Farrand created a temporary interface, and thus Finale was born. To appeal to the diverse needs of its customers, this product had to be an open landscape rather than a canyon. Its viability was absolutely dependent on its almost universal utility. A strict dedication to adaptability and robust user control has been at the center of Finale's development culture ever since, and not without consequence.

Ironically, market pressure and competition have often tested these principles, perpetually encouraging some sacrifice of user control for the sake of one specific type of customer or another. Development is a balancing act, and precious and limited resources require brutal sacrifice of one feature in favor of another; the refusal to compromise is not always easy. Ease of use, although of extreme importance, must never become a trap. Over the years this approach has lost some customers and gained others, but these fundamental factors stuck, have always shaped Finale's core development philosophy, and have proven the key to its distinctiveness.

I suspect it may have something to do with the spirit of creativity itself that permits an unrelenting dedication to individual choice, and Finale's longevity is evidence that this is popular. Competitors have come and gone and Finale somehow remains. I predict that so long as the many short-term temptations do not compromise the principles that have led to its success, Finale will continue to reign—not only as the engraver's standard, but also as the composing artist's chosen notation canvas.

The Playground

As Finale evolved, it became ever more attractive to all kinds of musicians, but especially composers. Although I can't claim to know the whole story, I can identify a few reasons, and they continue to this day. Composing Finale users call up and make feature requests, and sometimes Finale developers respond. At the same time, independent engineers develop their own plug-ins and share them with the Finale community. (Anyone with programming skills can use a Plug-in Development Kit to design their own Finale plug-ins.) Both of these factors attract more composers and more plug-ins, and the cycle continues; Finale's power continues to grow with each new innovation, ordained or rogue. One remarkable plug-in, FinaleScript, gives even programming muggles an interface to develop their own quasi plug-ins. (More on that later.) Perhaps most effectual, many of the people who create and shepherd Finale are composers themselves. Finale's most senior engineer, Randy Stokes, even has his own custom version, probably fraught with incomprehensible doodads and widgets that suit his compositional style. In a way, Finale itself is a composition in progress, benefiting from many contributors from all colors of the musical spectrum, and yes, this is our playground.

You Want Me to Play What?!

Of course, the goal is not just one of innovation, but also of communication—to transfer your thoughts to sound through the performer. Your creations must be legible or, at the very least, comprehensible to your engraver (if you are lucky enough to have one). Imaginative musical ideas are good; imaginative notation practices are bad. I will include some practical information to help make your score conform to the general standards, but remember that engraving is an art all to itself, and crafting publisher-quality scores is a topic beyond the scope of this book. (See Powell's *Music Engraving Today* for a good overview of engraving.) In other words, I will try to save your engraver a substantial amount of grief, but I cannot replace her entirely.

Reaping the Rewards

Now that you have a very basic understanding of Finale's resolute yet untamed history, it's time to discover the many rewards. This book demonstrates composing methods, and that means working with the development of real music—from delightful classical masterpieces to head-rattling marching percussion to my dark personal archives. I will be pulling apart examples of several styles to demonstrate techniques you can add to your composer's toolbox.

In some ways, this book begins where the *Finale Installation and Tutorials Manual* leaves off. If you are new to Finale, I recommend running through that first to get a basic view of the program. This is not a comprehensive guide to learning Finale, so if you're a beginner you need a general idea of Finale's framework and the basic fundamentals to get the most out of this book.

It's worth mentioning that Finale is not as hard as it used to be . . . really! When Finale becomes a friend, the possibilities become endless, which brings me to the many methods that can inspire ideas regarding orchestration, arranging, accompaniment, rhythm, and even make harmonic and melodic suggestions. Let's get started.

1 Taking the Wheel

You may not need to know precisely how a car works to drive it properly, but you do need to know how to shift gears, read the speedometer, and turn on the windshield wipers. While you're at it, you might as well take a look around and find the emergency brake and hazard lights just in case. That's the idea here: I'll describe a brief overview of some basic controls necessary to any Finale user, but especially to composers. These skills should become second nature so you can focus on your composition rather than on Finale.

Everyone knows it's not good to drive angry. And, while I'm sure many a frustrated Finale user has allowed rage to contribute a delightful edginess to his composition, try your best to leave the mechanics of the tool itself out of the creative process. In fact, let's see what gizmos we can find to make the ride that much smoother.

Here's a summary of what you will learn in this chapter:

- An approach to using Finale's main tools
- Super-charging Finale using shortcuts, plug-ins, and other utilities

Your Implements

In this section I will discuss Finale's basic framework from a composer's perspective. But first, from a learning perspective, you need to take care of a couple things for me. To be sure your system is primed and ready, do the following:

- From the Help menu, choose Check for Updates. Download the update if one is available. This is how you can be sure you are using the latest and greatest version of Finale 2009.

- I refer to Finale's sample files, located in the Finale 2009/Sample Files folder. If you do not see a Sample Files folder, download the sample files at www.composingwithfinale.com. (These were not included in the original Finale 2009 release.)

Alright, now that our seatbelts are securely fastened, it's time to begin accumulating traffic violations. When you step back and analyze the functions most beneficial to creating, a certain set of utilities and tasks take the foreground. Smooth pavement can take you far. With this in mind, let's review some essential skills.

The Standards

Finale contains seemingly millions of keyboard shortcuts and little usability tricks. Some are essential and useful in any project, so let's open a score and play with those.

1. Launch Finale. (Or, choose File, Launch Window.)

2. Click the Open button.

3. Navigate to the Finale 2009/Sample Files folder and open the file Beethoven.mus.

Ah, Beethoven's Moonlight Sonata: What better musical excerpt to demonstrate the technical mechanics of a software product? Ah, to ponder the contrasting duality of our real lives compared to our formulaic pixilated ones (if there is a difference—but I digress). Suffice it to say, Table 1.1 lists things possible in Finale....

Table 1.1 Essential Finale Shortcuts

Command	Windows Shortcut	Macintosh Shortcut
Undo	Ctrl+Z	Command+Z
Select All	Ctrl+A	Command+A
Save	Ctrl+S	Command+S
Context click	Right-click	Control+click (or right-click)
Zoom in	Middle mouse button*	Command+Shift+click
Zoom out	Ctrl+middle-click**	Command+Option+Shift+click
Drag the score around	Right-click+drag	Option+Command+click+drag
Switch documents	Ctrl+Tab	Command+'
Switch programs	Alt+Tab***	Command+Tab***
Go forward pages (Page View)	Page Down	Page Down
Go back pages (Page View)	Page Up	Page Up
Go forward (Scroll View)	Ctrl+Page Down	Command+Page Down
Go back (Scroll View)	Ctrl+Page Up	Command+Page Up

*Or Alt+Shift+right-click.
**Or Ctrl+Shift+right-click.
***Operating system commands, but important nonetheless.

Tip: Take a peek at Finale's menus to reference keyboard shortcuts. They are listed to the right of the command. Windows users can access every menu command using mnemonics: Just hold down Alt and look for the underlined letter. For example, press Alt+O+I to check/uncheck Display in Concert Pitch.

Go through and try out the shortcuts listed in Table 1.1. There are many other useful shortcuts that you will adopt into your regular workflow, but these are useful regardless of the tool chosen. They can save plenty of time throughout the score-creation process. I discuss many other important viewing and navigation tricks in the next chapter. But first, let's step forward into some regular controls: the pedals and levers that will be worn from constant use.

The Eight Kahunas

Whether you are composing a multi-movement orchestral score for the New York Philharmonic or a kazoo trio for your friend's birthday party, you will be using the main tools. You see them across the top of your screen. And if you use Finale with any regularity, you also see them gleefully dancing in your dreams and nightmares. Let's try to remove them from your nightmares. First, make sure they look really good.

1. Windows users, press Alt+E to open the Edit menu; then press G.

    Mac users, press Command+, (comma). The Program Options dialog box appears.

2. Click Save.

3. Check Auto-save File(s) Every. Enter a duration if you like.

4. Choose the Folders category of this dialog box.

5. Select a specific folder for your Auto-Save files.

    Losing all your hard work in case of a crash is never fun. Speaking of fun...

6. Click Palettes and Backgrounds.

7. Under Palettes, click the Style drop-down menu and choose Jazz Maroon.

    I prefer the sizzle of Jazz Maroon myself (see Figure 1.1). I think you'll agree.

8. Click OK. If you are using Windows you will see the new style next time you start Finale.

Caution: Escape the artist's death spiral. Please turn on Auto Save. Yes, you *can* conceive a heart-wrenching aria without the pain of watching original work permanently vanish before your eyes.

Figure 1.1 The Main Tool Palette is most attractive in Jazz Maroon.

Whew, isn't that better? Windows users have to close and launch Finale if you want to see the improved palette appearance.

How should you approach these? Well, for the purposes of composition, it is particularly important to familiarize yourself with eight tools: the eight kahunas.

The Selection Tool

This is your home tool. Yes, the Big Kahuna; see Figure 1.2. Press Esc a couple times to automatically return to this tool at any time. Remember that with it, you can:

- Select measures for copying and editing
- Select text and markings for editing
- Easily navigate to other tools

The third point is powerful since the Selection Tool basically turns everything in your score into a tool selector…just double-click an item to select its tool. Yes, the Selection Tool replaces the method of beating your head against the keyboard until the proper tool is selected to edit an item.

Click and drag to select regions of measures

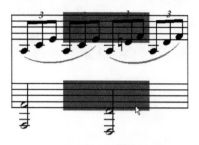

Selection Tool

Select, move, delete, and edit markings

Double-click to select the marking's tool for more editing options

Figure 1.2   Use the ubiquitous Selection Tool to select and edit anything in the score, and easily access any item's more specific editing functions.

Before you double-click a time signature to select the Time Signature Tool, remember that you can change time signatures without leaving the Selection Tool. In fact, you can change many items including clefs, key signatures, measures, and many others using context menus (some shown in Figure 1.3).

Context menus were listed earlier as well because they are important. Almost every tool includes its own context menu, some not available with the Selection Tool. They are great because they allow easy access to an arsenal of options. If you haven't ingrained these into your Finale work

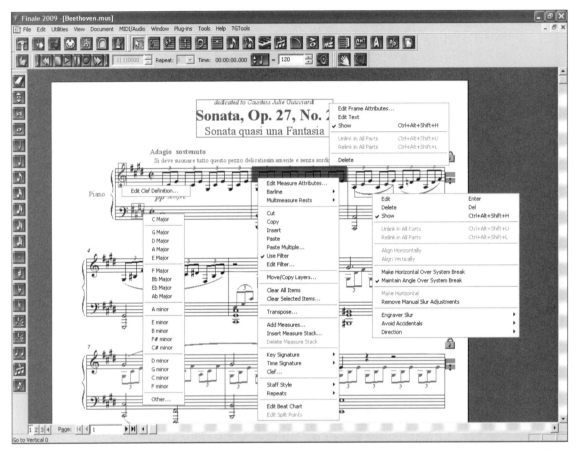

Figure 1.3 Windows users, right-click and Mac users Control+click to display context menus with a variety of options, all without leaving the Selection Tool.

already, I recommend experimenting with them so new meters, key signatures, and measures are even closer to your slightest whim.

And, just as commands accessible in many tools are available in the Selection Tool, commands often associated with the Selection Tool, such as copying and pasting, can be performed in other tools as well. I discuss those functions later.

Entry Tools: Simple Entry, Speedy Entry, and HyperScribe

Entry tools are used in so many different ways that volumes couldn't describe them all. For an excellent description of the essentials, consult the Finale Installation and Tutorials manual and the EntryExercises.mus file in the Finale 2009 folder. Note that Simple can be as fast as Speedy and HyperScribe isn't just for pianists. The best possible method for your creation will depend on the type of music you're composing and your unique preferences. See Figure 1.4.

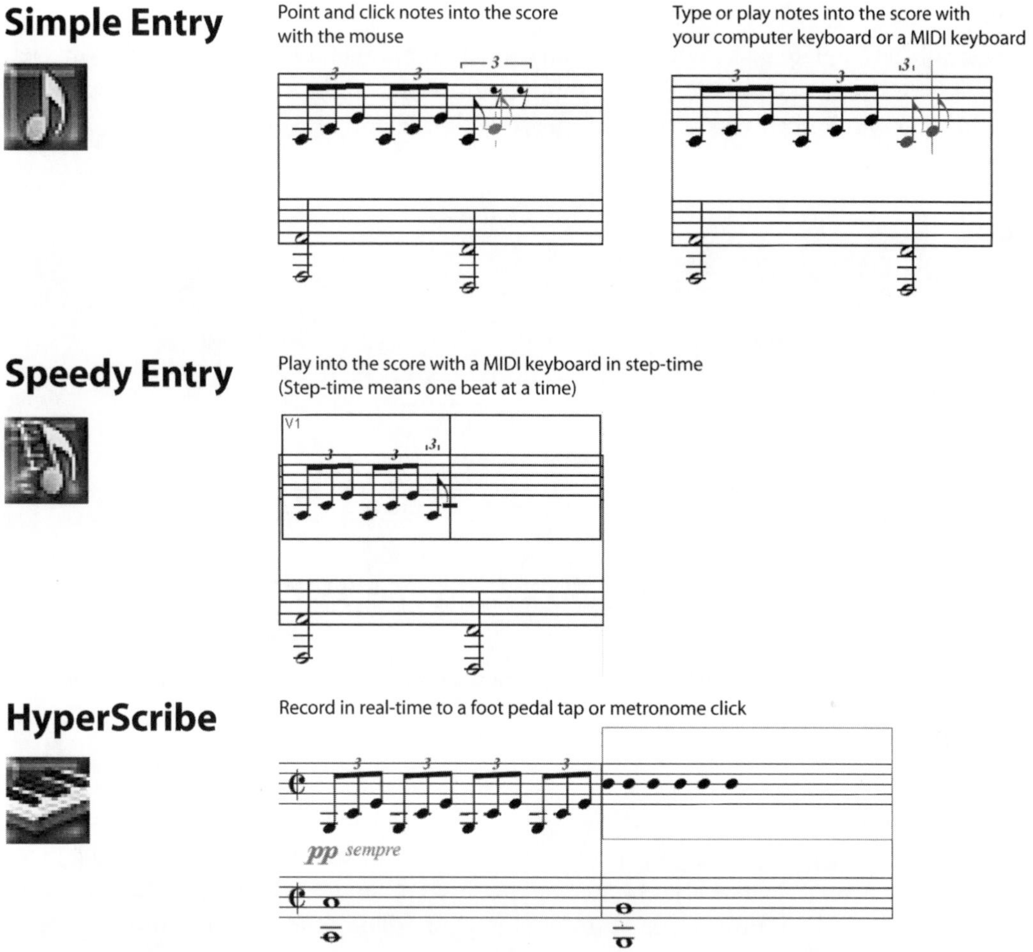

Simple Entry

Point and click notes into the score
with the mouse

Type or play notes into the score with
your computer keyboard or a MIDI keyboard

Speedy Entry

Play into the score with a MIDI keyboard in step-time
(Step-time means one beat at a time)

HyperScribe

Record in real-time to a foot pedal tap or metronome click

Figure 1.4   Use the entry tools to enter and edit music. The one you choose should depend on the music type, your compositional style, and perhaps your keyboard facility.

For me, the creative process is usually much slower than whatever mechanical process I use to enter notes. If this is the case for you as well, mastering the quickest way to type and play notes into a staff isn't particularly useful. Why learn to type 1,000 words a minute when your brain runs at a significantly slower speed? On the other hand, if a large piece is already composed in your noggin, you may indeed treat Finale like a copyist, transcribing directly from your brain to the score.

Choose whichever method allows you to place the music before the program. If you are distracted because Simple Entry is too slow, use HyperScribe instead. If you find yourself spending hours cleaning up HyperScribe recordings, try step-time with Speedy entry.

If you don't want to worry about the notation at all during entry, play it into a MIDI sequencer and import the MIDI file. This isn't cheating...and it's what a lot of the pros do. (I discuss importing MIDI files later.)

Staff Tool

A **staff** is basically a template upon which each instrumental part is built. The transposition, clef, notation style, number of staff lines, and anything else specific to the staff is handled with this tool, for either the whole staff or a region of measures; see Figure 1.5.

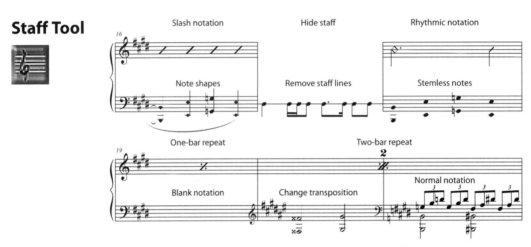

Figure 1.5 Use the Staff Tool to adjust staff settings. These common adjustments are applied as Staff Styles.

Staff settings are another mere formatting concern, not a creative one, but when you need to add a one-bar repeat or change the staff transposition, it isn't obvious that the Staff Tool is the place to go. So, review the available Staff Styles (most are pictured in Figure 1.5). Know that whenever you need to add one of these things, the Staff Tool is your friend, and all other tools are temporarily your arch nemesis.

The Staff Tool is certainly a capable implement, but the most regular functions are distinctive enough to mention. Here are some regular, everyday Staff Tool uses:

- Add a staff. Select a staff handle from the upper-left corner of the staff. From the Staff menu, choose New Staves (with Setup Wizard). The new staff appears above the selected staff.

- Delete a staff. Right-click (Control+click) the handle and choose Delete (or Delete and Reposition).

- Change staff settings. Double-click a staff to open the Staff Attributes dialog box.

- Apply a Staff Style (one of the styles shown in Figure 1.5). Select the desired region of measures, right-click (Control+click), and choose the style.

- Copy and paste measures just as you would with the Selection Tool.

Expression Tool

Basically, any text item that applies to a particular point in the music should be added as an **expression**; see Figure 1.6. Dynamics are the primary function of the Expression Tool.

Expression Tool
Dynamics, style indications, tempo markings, and rehearsal letters

Figure 1.6   Use expressions when text is required to express your intentions.

As you think about dynamics, style, and overall balance, you are gracefully negotiating the many helpful functions of the Expression Tool. As you do so, you will often switch to the Smart Shape Tool to add slurs and hairpins. Yes, your performers do need to know the dynamic level of your music. Remember, nothing is obvious to your esteemed instrumentalists. As capable as your virtuosos are, they have enough work to do without reading your mind. They need your guidance, and that means specifying the dynamic level throughout your piece. Yes, thou shalt sandwich thy hairpins.

But, expressions are also necessary for tempo/metronome markings and rehearsal letters. These items often appear at the top of the score only, or perhaps on the top staff of each instrumental group in a conductor's score.

Articulation Tool

Any marking attached to a single note can be added as an articulation, applied with the Articulation Tool. See Figure 1.7.

Articulation Tool
Accents, staccattos, fingerings, and other markings attached to notes

Figure 1.7   Use articulations when a marking must be added to a note to communicate a type of performance practice.

This includes staccatos, accents, fermatas, fingering numbers, and so on. You can enter these items naturally and transparently in lots of ways, which I discuss later. Again, you will likely switch back and forth from the Smart Shape Tool, as articulation is also communicated with slurs.

As with expressions, your performers generally won't play it if you don't mark it. Your engraver may loathe seeing a *fz* marking over every note in a phrase. But, if they are required, you must add them. Remember, notation works for you, not the other way around. Make it great, articulate.

Smart Shape Tool
Slurs and hairpins are the primary functions of the SmartShape Tool. Whenever you need to enter a shape that needs to adjust according to spacing changes in the score, enter a Smart Shape. See Figure 1.8.

Smart Shape Tool

Slurs, hairpins, ottavas, brackets, and other shapes

Figure 1.8 Use the Smart Shape Tool to add markings that require a unique shape for each occurrence, like slurs and hairpins.

Of course, slurs mean different things depending on the type of music and the instrument. They can indicate phrasing, bowing, feel, and when not to take a breath. As you are deciding how you want a phrase performed, as mentioned earlier, you will likely jump to and from the Smart Shape Tool. Expressions are often accompanied by hairpins, and articulations are often accompanied by slurs. So, you can see how these three tools are somewhat intertwined and often used together.

TNT for Your Tools
Bang for your buck, trinitrotoluene for your tools—you get the idea. How do you get the most out of these? You might ask, "Why isn't it simple? Why doesn't each tool have autonomous and specific functions?" Well, as the sands of time washed over Finale, the tools began morphing in scope, even overlapping. Wouldn't you know it? Some folks didn't care to memorize every

function of every tool. To lighten the load a little, functionality started to bleed across the main tools. Several tasks that used to require one specific tool can now be accomplished with many. The result is a way of working with Finale that is faster and easier than before.

Earlier, I introduced this concept by describing the long arm of the Selection Tool. Well, other tools can play that game too. For example, copying and pasting is a task so common, it is available in every tool that allows measure selection, including these:

- Selection Tool
- Staff Tool
- Key Signature Tool
- Time Signature Tool
- Clef Tool
- Measure Tool
- Repeat Tool
- MIDI Tool
- Mirror Tool

In fact, in addition to Copy and Paste, every item under the Edit menu is available whenever a region is selected, including Insert, Paste Multiple, Move/Copy Layers, Clear, Insert Measure, and Edit Measure Attributes.

Additionally, every item under the Utilities menu is also available whenever a measure region is selected; see Figure 1.9.

Make the most of all the tools by taking advantage of the overlapping functionality. The extra capabilities of these tools give even the least of them little kahuna status. If you ever need to copy something, or edit a measure region with one of the Edit or Utilities menu commands, don't bother choosing the Selection Tool unless you need to. Every tool that supports measure selection is equally qualified to copy, paste, insert, and perform all other Edit and Utilities commands. This shortcut is a great way to save you time. An extra mouse click to change tools may sound trivial, but if you are chopping down a giant sequoia, every whack counts.

Super-Charging Finale

If you like customizing things as much as I do, you'll love this section. Everyone uses Finale a little bit differently, and here I expose some practical ways to mold Finale to fit your unique work style. When you are bushwhacking through the dense jungle of your score and need quick, easy access to a variety of tools, it is fine to...

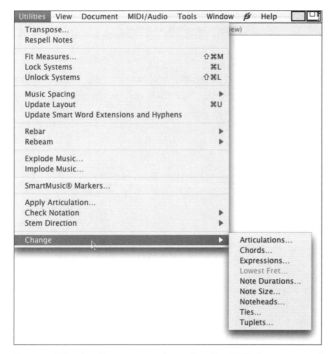

Figure 1.9 Apply commands under the Utilities menu whenever a measure region is selected.

Be a Control Freak

Prefer manual to automatic transmission? Do your own plumbing? Use Linux? Being a control freak isn't just a pastime. For some, it's a way of life. Every Finale user can benefit from learning a few tricks that improve accessibility, and some couldn't imagine using Finale without them.

Even if you stretch each tool to the limits of efficiency, you still need to move between them sometimes. You could click them when you need to do this, but why not assign them to a key command? Earlier I discussed the strong possibility of needing to switch between the Articulation, Smart Shape, and Expression Tools. So let's program these three tools to adjacent keystrokes for easy access.

To assign a tool shortcut on Windows:

1.   Choose the Articulation Tool .

2.   Press Shift+F4.

You have just assigned the Articulation Tool to the F4 key.

3.   Choose the Smart Shape Tool.

4.   Press Shift+F5.

     The Smart Shape Tool is now assigned to F5.

5.   Press Shift+F6.

     You've assigned the Expression Tool to F6.

6.   Press F4, F5, and F6 to select the Articulation, Smart Shape, and Expression tools (respectively).

I used these F keys because 4 kind of looks like an accent, 5 kind of looks like an S for Smart Shape, and 6 kind of looks like a G, which flipped horizontally resembles a lower case e for expression. Makes perfect sense! Now you're thinking like a composer. You can program tool shortcuts to F2 through F12 on Windows. F1 is reserved for opening the user manual.

To assign a tool shortcut on Macintosh:

1.   Press Option+Control+ F.

     The Master Tool Palette appears.

2.   Click the Articulation Tool and then click OK.

     You have just assigned the Articulation Tool to the F key.

3.   Press Option+Control+G.

     The Master Tool Palette appears.

4.   Click the Expression Tool and click OK.

     It is assigned to the G key.

5.   Press Option+Control+H.

     The Master Tool Palette appears.

6.   Click the Smart Shape Tool and then click OK.

     You have just assigned the Smart Shape Tool to the H key.

7.   Use Control+*letter* to select the tool.

     Press Control+F for the Articulation Tool, Control+G for the Expression Tool, and Control+H for the Smart Shape Tool.

The letter G flipped horizontally looks like a lowercase e for expression. You'll just have to memorize the other ones using your own clever mnemonic. You can program any of the home row keys between F and ; to a tool.

Windows-Only Menu Shortcuts

At the beginning of this chapter I mentioned some valuable keyboard shortcuts, and noted that you will almost certainly find some favorites of your own. When you do, assign them to your own convenient keystroke using the Menu Shortcuts plug-in (Plug-ins/ 🖋, TGTools, Menu Shortcuts). See Figure 1.10.

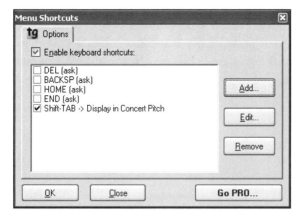

Figure 1.10   Assign menu items to your own custom keyboard shortcuts using the Menu Shortcuts plug-in.

You might use this to map, for example:

- Shift+Tab to Document > Display in Concert Pitch
- F12 to a particular staff set you have defined under the View menu
- F11 to Show > Rulers
- Ctrl+down arrow to Help > User Manual > Keyboard Shortcuts

Caution: TGTools menu shortcuts override main tool shortcuts you have assigned, so be sure there aren't conflicts. Use modifiers (Shift/Alt/Ctrl) for a multitude of choices.

The possibilities are virtually endless. If you find yourself navigating to a specific menu item often, this is one way help maintain your sanity.

Note: If you are using the full version of TGTools, you can view the keyboard remapper by choosing TGTools > Options. You will learn more about the full version of TGTools soon.

Programming and Using Metatools

In Finale, metatools are perhaps the single feature that saves you more time than all others. You already learned how to program tools to a keystroke. You can do the same thing to program an accent, dynamic marking, slur, time signature, clef, repeat bar, or just about any other item to any key for easy assignment. Let's program and use a few metatools. Open the Beethoven sample file if it isn't already.

1. Choose the Articulation Tool .

2. Hold down A and click directly on a note.

    An accent appears. You have just used a metatool to enter an articulation.

3. Now, hold down A and drag a box around a few notes.

    You have just entered several articulations using a metatool.

Finale has preprogrammed dozens of metatools. Let's take a look at what they are and how to program them.

1. Click a note.

    The Articulation Selection dialog box appears. Metatool assignments are in the upper-right corner as shown in Figure 1.11. You can reprogram these to any key you wish.

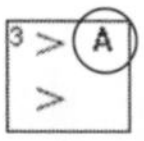

Figure 1.11 Reference metatools by looking in the selection dialog boxes (Articulation/Expression Selection, for example).

2. Click Cancel.

    Go to Step 3 to program ⌢ to the F key.

3. Press Shift+F.

    The Articulation Selection dialog box appears.

4. Double-click the ⌢.

    You return to the score.

5.   Now, hold down F and click a note.

The fermata appears in the score.

The same basic concept applies to programming metatools for:

- Expressions (dynamics)
- Smart Shapes (slurs, hairpins)
- Key signatures
- Time signatures
- Repeats
- A whole bunch of other things

Let's experiment with metatools, shall we? Try Smart Shapes.

1.   Choose the Smart Shape Tool ◣.

2.   Hold down S and double-click a note (or double-click and drag to another note).

3.   Try < for a crescendo, G for a gliss, or 8 for an 8va.

Where do you reference Smart Shape metatools? The user manual (since there is no selection dialog box). Now, program a Smart Shape metatool.

4.   Click the Trill Tool 🎵 in the Smart Shape Palette.

5.   Press Shift+T. Click Yes.

6.   Hold down T, double-click, and drag to create a trill extension.

T was already assigned to the Trill Extension Tool, so you really haven't changed the default setting.

These are really powerful, and they apply to so many things. Now try time signatures:

1.   Choose the Time Signature Tool ▦.

2.   Drag+select the first three measures (top system) so they are highlighted.

3.   Hold down 4 and double-click somewhere within the highlighted region.

The time changes to $\frac{4}{4}$. Now program one.

4.   Press Shift+6.

The Time Signature dialog box appears. Right now the 6 metatool is set to $\frac{6}{4}$. Change this to $\frac{6}{8}$.

5.   Next to Number of Beats, click the arrow to the left of the scroll bar four times.

6.   Next to Beat Duration, click the arrow to the right of the scroll bar once.

You should see two dotted quarter notes in the preview display.

7.   Click OK.

Now, use your new metatool.

8.   Drag+select the first three measures (top system) so they are highlighted.

9.   Hold down 6 and double-click within the highlighted measures.

The time signature changes and Finale rebars the music accordingly. But, for the performer's sake, you probably don't actually want to do this, so go on with Step 10.

10.   Press Ctrl+ Z /(Command+Z) to undo.

This may seem a bit advanced and involved right off the bat, but the idea is to demonstrate what a far-reaching thing metatools are. Like context menus, integrate them into your workflow to simplify things.

Tip: Metatool assignments are saved along with the document, and, unfortunately, cannot be transferred between documents. If you like a certain file's metatool setup and want to use it in new files, save it as a template. Or, better yet, save it as a Document Style for future use with the Document Setup Wizard. (Simply save it to the Finale 2009/Document Styles folder.) For more information about these features, see "Templates" and "Super Templates—Document Styles" in Chapter 5, "Managing Your Instrumentalists."

Plug It In

Finale includes an expansive Plug-ins menu. On a Mac, the menu is displayed as a picture 🗪 to the perpetual chagrin of Finale's documentation editor. As plug-ins, you might expect these are bonus utilities included for obscure tasks. Some are. But, under this menu you also find the preferred method to accomplish the following:

- Create a metronome/tempo marking (Create Tempo Marking)
- Create a coda system (Create Coda System)

- Split a measure over a system break (Split Measure)

- Beam across a barline (Patterson Beams)

- Easily achieve high-quality beaming (Patterson Beams)

- Add cue notes (Smart Cue Notes)

- Check to ensure notes fall within an instrument's range (Check Range)

- Change staff attributes for several staves at once (Global Staff Attributes)

- Create a piano reduction (Piano Reduction)

- Identify and remove awkward page turns (Smart Page Turns)

- Edit brackets after optimization (Update Groups and Brackets)

- Create cross-staff notes for keyboard music (TGTools: Cross Staff)

- Notate string harmonics (TGTools: Easy Harmonics)

- Notate string tremolos (TGTools: Easy Tremolos)

- Separate a multi-part staff into two separate staves (TGTools: Process Extracted Part)

The plug-ins are not outcasts. These are rogue features just as much a part of working with Finale as an ordained Utilities menu command. Sure, you can accomplish every function in the preceding list via painstaking manual editing, but you have music to write. Familiarize yourself with the list, as I would hate to see you dilly dallying with the Special Tools when you could be composing.

The existing plug-ins aren't the only thing super-charging Finale. Remember the third-party plug-ins I mentioned in the intro? I recommend reviewing their functionality and downloading them if you think they might be helpful. You can find complete descriptions and download/installation instructions at the following Web sites:

- TGTools. This is a collection by Tobias Giesen. A limited edition is already available under Finale's Plug-ins 🎵 menu. Features include an expression browser, layout functions, parts handling, and much more. A fully functional trial version is available at http://tgtools.de.

- Patterson Plug-in Collection. These are Robert Patterson's plug-ins, and you also see some of his work in Finale's regular Plug-ins 🎵 menu (Patterson Beams and Beam Over Barlines). See www.robertgpatterson.com/-fininfo/finmain.html.

- JW Plug-ins. Jari Williamsson's plug-ins are available for free! Note that Search and Replace and the Score System divider are already included with your Finale package. See www .finaletips.nu/plugins.php for these, as well as a directory of plug-ins from other authors.

Start the Engine

You may want to change some additional Finale settings right from the start.

Laptop Users

Finale includes a separate set of Simple Entry keystrokes specifically for laptop users.

1. Choose the Simple Entry Tool .

2. From the Simple menu, choose Simple Entry Options, then click Edit Keyboard Shortcuts.

3. Click the drop-down menu under Keyboard Shortcut Set and choose Laptop Shortcut Table.

   This set was designed for the abbreviated keyboard sans number pad. If you ever need to edit the Simple Entry keystrokes, you can do so here. To reference keystrokes, it's easiest to just open the Simple menu.

4. Click OK twice to return to the score.

Tip: Laptop users with an abbreviated keyboard can use the fn modifier key to access the extra keys of a full keyboard. For example, on a Macintosh laptop, to access the Clear key, use fn+6. Consult your laptop's documentation (and hints printed on the keys themselves, usually in purple) for fn key functionality.

Turn Off Fill with Rests

Finale automatically completes unfilled measures with rests anytime you switch focus to another measure or change tools. Some composers find this annoying and, although it protects against missing beats, they turn this feature off. If you also find this feature annoying, follow along:

1. Choose the Simple Entry Tool .

2. From the Simple menu, choose Simple Entry Options.

3. Uncheck Fill with Rests at End of Measure.

4. Click OK. Choose the Speedy Entry Tool .

5. From the Speedy menu, choose Speedy Options.

6. Uncheck Fill with Rests at End of Measure.

7. Click OK.

To fill regions of measures with rests manually, select a region, go to the Utilities menu, and choose Check Notation > Fill with Rests.

Default View

Finale always starts in Page view, which is great for some scores, but many composers prefer Scroll view for general editing (which I cover in the next chapter).

To change the default view to Scroll view:

1. Windows users, press Alt+E to open the Edit menu and then press G.

    Mac users, press Command+, (comma). The Program Options dialog box appears.

2. Click New if it isn't chosen already.

3. In the New Document Windows section, select the Scroll View radio button.

4. Click OK.

2 Getting the Best Angle

I've got an uncle who records sound for motion pictures. His technical title is Production Sound Mixer. He's basically the guy who makes sure you can hear what's going on as you munch on popcorn at the theater. I'm told the job requires an expert sense of acoustics, highly specialized technical knowledge, and really expensive equipment. On the set, or on location, he has the luxury of shutting out a lot of the mayhem going on around him and devoting all of his attention to things like microphone placement and real-time mixing. He has, no doubt, a unique perspective of the film being produced, and one necessary to capture the proper balance and subtlety for the viewer.

Like a film, a musical composition has many distinct dimensions. One moment you are deciding whether the second violin should be resting, and the next you are covering a giant swath of your score with *sfz* markings. One moment you are tweaking the system spacing, and the next you are tapping out the tempo changes. As you work, you will find that different views are better suited for different tasks. Finale has no shortage of ways to get the best angle, and it's important to include them in your bag of tricks.

So, if you are directing a film, and need to hear every last piece of shattered glass erupt from the crashing chandelier, you should consult the individual who does that sort of thing—your Production Sound Mixer. If you are composing with Finale and need to adjust the volume of staves in real time, use the view designed for that sort of thing—Studio View. Take advantage of specialization whenever you can...that's what it's there for.

Here's a summary of what you will learn in this chapter:

- How to get the most out of Finale's general navigation features
- How to approach Finale's three views
- How to use wormholes (viewing shortcuts)

A Closer Look: Zooming

Regardless of the view you are using, zooming in and out and moving your score around are staples of composing in Finale, so I cover them first. These skills are so important, I included the bare essentials at the beginning of the first chapter. Take a closer look at zooming and navigation to magnify these capabilities.

Continue using the same Beethoven.mus document from the Finale 2008/Sample Files folder (also available at www.composingwithfinale.com). Follow these steps to learn how to easily navigate to any part of the page at any view percentage.

Windows users:

1. Click the middle mouse button to zoom in.

    Or press Alt+Shift+right-click.

2. Hold down Ctrl and press the middle mouse button to zoom out.

    Or, press Ctrl+Shift+right-click.

3. Press Shift+right-click and drag a box around a region, then release the mouse button to expand the region to the size of the window. See Figure 2.1.

4. Press Ctrl++ (plus sign) to zoom in.

5. Press Ctrl+− (minus sign) to zoom out.

6. Press Ctrl+1, Ctrl+2, and Ctrl+3 to zoom to 100%, 200%, and 75% respectively.

Macintosh users:

1. Press Shift+Command to display the ⊕ cursor, then click to zoom in.

2. Press Shift+Option+Command to display the ⊖ cursor, then click to zoom out.

3. Press Shift+Command and drag a box around a region, then release the mouse button to expand the region to the size of the window. See Figure 2.2.

4. Press Command++ (plus sign) to zoom in.

5. Press Command+− (minus sign) to zoom out

6. Press Command+1, command+2, and Command+3 to zoom to 100%, 200%, and 75% respectively.

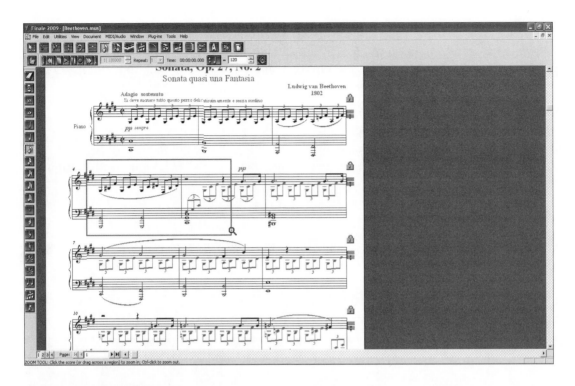

Figure 2.1 In Windows, hold down Shift and right-click to quickly zoom in to a specific region.

To zoom in, I prefer the middle mouse button in Windows. In fact, it's definitely worth the cost of a mouse with a middle button (preferably a clickable scroll wheel) if you don't have one. On Mac, I prefer Shift+Command+click and Option+Shift+Command+click to zoom in and out.

Custom Zoom Percentages

My wife, Kami, handles some interface design at MakeMusic. She has been heavily involved in designing the user interface for such monstrosities as Linked Parts and the Finale 2008 Selection Tool updates. But for some reason, whenever I mention the updated View menu during our strolls around the lake, she puts a bounce to her step and reminds me who designed it. So, with pleasure, here's a nifty zoom capability courtesy of Kami.

There were once several more zoom percentage shortcuts, but they were fixed (50%, 100%, 200%, and so on). Now, you only have three, but you can set them to any percentage you want.

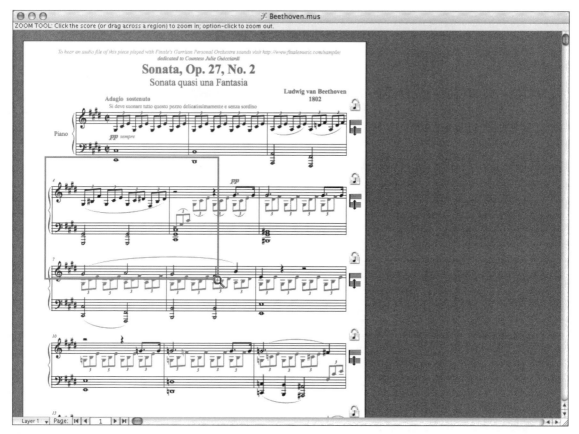

Figure 2.2 On Macintosh, Shift+Command+click+drag to quickly zoom in to a specific region.

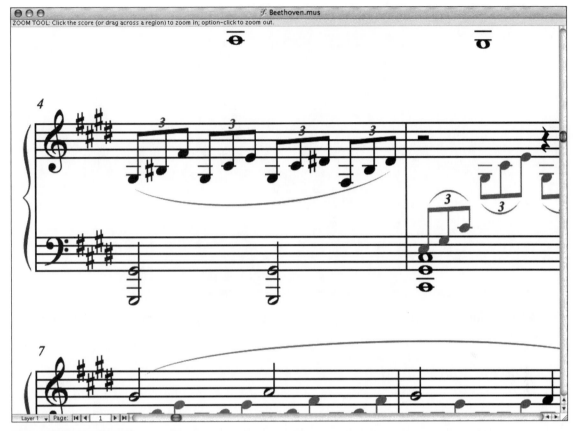

Figure 2.2 Continued

1. From the View menu, choose Zoom > Define Custom Zooms.

    The Program Options–View dialog box appears, as shown in Figure 2.3.

2. In the Custom Zoom percents section, enter the desired percentages.

3. Click OK.

    Ctrl/Command+1/2/3 are now assigned to the view percentages you entered. This is a program setting, so it applies to all documents.

Customizing these shortcuts is especially nice because the size of the music on the page is often different from one score to the next (depending on changes applied with the Resize Tool, for instance). You might even make adjusting the three preferred zoom percentages a routine part of your preparation whenever you begin a new project.

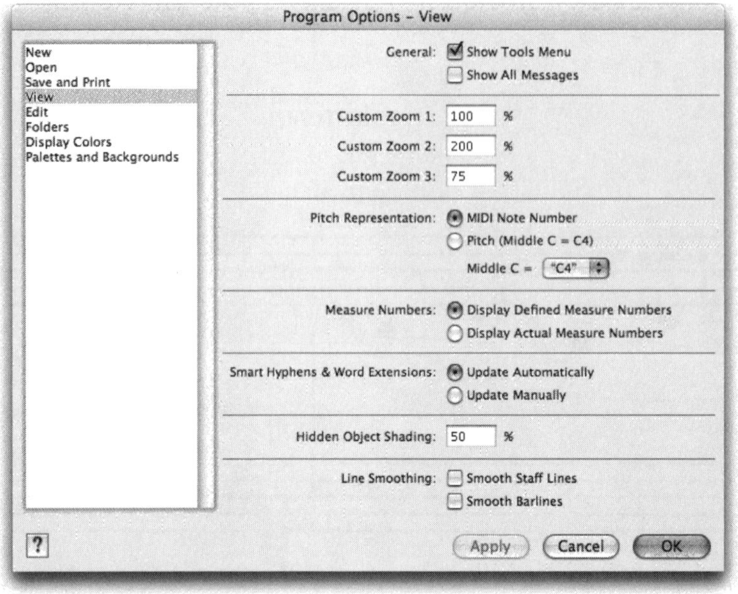

Figure 2.3 Assign custom zoom percentages to the zoom shortcuts (Ctrl/Command+1/2/3) in Program Options–View.

Dragging the Score Around

The Hand Grabber Tool ✋ shares a cozy spot next to his sister, the Zoom Tool. In Windows, both of these tools are in the Navigational Tools Palette. In the previous sections, you learned how to use every function of the Zoom Tool without its mention. The same could be true for the Hand Grabber Tool, except I just mentioned it. In Windows, to eliminate these tools from your screen, from the Window menu, uncheck Navigational Tools Palette.

Dragging and zooming go hand-in-hand as viewing/navigation functions, so it's appropriate to reach out and discuss this here.

- Windows users, right-click (not directly on a staff) and drag.

- Macintosh users, hold down Option+Command. Your cursor changes to ✋. Now click+ drag to move the score.

Seldom, if ever, will you need to manually drag the horizontal and vertical scroll bars. Use the preceding technique instead.

Tip: Macintosh laptop users, newer models have a nifty two-finger scroll feature (drag two fingers up/down/left/right on your track pad). See System Preferences > Keyboard & Mouse 7 > Trackpad: "Use two fingers to scroll" checkbox.

Note: In Scroll and Studio View, only use Hand Grabber functionality for vertical navigation (up and down).

The Scroll Wheel

Again, I recommend you purchase a mouse with a clickable scroll wheel if you don't have one. You can also use the wheel to easily scroll through the score vertically or horizontally (like most word-processing documents). Macintosh users, to scroll horizontally, press the Shift key while scrolling.

Room with a View

You could think of Finale as a powerful notation observatory. But, rather than a supernova or distant galaxy, the subject is your composition. You might imagine your project is a statue resting in the middle of an observatory, a square room with giant windows on all sides. Rather than looking out, this observatory requires you to look in, like an exhibit. Each of the statue's features are visible from one of the windows, or maybe even up to three of them, but each window gives you a unique perspective.

In Finale, these windows are Scroll View, Page View, Studio View, and the MIDI window. Each allows you to view at least one aspect of the music undetectable from the other three. They may not all be required for every project, but, no one ever found a four-leaf clover without taking off the gorilla suit. So, let's turn a discerning eye to each window to see what we find.

Note: In this chapter I focus on the three main views: Page, Scroll, and Studio View. The need for the MIDI window has been eclipsed somewhat by advancements in Finale's Human Playback feature. See Chapter 4, "Listen."

Scroll View

In Scroll View, your music appears in a continuous horizontal band as shown in Figure 2.4. You might also describe this as "one long system stretching into infinity," or "the everlasting void of silent dreams that will never be heard," whatever the case may be. This view offers a potpourri of advantages, and although it is the eldest view, it continues to be favored by many composers.

Press Ctrl+E (Command+E) to move to Scroll View; Ctrl+E (Command+E) toggles between Scroll and Page View.

Working in Scroll View has several advantages from a composer's perspective.

■ Scroll View is zippy compared to Page View, with fast screen redraws while editing.

■ Scroll View allows you to completely ignore system and measure layout concerns while thinking about the music. Out of sight, out of mind, which can eliminate unwanted distraction.

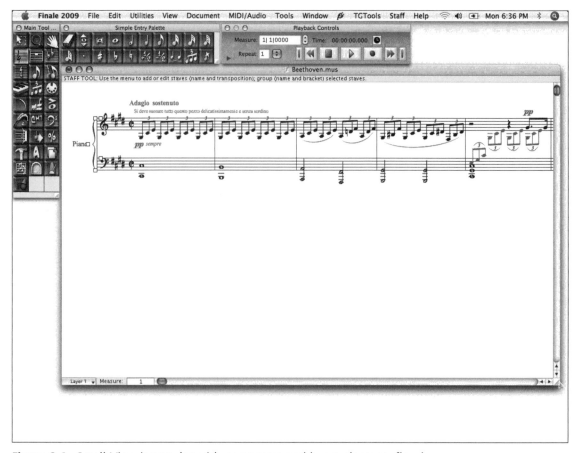

Figure 2.4 Scroll View is popular with composers and has a pleasant, floral aroma.

- Scroll View allows you to easily navigate forward and backward without changing the vertical positioning of onscreen staves.

- Scroll View has several robust navigation and viewing options.

I, as you might have guessed, prefer Scroll View for composing. If you are comfortable using MIDI or pro audio sequencers, this view allows you to treat staves kind of like tracks (without worrying about the page formatting). And, it has a lot of flexibility with regard to viewing and navigating staves, which I cover next.

Tip: Convenient playback can also be a benefit of Scroll View. To instruct Finale to begin playback at the leftmost measure on the screen, check Leftmost Measure in the Playback Settings dialog box (Playback Controls dialog box). Windows users, click the speaker icon on the Playback Controls. Macintosh users, expand the Playback Controls by clicking the triangle in the lower-left corner.

Navigating in Scroll View

Right now you should be viewing your Beethoven example in Scroll View; see Figure 2.4. If not, press Ctrl+E (Command+E). Now, play a little.

1.   Right-click+drag (Option+Ctrl+click+drag) to move the staff to the right a bit so the staff name is in view.

2.   You can also use this method to move up and down among the staves. (Notice the scroll bar on the right move as you do this.)

Caution: In Scroll View, never drag the system laterally with the mouse except to position the left edge so the staff names are visible. You should always see the staff name and measure number on the left edge of the system in Scroll View.

Macintosh users, if you have a mouse with a scroll wheel, hold down Shift and scroll to navigate horizontally. The scroll wheel by itself allows you to navigate vertically. This is enough reason to buy a mouse with a scroll wheel (if not switch to using Finale on a Macintosh altogether).

3.   Press Ctrl+Page Down (Command+Page Down) to move forward a length of measures.

     Press Ctrl+Page Up (Command+Page Up) to move in reverse a length of measures. A length refers to the number of measures that fit within the document window's width.

4.   To move by increments of a single measure, use the left and right arrows on the scroll bar at the bottom of the document window.

5.   To navigate to a specific measure, type the measure number in the Measure text box (lower-left corner of the Finale window) and press Enter.

6.   To change the space between staves for editing convenience, choose the Staff Tool and drag the staff handles up and down as necessary. You can restore appropriate staff spacing later as you prepare the layout for printing. For now, you need to be sure all items are attached to the correct staff, and that may mean distancing them a bit to be sure.

Tip: You will learn about respacing staves for layout and printing in Chapter 15, "Wrapping Up."

All the zooming options mentioned earlier also work in Scroll View—except the ability to zoom in by dragging a box around the target region.

Assigning and Using Staff Sets

I didn't fall for Scroll View completely until I discovered Staff Sets. From a composer's perspective, these things are fantastic. If you work with large ensembles, you may find yourself moving up and down repeatedly from the woodwind section to the strings, or from the trumpets to the percussion, unless you assign Staff Sets. Staff Sets allow you to eliminate staves from the screen so you can focus on a hand-picked collection for editing in the same viewable region. See Figure 2.5.

In the excerpt in Figure 2.5, the woodwinds and strings share a similar passage, but they are separated by an ocean of intermediate staves. So, I created a Staff Set, including the six relevant staves, so they can be edited in the same viewable region at a higher view percentage. Now you can easily copy and paste material between these staves. Here's what I did to create the Staff Sets:

1. From the File menu, choose Open.

2. Navigate to the Finale 2009/Sample Files folder and open the file Puccini.mus. If you do not see the Sample Files folder, go to www.composingwithfinale.com to download the sample files.

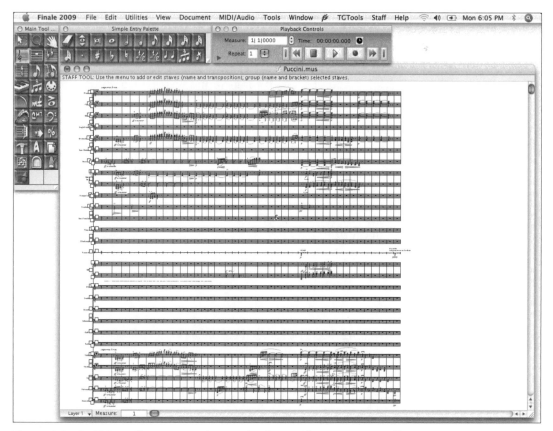

Figure 2.5 Staff Sets allow you to view and edit specific staves in Scroll View when you don't need to view the full score.

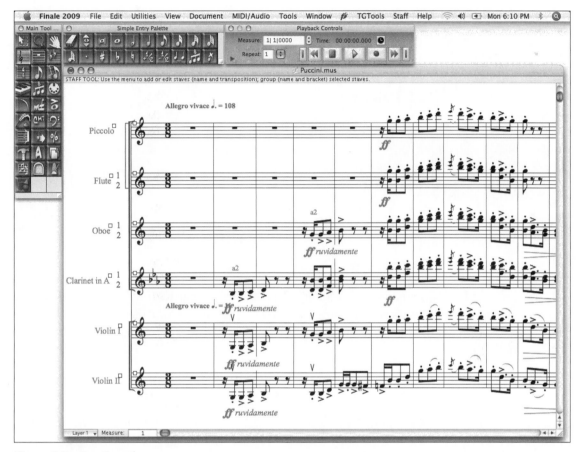

Figure 2.5   Continued

3. Press Ctrl+E (Command+E) to move to Scroll View.

4. Press Ctrl+0 (Command+0), enter 50, and click OK. The view percentage changes to 50%. Notice the staves that include the ascending then descending passage between measures 5-9. Assign those to a Staff Set.

5. Choose the Staff Tool ▦. A handle appears on each staff.

6. Shift+click the handle on each staff you would like to include (as shown in Figure 2.5). Ignore the handles to the left of the staff handles; they are for the group brackets and staff names.

7. Press Ctrl and choose the View menu (press Option and choose the View menu). You see a new option: Program Staff Set. See Figure 2.6.

8. Choose Program Staff Set > Staff Set 1. Staves you didn't select disappear.

Figure 2.6 Hold down Ctrl/Option while choosing the View menu to display the Program Staff Set command.

9. Press Ctrl+1 (Command+1) to change the view percentage to 100%. Notice the allegro vivace marking on the violin staff collides with *ff* on the Clarinet staff. You can use the Staff Tool to change the staff positioning without changing the appearance of the full score view.

10. Drag the handles on the violin staves to move them down for more breathing room. Respace all the staves if you want so they are optimal for viewing and editing.

11. From the View menu, choose Select Staff Set > All Staves to return to the full score. Notice the spacing changes made in the Staff Set do not apply to the full score view. (They do not apply to other Staff Sets, either.)

12. Press Ctrl+S (Command+S) and save this file. You can choose a new name if you don't want to overwrite the original file. We will be coming back to this file (with the Staff Set assigned) later.

You can assign up to eight different Staff Sets. Then, select them from the View menu to navigate to them. You will learn how to make Staff Sets even more powerful in the "Using Bookmarks" section later in this chapter.

Tip: Windows users, use Plug-ins > TGTools > Menu Shortcuts to assign Staff Sets to keyboard shortcuts (Shift+F2, Shift+F3, and so on, for example). Macintosh users, press Ctrl+1, Ctrl+2, etc. to navigate to the respective Staff Set. Press Ctrl+0 to view all staves.

Page View

Page View has exclusive reign over all the system and page-layout options you will ever need to produce lovely, evenly spaced, professional-looking sheet music. Although it has been greatly improved in Finale 2009, it has few advantages for a composition in progress.

Page View displays a preview of the printed page (see Figure 2.7), and allows you to do things like adjust the system margins and spacing, assign text and graphics to fixed positions on the page, and insert title pages. Its unique capabilities, although necessary, are limited to aspects unrelated to composition itself. While you can certainly craft your opus in this view, it's kind of like boiling water with a blow torch.

For large ensembles, I recommend thinking of Page View as the utility for perfecting the appearance of the measures, systems, and pages for the conductor and performer after the audible

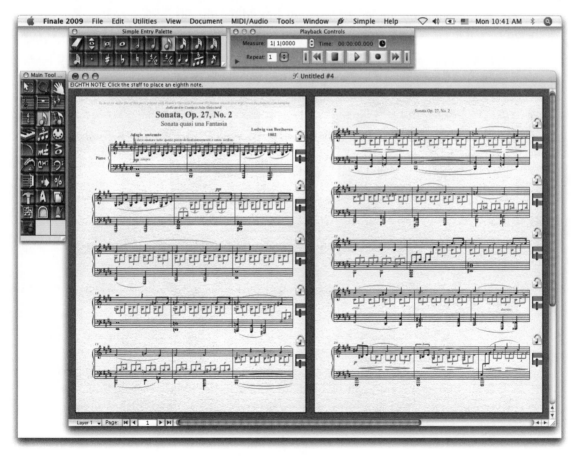

Figure 2.7   Composing in Page View is like boiling water with a blow torch.

creative activity has ceased. Or, let a qualified engraver or copyist deal with it. (As mentioned earlier, the visual art of engraving is a rich subject all to itself.)

But, I know some of you are saying, "I like composing in Page View!" Okay, okay, to each one's own. I know some like the pages to look pretty right away, and you can see more content at a time with scores with few staves per system. In addition to the important navigation/zooming suggestions explained earlier in this chapter, here are some suggestions.

- Press Page Down to move forward pages and Page Up to move backward pages. Press these keystrokes multiple times. They scroll to the top/bottom of the page before moving to the previous/next.

- Press Ctrl+Page Down (Command+Page Down) to move directly to the next page and Ctrl+Page Up (Command+Page Up) to move directly to the previous page.

- Use the Fit in Window Ctrl+] (Option+Command+]) and Fit Width Ctrl+[(Option+ Command+[) commands under the View menu to resize the entire page or the page width to fit the viewable area.

- Use Bookmarks to automatically navigate to specific points in the score. (You will learn more about Bookmarks soon.)

There could be a book this size devoted to engraver standards for page layout and how to accomplish them with Finale. I will refer you to the Finale user manual for a good reference. But, keeping the page formatting relatively attractive as you work is irresistible in Page View, so here are a few tips to mind your Ps and Qs along the way.

- To move a measure to the next system, select the measure and press the down arrow. Use the up arrow to move a selected measure to the previous system.

- To update the music spacing, highlight a region and press Ctrl+4 (Command+4) to apply Finale's Note Spacing feature.

- If Note Spacing doesn't cut it, to change the width of measures manually, select the Measure Tool . Then, drag the top handle on the barlines horizontally.

- Multimeasure rests are visible only in Page View. So, if, in Scroll View, you add music into a multimeasure rest region, Finale breaks the multimeasure rest automatically. But, if you subsequently clear the measures, Finale does not re-create the multimeasure rest. Worse, notes that should be showing can be hidden behind multimeasure rests. The point? Always review your parts for missing multimeasure rests and create them accordingly when they are missing (with the Measure Tool).

Studio View

Like Scroll View, Studio View also displays the music in a continuous horizontal band. By using it, you will trade off a bit of viewing convenience for better control over playback. Studio View is like Scroll View's roadie cousin. It looks a lot like Scroll View, but made some interesting choices as it came into its own.

Although Studio View may seem like "the view to listen to your score," you will find all of the generally required playback functions in all of the views. (See Chapter 4 for extensive details.) Auditioning the music as you write is a luxury so ingrained these days that scarcely does a composer consider using a view that doesn't include it. In practice, Studio View is sometimes used as an alternative to Scroll View, and is required in certain situations.

Press Ctrl+Shift+E (Command+Shift+E) to move to Studio view. The staff controls on the left side of the score and the TempoTap staff at the top are the distinctions of Studio View. See Figure 2.8.

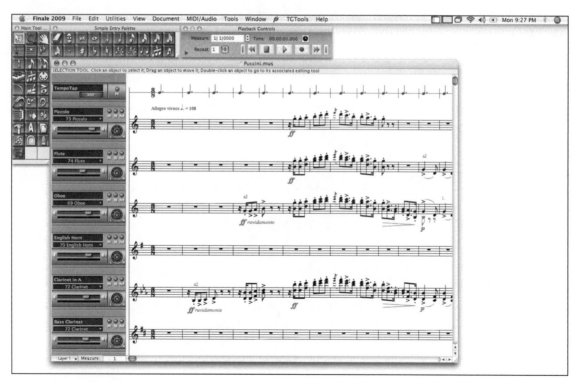

Figure 2.8 Studio View is like Scroll View's roadie cousin, sacrificing a few practical things for the love of the music.

Although very similar to Scroll View in appearance, the following things prevent some composers from adopting Studio View as their primary view:

- You cannot program or view Staff Sets in Studio View.

- You cannot define Bookmarks to display the score in Studio View (more on Bookmarks soon).

- The staff controls on the left occupy valuable screen real estate. This is particularly noticeable without a widescreen monitor.

Studio View does include convenient access to the Instrument List's playback functionality, including the ability to adjust the volume, mute, solo, or pan settings for individual staves (during playback). These are available from the staff controls to the left of each staff. They also allow you to change some other properties as well, such as the Finale instrument's General MIDI patch and channel.

Whether the advantages of Studio View make up for the drawbacks is a matter of individual preference, but certain situations require Studio View:

- When you need to "conduct" tempo changes (ritardando/accelerando) with TempoTap.

- When you need to add, edit, or remove an audio track.

A composer's ear is an important tool, and Studio View can definitely be used to complement it. With that, I leave the choice to you. Finale's views will be combined and applied in a unique way for every composition. The full weight of their power will be a bit more apparent after the next section.

Note: Chapter 4 details conducting tempo changes, and adding an audio track is described in Chapter 16, "Unleashing Your Masterpiece."

Wormholes

Quantum theory suggests space-time can be folded to allow instant passage from one point in the universe to another. If your score were the universe, Finale includes several different types of wormholes to allow for instant transport between any two points in your score. Furthermore, you can approach your destination from any side of the observatory I described earlier.

Using Bookmarks

Bookmarks are the first type of wormhole. They are specific views of the score that you can define using all the viewing and navigation capabilities this chapter explains, including

- Zoom percentage (Page and Scroll View)

- Measure (Scroll View)

- Staff Set (Scroll View)

- Staff (Scroll View)

- Page (Page View + specific horizontal and vertical position)

Although you can assign Bookmarks to Page or Scroll View at any score position and view percentage, they can also be integrated beautifully with Staff Sets to allow a custom display of any combination of staves as well.

Assign a Bookmark to the Staff Set you applied earlier (under "Assigning and Using Staff Sets").

1. If the Puccini score you edited earlier isn't open, open it now.

2. Press Ctrl+E (Command+E) once or twice to display the score in Scroll View.

3. From the View menu, choose Select Staff Set > All Staves.

    You will assign a Bookmark to display the violin staves at their entrance on measure 2, at 100%, and in Staff Set 1 (which you assigned earlier). This gives you a nice view of the violin staves as well as the other instruments that include a similar passage.

4. From the View menu, choose Bookmarks > Add Bookmark. The Add Bookmark dialog box appears.

5. For Name, enter Violins m. 2 and ensure the Scroll View radio button is selected.

6. Under Settings for Scroll View, for Measure:, enter **2**.

7. Check all three checkboxes.

8. Set Zoom To to 100, Staff Set to Staff Set 1, and Staff to Violin 1 (as shown in Figure 2.9).

Figure 2.9 Define the destination of your wormhole in the Add Bookmark dialog box.

9. Click Add to return to the score.

10. Choose Bookmarks from the View menu. You see a new option, Violins m.2, as shown in Figure 2.10.

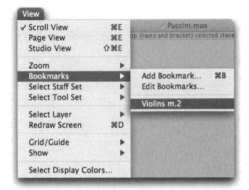

Figure 2.10 New Bookmarks appear at the bottom of the Bookmarks submenu.

11. Choose Violins m.2. You snap to Staff Set 1, measure 2, as shown in Figure 2.11.

You might regard Staff Sets and Bookmarks like a scaffold built around your composition. They complicate the building process up front to a small degree, but they make up for it tenfold by allowing easy access once the project is in full swing. Of course, as your composition progresses, you might update the Bookmarks to adjust them according to the parts of the score that require attention.

Tip: Windows users, use Plug-ins > TGTools > Menu Shortcuts to assign Bookmarks to keyboard shortcuts (Ctrl+F2, Ctrl+F3, and so on). Macintosh users, consider using QuicKeys (www.startly.com) to assign Bookmarks and other menu items to keyboard shortcuts.

Between Score and Parts

Where was Linked Parts ten years ago?! I remember spending two straight days locked in a tiny music lab with a laser printer plowing through reams of paper in a futile effort to perfect parts for the reading of my first concert band score. My, have things changed since then.

Working with parts is another incidental formatting concern for the composer (albeit an important one), but their mere availability during the score-editing process warrants a word about their utility and accessibility from a composer's perspective (read: how to avoid really messing things up).

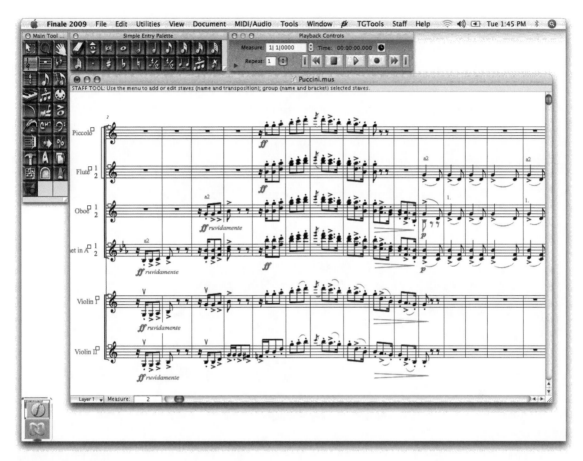

Figure 2.11 Select a Bookmark to navigate to your specified measure, staff, view percentage, and Staff Set.

You can completely ignore Linked Parts until you have finished composing your score. In fact, you can wait to generate parts until after your score is complete if you want to. Although there is disagreement as to whether it is appropriate to do this, I see no reason parts must be generated prior to the formatting stage of your composition project. I have difficulty seeing how the distraction of part formatting can increase creative productivity. But, it is far more difficult to understand the unique and mysterious ways of any of my composing brethren. Here are tips for using Linked Parts.

- Press Ctrl+Alt+> or Ctrl+Alt+< (Command+Option+> or Command+Option+<) to move to the next or previous part.

- Navigate to a specific part by choosing Document > Edit Part > *part name*.

Between Documents

Like most programs, Finale allows you to open as many documents as you want at one time. You may need to do this to copy between documents or reference one document while composing another.

Here are the important wormholes between documents.

- Select an open document from the bottom of the Window menu.

- Press Ctrl+Tab (Command–') to toggle between open documents.

- From the Window menu, choose Tile Horizontally/Vertically (Tile Windows) to display the open documents beside one another or on top of one another. See Figure 2.12.

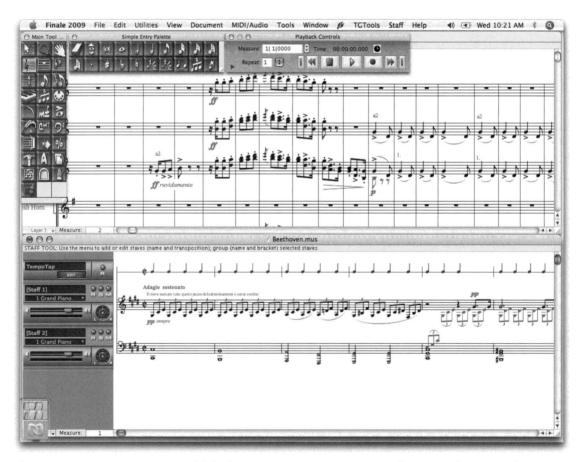

Figure 2.12 You can arrange multiple documents in any onscreen configuration for easy reference or copying.

■ From the Window menu, choose Cascade (Stack Windows) to display the document windows so they slightly overlap, offering more convenient access to them.

Note: I explain some more advantages regarding multiple open documents in Chapter 7, "The Composer's Wild Kingdom."

Between Programs

Believe it or not, a wonderful world of software products is out there in addition to Finale. There are so many situations you may need to quickly switch between Finale and another programs. Here are a few:

■ You are writing a book about Finale. (Hey, it's kind of like composing.)

■ You need to reference the user manual.

■ You need to reference a font character map, e-mail message, MIDI sequencer, graphics editor, PDF, or the like.

Alright, you get the picture. Here are the essential general OS keyboard shortcuts when you are working with multiple programs. Forgive me if you already use these continuously, but I couldn't leave them out—they are just too important.

Windows:

■ Press Alt+Tab to switch back and forth between programs.

■ Press Alt+Tab to display the program icons. Then, continue holding down Alt and press Tab until the desired program is selected. Then, release Alt to switch to the chosen program. (You can add Shift to reverse the tab direction).

■ Press Alt+Esc (or Alt+Shift+Esc) to advance through program windows without displaying the program icons.

Macintosh:

■ Press Command+Tab to switch back and forth between programs.

■ Press Command+Tab to display the program icons. Then, continue holding down Command and press Tab until the desired program is selected. Release Command to switch to the chosen program. (You can add Shift to reverse the tab direction.)

■ While holding down Command, press the H key to hide the selected program.

3 Moving Stuff Around

At school, in the frozen tundra of Minnesota, Dr. Tim Mahr's first assignment in Composition 101 was this: Compose a piece using one pitch. We soon realized the plethora of choices even under very limited circumstances. What is the timbre/instrument? What octave should I choose? What is the dynamic level? How will it be articulated? What is the rhythm? What is the tempo? Should I add rehearsal letters? Will this require circular breathing?

As fledgling composers, we recognized how easy it is to make assumptions about these aspects—assumptions we must at least recognize and notate if we have any chance of communicating them to our performers and audience. More importantly, we recognized that we should ask ourselves questions like, "Did I compose this passage's phrasing or overlook that aspect?" Or maybe even, "Could a completely different combination of pitches satisfy my requirements better given all my other options?"

My point is that pitch is only one aspect of any composition, and yes, only one of the many aspects you are allowed to copy and paste in Finale. Sure, your motivic development may require a gazillion copies of one five-note figure, and yes, Finale will make this easy; but it's the tip of the iceberg. By applying an aspect from one region of music to another you can quickly, exponentially expand your options. For example, you might notice that the delightful series of articulations from your snare solo would also apply to the marimba feature later on. Or, perhaps you want to change the slurring on every occurrence of a particular theme throughout your opera; it only takes a minute.

"Moving stuff around" refers to all the musical elements, including notes, voices (layers), markings, notation styles, and measure settings such as meters. So, while you continually ask yourself the essential questions, you can also draw on aspects of your existing creations and apply them as you see fit. Not only can you eliminate redundancy, but also consider new avenues that you may have otherwise overlooked.

Here's a summary of what you will learn in this chapter:

- How to select measure regions
- How to copy measures (move everything)
- How to copy specific elements (move particular things)

Selecting

I find the whole association between time, sound, and visual/spatial figures most engaging when thrashing through the midst of a busy score. We fast forward and rewind in our minds as we consider which chunk of music goes where. It goes without saying that some compositional styles benefit from copying and pasting more than others, but we probably all use some degree of repetition in our creations.

Whether you intend to copy, change, or delete a measure region, you first need to select it. The following are some methods you can use to quickly identify the intended target. The steps in this section assume the Selection Tool, or a tool that supports regional selection, is chosen.

Drag-Selecting

Click and drag a box around the desired measure region to select it; see Figure 3.1. Do not click directly on a measure, note, or marking. If you do, you select it instead. Even in the most crowded score you should be able to find some white space.

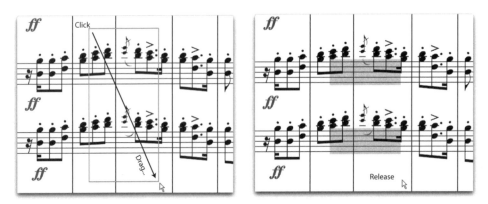

Figure 3.1 Click and drag to select any measure region (full or partial measures).

Notice the region includes partial measures. You can pinpoint any region for selection, down to the twelfth 128th note in a run. Zoom in to select precise regions.

Shift+Drag-Selecting

When you hold down Shift and drag-select, Finale always selects full measures (see Figure 3.2).

Click-Selecting

You can use your mouse to select a single measure or hold down Shift to expand and contract selected regions.

- Click empty space in a measure to select the measure. A single click in a measure always highlights the full measure.

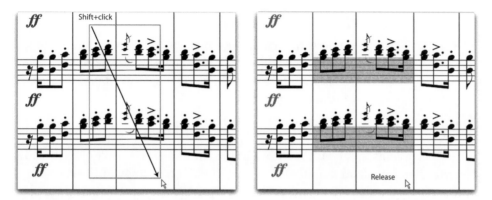

Figure 3.2   Click and drag while holding down Shift to select any measure region (full measures only).

- Shift+click to extend the selected region in any direction.
- Click to the left of a staff (or to the left of the time signature) to select the entire staff.
- Shift+click to the left of another staff (or to the left of the time signature) to include additional staves in the selection.
- Double-click to extend a partial measure selection to include the full measure(s).
- Double-click a full measure to select the measure stack. A **stack** is a vertical slice of the score, and always consists of full measures.

Selection Keyboard Shortcuts

Remember these important selection keyboard shortcuts. They come in handy:

- Hold down Shift and press the arrow keys to extend the selection incrementally (by note, empty measure, or by staff).
- Hold down Shift+Ctrl (Shift+Option) and press the left or right arrow keys to extend the selection incrementally by full measures.
- Hold down Shift and press the End key to extend the selection to the end of the score.
- Hold down Shift and press the Home key to extend the selection to the beginning of the score.
- Hold down Shift and press Page Up or Page Down to extend the selection to the top or bottom staff.
- Press Ctrl+A (Command+A) to select all.

Moving Things Around

Whenever you move things around you need to specify both the source material and the **target region** (where you want the material to go). Now that you've mastered selecting a precise region of measures, it's time to learn the most basic method of copying/moving all the notes and markings within that region from one place to another.

In the following steps, you will

1. Open the file Puccini.mus in the Finale 2009/Sample Files folder if it isn't open already. Remember, you can download this file by visiting www.composingwithfinale.com.

2. Press Ctrl+E (Command+E) to move to Scroll View and move to measure 1, so the top staff is visible.

3. Press Ctrl+1 (Command+1) to zoom to 100%.

4. From the View menu, choose Select Staff Set > All Staves (in case you were viewing the Staff Set you defined earlier).

5. Choose the Selection Tool.

6. From the Edit menu, make sure Use Filter is unchecked.

7. Hold down Shift and drag a box, including measures 6-10 of the Oboe staff, as shown in Figure 3.3. Whenever you want to select whole measures, hold down Shift. Alternatively, click measure 6 to select it, then hold down Shift and click measure 11.

8. Press Backspace (Delete) to clear the measures.

   Now you'll copy the identical passage in the Clarinet in A staff up to the Oboe staff. They are the same notes. If you want to make this apparent, view the score in concert pitch: Choose the Document menu and select Display in Concert Pitch.

9. Select measures 6-10 in the Clarinet in A staff (5th from the top).

10. Click-drag the highlighted measures so a black border appears around measures 6-10 in the Oboe staff (as shown in Figure 3.4).

11. Press Ctrl+Z (Command+Z) to undo. The copied music in the Oboe staff disappears. Measures 6-10 in the Clarinet staff are still highlighted.

12. Press Ctrl+C (Command+C).

13. Click measure 6 in the Oboe staff to highlight the measure.

14. Press Ctrl+V (Command+V). Finale pastes into measures 6-10 even though only measure 6 was selected.

15. Press Ctrl+Z (Command+Z) to undo.

Figure 3.3 Select a region of measures by drag-selecting or Shift+clicking. While drag-selecting, hold down Shift to select full measures.

16.   Highlight measures 6-10 in the Clarinet staff again.

17.   Ctrl+click (Option+click) measure 6 in the Oboe staff. The music appears in measures 6-10.

All of the preceding methods of copying are identical in function. Whether you are copying between documents or within the same document, all of these methods yield the same results. (This was not the case in Finale versions prior to Finale 2008.)

Tip: Hold down Alt (Command) while drag-copying to insert rather than paste (or, select Insert from the Edit menu to insert from the clipboard). When you insert, subsequent music in the staff (or staves) is nudged the duration of the inserted material.

Figure 3.4 While drag-copying, surround the target region with a black border, then release the mouse button to paste.

Making Sure You Move Everything

Well, you did move everything you wanted to, right? Perhaps, but Finale completely ignored several aspects of the selected region, including

- Time signatures

- Key signatures

- Barline styles

- Clefs

- Repeats

- Note positioning

- Some other aspects of the measure

Had any of these elements existed in your source region, they would not have transferred to the target measures. Why? Because if Finale did copy the clefs, time signatures, and key signatures whenever you dragged-copied some music, MakeMusic's Customer Support department would be completely overwhelmed with calls and e-mails. These are, for the most part, settings that apply to every staff, and only full measures. As such, a particular type of selection (called a **stack**) accommodates these things, which, as mentioned earlier, consists of full measures in all staves (a vertical slice of the score).

To see all the elements that require a stack selection, from the Edit menu, choose Edit Filter. (The Edit Filter dialog box is shown later in Figure 3.9.) In the Edit Filter dialog box, refer to the items under Measure Settings (Stack Selection Only).

Moving Everything

Okay, let's review. To select a stack, double-click a full measure selection (with the Selection Tool chosen). You can confirm that a selection includes the entire stack if highlighting extends between staves. In scores with a single staff, all full-measure selections are always stacks.

But to copy stacks, along with their measure settings, the target region must also begin at a barline; see Figure 3.5.

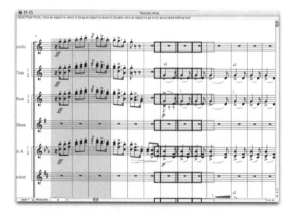 

A target region not compatable with stack-pasting   A target region compatable with stack-pasting

Figure 3.5   To really copy *everything* (including measure settings), you must select a stack and paste (or insert) to a region beginning on a barline. Look for green to paste (or insert) a stack.

Tip: When drag-inserting a stack, a green vertical bar appears. The bar changes color to green when positioned at a point eligible for stack insertion.

Moving It More Than Once: Multiple Copies

Finale makes it easy to repeat the same passage twice, a hundred, or, if you're Steve Reich, thousands of times. (I'm listening to "Music for 18 Musicians" now. What pleasant inspiration for this short section.) Once learned, I trust you will employ these steps in as many unique and fascinating ways possible.

To copy multiple times horizontally:

1.   Select the source region.

2.   Press Ctrl+C (Command+C) to copy or Ctrl+X (Command+X) to cut.

3.   Select the target region, so the left edge begins where you would like to paste.

4.   Press Ctrl+Alt+V (Control+Command+V). The Paste Multiple dialog box appears.

5.   Enter the number of times you want to repeat the material in Paste Horizontally, then click OK. The music appears in the number of repetitions specified; see Figure 3.6.

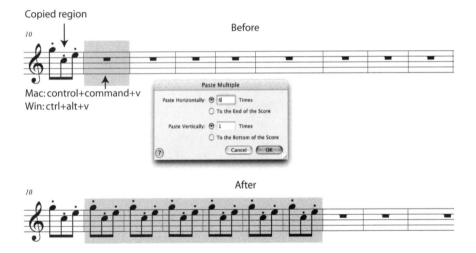

Figure 3.6   Specify the number of iterations in the Paste Multiple dialog box.

You can use the same procedure to copy vertically (to subsequent staves). See Figure 3.7.

Tip: To indicate one- or two-bar repeats, use a Staff Style. See the section "One- and Two-Bar Repeats" at the end of Chapter 14, "Jazz Band."

Moving Specific Things

Now that I have covered selection, and copying "everything," let me explain some of those other musical elements I talked about earlier. How do you transfer things about the music other than notes, or copy *just* the notes and leave the markings behind? Also, how do you do this easily,

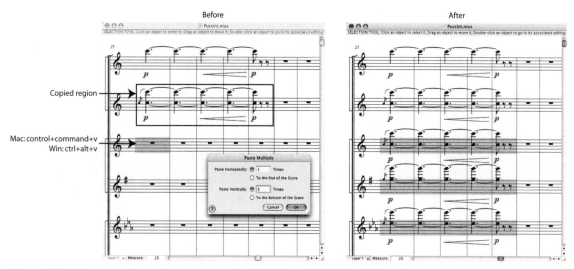

Figure 3.7 Copy to subsequent staves using the Paste Multiple dialog box.

without becoming confused with the interrelated web of various types of elements? In this section, I'll answer these questions to the best of my ability, and certainly at least point you in the right direction.

I must note that Finale suffers from a deficiency with regard to copying and pasting specific score elements. Intuition suggests that one should be able to select multiple elements with the Selection Tool (slurs, articulations, or dynamics, for example), copy them, and then paste them to your desired target region. The markings that find a corresponding note should just fall into place, right?

Unfortunately, this is not the case. You must manually filter the items you want by choosing them in a dialog box. That means you need to know that slurs are technically Smart Shapes, dynamics are technically expressions, and one-bar repeats are probably Staff Styles. Becoming familiar with the technical terms of these items is important. If you are unaware of a marking's identity, double-click it with the Selection Tool. The name of its tool should reveal the element type, and the appropriate box to check or uncheck in the Edit Filter dialog box.

Moving Specific Markings

How your music is articulated is generally a very important aspect of the performance. Now you will learn how to copy some articulations and dynamics and leave the notes alone.

1. Puccini.mus should still be open. If not, open it (Finale 2009/Sample Files folder).

2. Press Ctrl+E (Command+E) to move to Scroll View and move to measure 1, so the top staff is visible.

3. Press Ctrl+1 (Command+1) to zoom to 100%.

4. If you see an *ff* marking beneath measure 6 of the Oboe staff, click it and press Delete.

5. Choose the Articulation Tool.

6. Delete+click-drag over measures 6-12 in the Oboe staff. (See Figure 3.8.) The articulations disappear. The same applies for expressions, Smart Shapes, and text.

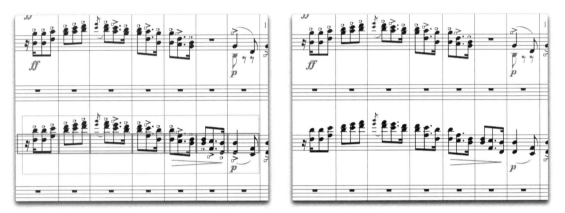

Figure 3.8 To delete multiple occurrences of the same kind of marking, use its tool—in this case, the Articulation Tool.

7. Choose the Selection Tool. (It's advisable to use the Selection Tool to copy, even though you can do so with other tools.)

8. From the Edit menu, choose Edit Filter to bring up the Edit Filter dialog box.

9. Click None to uncheck everything.

10. Check Articulations; Expressions: Dynamics, Expressive Text, Technique Text; and Miscellaneous. The Edit Filter dialog box should now look like Figure 3.9.

11. Click OK.

12. Click the Edit menu. While copying and pasting, you can see if the filter is enabled here. Right now, Use Filter should be checked.

13. Select measures 6-12 in the Clarinet in A staff.

14. Copy to measures 6-12 of the Oboe staff. Drag-copy, Ctrl+click (Option+drag), or use the clipboard (as described previously). In this case, I prefer to Ctrl+click (Option+click) measure 6. The articulations and the *ff* expression appear.

Notice, in the preceding steps, that the *p* marking in measure 12 of the Clarinet in A staff was overwritten with new positioning settings. (Press Ctrl+Z [Command+Z] to undo the copy and

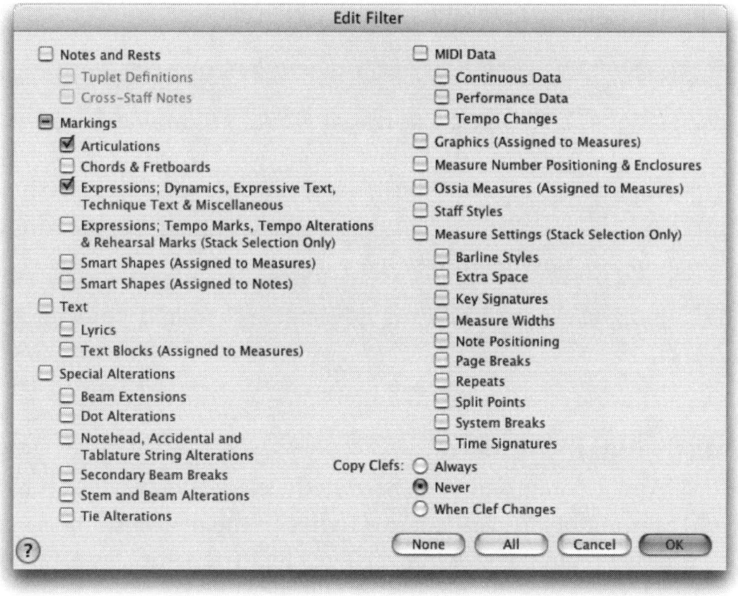

Figure 3.9   Choose the elements you would like to copy in the Edit Filter dialog box.

review the positioning change). While copying, Finale replaces expressions in the target region with those from the source region. This is important to remember when copying music in general; if you do not want to bring the expressions along, uncheck the appropriate Expression checkbox(es) in the Edit Filter dialog box.

Moving Specific Markings Faster

Settings you make in the Edit Filter dialog box remain active the next time you copy (unless you remember to uncheck Edit Filter under the Edit menu). If you have ever copied music and found yourself confused because nothing happened, you probably forgot to uncheck Edit Filter under the Edit menu (with something like Articulations and Expressions checked in the Edit Filter dialog box).

Fortunately, there is a better way to handle moving specific elements than constantly checking and unchecking Edit Filter under the Edit menu. Whenever you copy, Finale *always* copies *everything* in the region. Finale filters out chosen elements when you paste. Therefore, simply invoke the Edit Filter dialog box while pasting if you want to paste something other than the default settings.

1. From the Edit menu, ensure Edit Filter is unchecked. (This is perhaps a good habit to adopt until your Edit Filter state is a fixture in the back of your mind.)

2. Select measures 4-5 of the Oboe staff, then press Ctrl+C (Command+C) to copy. Say you want to copy the notes and articulations to measure 4 of the English Horn staff, but not the dynamic.

3. Click measure 4 of the English Horn staff.

4. Press Ctrl+Shift+V (Command+Shift+V). The Edit Filter dialog box appears.

5. Click All, then uncheck Expressions: Dynamics, Expressive Text, Technique Text.

6. Click OK.

The notes appear in measures 4-5. Finale assumes you want to continue using the filter, so uncheck it. Don't bother going to the menu; just use a keystroke.

7. Press Alt+Ctrl+F (Option+Command+F). Use Filter is now unchecked and you can go back to copying everything.

Moving Specific Markings with Blazing Speed

SmartFind and Paint is a great utility from a composer's perspective. It allows you to search for rhythmically identical passages and automatically articulate ("paint") them according to a source region you have already selected. Pretend you want change the articulation of one of the motifs in the Puccini score at just about every occurrence.

1. The Selection Tool should still be selected.

2. Click each accent in measure 4 of the Oboe staff and press Delete.

3. Choose the Smart Shape Tool .

4. Hold down S and double-click the eighth note on beat 2, measure 4 of the Oboe staff. A slur extends to the eighth note on beat 3.

5. Press the Esc key twice to return to the Selection Tool.

6. Click and drag a box around the four notes in measures 4-5 of the Oboe staff. (Smart-Find requires a note at the beginning of the selection.)

7. From the Edit menu, choose SmartFind and Paint > Select SmartFind Source Region.

A black border appears around the selected notes, as shown in Figure 3.10. Now apply this newly articulated motif to other, similar figures in the score.

8. From the Edit menu, choose SmartFind and Paint > Apply SmartFind and Paint. The SmartFind and Paint dialog box appears.

9. Uncheck Smart Shapes and Expressions. Make sure Slurs, Articulations, and Delete Target Markings Before Paint are checked. The SmartFind and Paint dialog box should look like Figure 3.11.

10. Click Find. SmartFind locates and selects the first similar notes in measures 4-5 of the Piccolo staff.

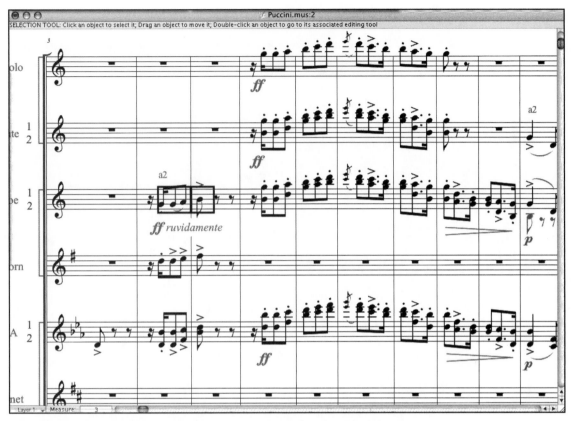

Figure 3.10   The SmartFind source region is indicated with a black border.

Figure 3.11   Uncheck elements that you do not want to alter/remove in the SmartFind and Paint dialog box.

11. Click Paint. Finale applies the markings from the source to the Piccolo region and selects the next identical rhythmic passage. See Figure 3.12.

12. Click Find Next to move to the next passage without making changes. Or, click Paint All to automatically replace every find in the document.

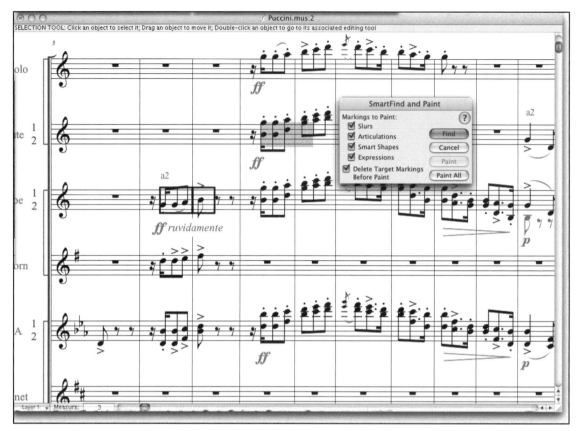

Figure 3.12   Click Find to navigate to the next similar passage and apply the new articulation.

I hope this section illustrates this utility's power. You could use this utility to apply any combination of slurs, articulations, and expressions to passages throughout a score.

Clearing, Copying, or Changing Specific Voices/Layers

Now that you know how to move specific markings, you will now learn how to edit specific notes. Scores, particularly keyboard pieces, are often composed using notes in multiple layers. You will likely need to clear, copy, or perform other operations (perhaps even SmartFind and Paint) to one layer, ignoring all the others. To do so, choose Show Active Layer Only from the Document menu. The following is an example.

To work with individual layers:

1.   Return to the Beethoven piece if it is still open. If not, from the File menu, choose Open, then navigate to Finale 2009/Sample Files, and open Beethoven.mus.

The notes in Layer 2 are red. Pretend you want to delete the triplets in measure 5. You can't just select the measure and press Delete, because you would delete all the notes.

2.   From the Document menu, choose Show Active Layer Only. Layer 2 disappears.

3.   Move to Layer 2 using the layer selection in the lower left of the document window. Layer 1 disappears and Layer 2 reappears. Although the menu item says *Show* Active Layer Only, it prevents you from making changes to other layers as well. See Figure 3.13.

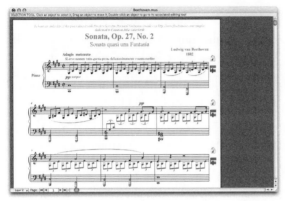

"Show Active Layer Only" Unchecked   "Show Active Layer Only" Checked (active layer = 2)

Figure 3.13   Use Show Active Layer Only under the Document menu when you need to clear, copy, or change layers independently.

4.   Select measure 5 in both staves and press Backspace (Clear) to remove the notes.

Tip: Select a stack and press Backspace (Clear) to clear the notes out of measure/s. Press Delete to remove the measure entirely.

---

5.   From the Document menu, uncheck Show Active Layer Only.

Tip: You will learn more about copying and moving layers around in Chapter 6, "Arranging and Rearranging."

Copying Tricks

The content in this chapter describes the general types of copy-and-paste operations common to most projects. Of course, copying, pasting, and inserting have multitudes of other uses.

Here are some tricks:

■   To change the instrumentation, create a new document with the Setup Wizard and copy material from another score into it. When you do this, be sure to copy the full stack to bring along the time- and key-signature changes (and other measure settings). You will learn more about this in Chapter 5, "Managing Your Instrumentalists."

■ Use a scratch document to store musical ideas, and copy between the two for convenient access to recurring material. This allows you to view the examples and crop the selections to size (unlike clip files).

■ Although it requires a perusal of the Finale user manual, you might consider trying to use Finale's Mirror Tool. This tool allows you to create duplicate measures that are dynamically linked to a source measure. Notes moved in the source also move in every mirrored measure.

■ Replace or merge notes from one region to another (within the viewable area) with the NoteMover Tool. See "NoteMover" in the Finale user manual for details.

■ Copy MIDI data with the MIDI Tool. (Choose the MIDI Tool, go to the MIDI menu, and choose Dragging Copies MIDI Data.) See "MIDI" in the Finale user manual for details.

4 Listen

Before Finale's sonoric revolution, countless phone calls to MakeMusic technical support revolved around the subject of playback. The main question being, "How do I make it sound pretty?" An honest response? "Find a good ensemble." Somehow users couldn't appreciate the unique tinny timbre of the Microsoft Wavetable Synth or the Macintosh internal speaker.

In the early years, an expensive sound module was really the key to quality playback from Finale. Then, the SmartMusic SoftSynth SoundFont and Human Playback ushered in the first wave leading to what you could consider a somewhat realistic synthesized performance.

Then, in the last few versions, an arsenal of new features was hauled onto Finale's deck. Playback now benefits from a world-class collection of Garritan sound samples courtesy of Gary Garritan. And, it performs as a live performer would, interpreting the score according to your chosen style courtesy of Human Playback by the maestro, Robert Piéchaud. You will find other features that satisfy most requirements for playback, including the ability to "conduct" tempo changes and even add a vocal line (by adding an audio file).

Of course, remember that Finale is primarily a notation utility, and if you don't need the sheet music, it can't compete with the robust features of a dedicated pro audio sequencer. In this chapter, you will learn the most applicable auditioning tricks useful to composers and, yes, how to make it sound pretty. Well, I guess no one can guarantee that, but I can certainly describe the bounty of possibilities.

Here's a summary of what you will learn in this chapter:

- How to make the most of Finale's auditioning capabilities
- How to make your music sound pretty

Auditioning Your Score

As I've mentioned before, a composer's ears are a very valuable asset. Being able to audition your composition in progress is just one of the many advantages of composing at a computer. While purists might consider this a crutch, even the most veteran composer can benefit from listening for subtle errors in a dense score rather than carefully analyzing every note visually. I prefer to use every tool at my disposal to review all aspects of the score throughout the creation process, and this includes Finale's robust set of auditioning capabilities.

To experiment with these capabilities, prepare a sandbox:

1. Open the file Bach.mus in the Finale 2009/Sample Files folder. If you do not see a Sample Files folder, visit www.composingwithfinale.com to download the sample files.

2. Press Ctrl+E (Command+E) to move to Scroll View. I usually recommend Scroll View rather than Studio View because when you are getting your hands dirty, it's really nice to see as much on the screen as possible at a reasonable view percentage and benefit from Staff Sets and Bookmarks.

3. From the MIDI/Audio menu, make sure Play Finale through MIDI is checked. This file is set up to use Finale's General MIDI SmartMusic SoftSynth SoundFont for playback.

4. If you don't see the Playback Controls on your screen, from the Window menu, check Playback Controls.

You should now be ready. Click the play button in the Playback Controls to make sure you hear something. If not, be sure the volume is up. Windows users, if you still don't hear anything, from the MIDI/Audio menu, choose Reload MIDI Driver.

You are using the MIDI SmartMusic SoftSynth playback device to demonstrate the basics because it takes less memory than the Garritan sounds. I recommend always using SoftSynth while composing for this reason. (Reserve the Garritan sounds for when they are practical—when wowing your commissioners and/or audiences.)

Starting Playback Whenever

Perhaps the universal requirement for any project is the ability to begin playback at any desired measure. You can do this several ways, but you want to familiarize yourself with the quicker and more transparent methods. The steps are different for each platform.

Starting Playback on a Macintosh

Mac users can start playback this way:

1. Click the arrow in the lower-left corner of the Playback Controls to show the additional options.

2.   Under Playback Region, choose Leftmost Measure. This option, shown in Figure 4.1, refers to the left-most visible measure of the score.

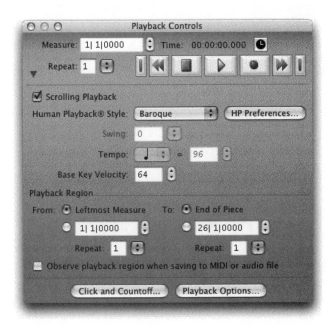

Figure 4.1   Choose Leftmost Measure to tell Finale to begin playback at the left-most visible measure.

3.   Press the spacebar. Listen to the first two measures, then press the spacebar again. You just paused playback (as if you had pressed the pause button in the Playback Controls). Finale continues where you left off when you start playback again.

4.   Position your cursor over the square stop button on the Playback Controls. Press the spacebar again. This time, let the green scrollbar advance past the right side of the screen, advancing to the next set of measures.

5.   Click the stop button when you reach about measure 7. (The left-most measure might now be measure 4 or 5.)

Click the stop button to cease playback if you want to begin playback next time at the left-most visible measure, rather than where you left off; see Figure 4.2. This is my preference and I recommend it. By pressing Shift and using my mouse's scroll wheel (to scroll horizontally), I can easily navigate to any measure quickly. Then, by clicking the stop button rather than pressing the spacebar, I know playback will start at the left-most measure next time (rather than some point off screen where I previously paused).

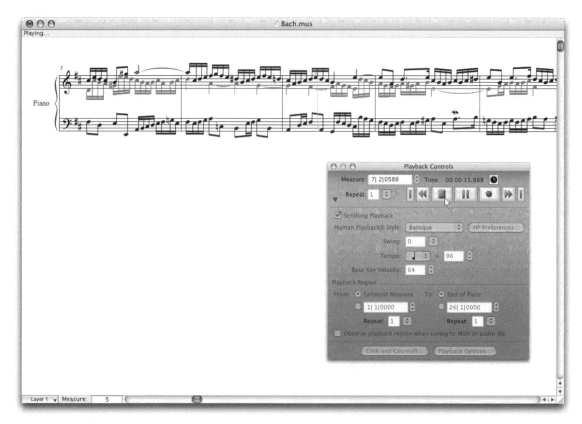

Figure 4.2 Click the stop button (instead of pausing) if you always want to begin listening at the left-most measure.

Starting Playback on Windows

Windows users can start playback this way:

1.   Hold down the spacebar to display the ear cursor shown in Figure 4.3.

Figure 4.3 Press the spacebar to display the ear cursor and click the measure you would like to play.

2.   Click the measure you would like to play.

3.   Click the score to stop playback.

Being able to immediately click any measure to begin playback, then click anywhere to stop (rather than having to click the stop button), is an advantage of playback with Windows over Macintosh. But, trading off the Mac's horizontal scroll capability in Scroll View (Shift plus the mouse scroll wheel) makes platform a matter of personal preference.

Listening to Specific Staves

Finale allows you to easily isolate specific staves for playback, both for audio spot-checking (scrubbing, which we'll cover soon), and in real time, covered here.

Listening to a Specific Staff on a Macintosh

You can audition a specific staff on a Mac with these steps:

1.   Hold down Shift+spacebar and click the top staff. Finale plays the top staff, in time, but without a scroll bar. The display does not advance along with the music, so you soon cannot see what Finale is playing.

2.   Click anywhere to stop playback.

This method is great for auditioning short, specific regions of (for example) instrumental parts.

Listening to a Specific Staff on Windows

You can audition a specific staff in Windows with these steps:

1.   Hold down Shift+spacebar and click the top staff. Finale plays the top staff, in time, and with a scroll bar (as long as Scrolling Playback is checked in the Playback Settings dialog box).

2.   Click anywhere to stop playback.

This method (as on the Macintosh) is great for auditioning short, specific regions of, for example, instrumental parts. But, since the scroll bar is available, you could review the entire contents of a staff using this method.

Audio Spot-Checking

If you really want supreme control over playback of every last note in your score, you may become addicted to **audio spot-checking**. This technique allows you to wave your cursor over a section of music and scrub to hear the harmonies of the full score or a specific staff at your own pace (instead of in real time at the prescribed tempo). For this reason, it is sometimes called **scrubbing** playback.

Let's explore a larger score to confront the benefits of audio spot-checking. If you haven't closed the Puccini.mus file, choose it from the Window menu. If it isn't already open, choose Open from the File menu, navigate to Finale 2009/Sample Files, and open Puccini.mus (also available at www.composingwithfinale.com).

Audio Spot-Checking on a Macintosh

Mac users, spot-check like this:

1. Hold down Option+spacebar to display the speaker icon.

2. Drag over the music. As you scrub, Finale plays the music aligned with your mouse cursor.

3. Add Shift (Shift+Option+spacebar) and drag over a staff to isolate the staff for audio spot-checking.

I usually place my ring finger on Option, my index finger on the spacebar, and then alternate between a single staff and the full score by pressing Shift with my pinky.

Audio Spot-Checking on Windows

Windows users, spot-check like this:

1. Hold down Ctrl+spacebar to display the ear icon.

2. Drag over the music. As you scrub, Finale plays the music aligned with your mouse cursor.

3. Add Shift (Shift+Ctrl+spacebar) and drag over a staff to isolate the staff for audio spot-checking.

On Windows, I usually place my ring finger on Ctrl, my index finger on the spacebar, and then alternate between a single staff and the full score by pressing Shift with my pinky.

Caution: Audio spot-checking on Windows sometimes wreaks havoc with the MIDI driver. When Finale goes silent while audio spot-checking, from the MIDI/Audio menu, choose Reload MIDI Driver. That should fix it.

Making It Sound Pretty

As you compose, you will probably use the procedures explained so far in this chapter to quickly audition your music as part of the composition process. However, a composer's job is not always done when the notation is complete. A suitable audio performance is sometimes required for demonstration purposes (if you don't have access to a full concert band, etc). And, even if you do, you might be anxious to produce a relatively close representation of what it's going to sound like before the world premiere.

Just as your score's appearance will always benefit from the expert skills of a qualified engraver, the audio will always benefit from the expert skills of a qualified digital audio specialist. In this section, I will describe some practical methods for making your score sound great without dilly dallying with every key velocity setting in the MIDI Tool window. I may sound like a broken record, but if you are specializing in composing, the key is to spend little time dealing with the peripherals and focus on the task at hand. Still, with any luck, a few tricks can result in a startlingly polished digital performance, whether you want it to sound pretty, powerful, pleasantly pitiful, or ponderous.

Using Garritan Sounds

Finale's included Garritan sounds are professionally sampled recordings of live instrumentalists, remastered and optimized for MIDI sequencing. Back when Garritan first became available with Finale, I remember applying the new sounds to all of my compositions. It was pure bliss! Here are some methods to make using Garritan sounds easy. (This is just the frosting on the cake. For complete information, see the Finale 2009 user manual.)

Note: The system requirements for Garritan are higher than for Finale proper. 1 GB of memory is recommended, but more is better.

Whenever you would like to play using the Garritan sounds, go to the MIDI/Audio menu and ensure that Play Finale through VST (Play Finale through Audio Units) is checked.

Adding Garritan Staves with the Setup Wizard

When you start a score with the Setup Wizard and choose Garritan instruments, Finale automatically assigns the appropriate VST (AU) instruments to the generated Finale staves. You can either choose a Garritan ensemble on the first screen or select the Garritan Instruments for Finale option on the second screen; see Figure 4.4.

The Garritan instruments are also available when you add new staves to existing documents with the Staff Tool using the Staff > New Staves (with Setup Wizard) option.

Applying Garritan Sounds to Existing Staves

You could use the included Aria Player to manually assign different Garritan sounds to the appropriate channels. But, there is a faster way: Start a new document with the Setup Wizard, adding the appropriate Garritan staves, and then copy and insert it into the new document. By doing this, you sort of tear off a different version of the file for playback purposes, which is a common practice anyway.

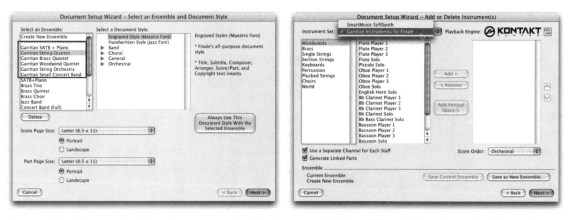

Figure 4.4 Choose Garritan instruments in the Document Setup Wizard to automatically configure staves for playback using the Garritan sounds.

1. From the File menu, choose Save As. Type SCRATCH or something that indicates this is a temporary document. You do not want to take any risks with your precious creation.

2. From the File menu, choose New > Document with Setup Wizard.

3. Choose the desired Garritan instruments on screen 2. Make sure they are in the exact same order as your original document. When you finish the Wizard, Finale opens the new document and loads the desired Garritan instruments.

4. From the Window menu, choose your SCRATCH document.

5. Press Ctrl+A (Command+A) to select all.

6. Press Ctrl+C (Command+C) to copy.

7. From the Window menu, choose your new document.

8. Press Ctrl+A (Command+A) to select all.

9. From the Edit menu, choose Insert.

When you play back the score, Finale uses the Garritan sounds. When you copy, Finale includes all the measure information including key signatures, time signatures, and so on. You will probably want to navigate to the end of the file and delete the extra measures.

Using Human Playback

Human Playback is another way Finale makes your music sound pretty automatically. Earlier you may have noticed a progress bar appearing before playback. This was Human Playback processing the score, applying temporary MIDI data to generate a nuanced, realistic performance. Human Playback's interpretation of your music depends on the style setting selected in the Playback Settings (Playback Controls) dialog box. You can choose a variety of styles including Baroque, Romantic, Jazz, or 21st Century, and Human Playback performs your score accordingly.

You can tweak Human Playback (HP) in an overwhelming number of ways to accommodate integration with custom MIDI data or other specifications. However, if you want to focus on your composition, you should know about two primary capabilities.

Applying Human Playback to the Entire Score

By default, Finale applies the Standard Human Playback style to all new scores. You can change to a different style or turn Human Playback off altogether if you want to. To do so, choose Human Playback from the MIDI/Audio menu and select the desired style from the submenu. See Figure 4.5.

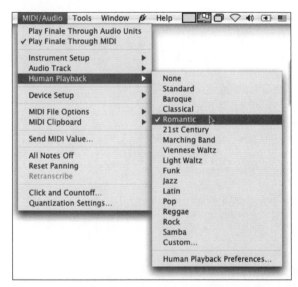

Figure 4.5   Change the Human Playback style directly from the MIDI/Audio menu.

Human Playback Preferences

To incorporate your own custom MIDI data into Human Playback's interpretation, specify techniques and effects for specific sound sample libraries, or tweak other aspects of the performance, you can do so in the Human Playback Preferences dialog box. To access these settings, from the MIDI/Audio menu, choose Human Playback > Human Playback Preferences. See Figure 4.6.

Tip: To create your own custom Human Playback style, from the MIDI/Audio menu, choose Human Playback > Custom.

Figure 4.6 The Human Playback Preferences dialog box allows you to tweak Human Playback's interpretation and tweak techniques to accommodate sound sample libraries.

Applying Human Playback to Parts of the Score

What if your score requires Standard Human Playback in one section, and Jazz Human Playback in another? Use the Apply Human Playback plug-in.

1. From the MIDI/Audio menu, choose Human Playback > None. Since this plug-in actually adds MIDI data to your score, HP needs to be set to None. (If you choose any HP style in the Playback Settings [Playback Controls], all existing MIDI data entered manually is ignored in favor of HP's interpretation during playback.)

2. Press Esc a couple times to choose the Selection Tool.

3. Select a region of measures containing the music you want to set to a particular Human Playback style.

4.   From the Plug-ins menu, choose Playback > Apply Human Playback. The Apply Human Playback dialog box appears, as shown in Figure 4.7.

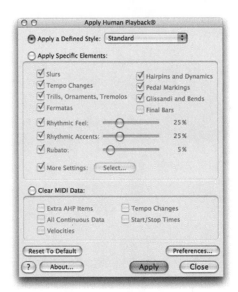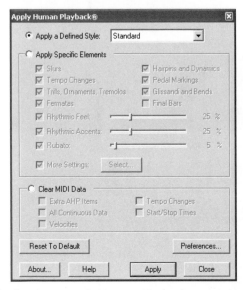

Figure 4.7   Use the Apply Human Playback plug-in to apply Human Playback to portions of your score.

5.   Choose an HP style or select Apply Specific Elements to specify which items you want HP to incorporate or ignore. Select Clear MIDI Data to specify types of existing MIDI data to clear from the selected region.

6.   Click Apply to apply these settings to the selected region.

7.   Click the play button in the Playback Controls. Repeat steps 5–9 for additional regions that require a Human Playback style.

Note: The Apply Human Playback plug-in includes its own set of Human Playback preferences. In the Apply Human Playback dialog box, click Preferences to open the plug-in's own Human Playback Preferences dialog box.

The Mixer

If you want to view all of the nifty Playback Controls available in Studio View, but work with your score in Page View or Scroll View, open the Mixer (see Figure 4.8). The controls in the Mixer are the same (and dynamically linked) to the staff controls of Studio View (as well as the settings in the Instrument List). They include volume, panning, mute, solo, and instrument sound settings.

Figure 4.8 Use the Mixer to adjust playback settings such as volume in Page or Scroll View (as an alternative to the staff controls of Studio View).

To open the Mixer, from the Window menu, choose Mixer.

"Conducting" Tempo Changes

Yes, Finale allows you to conduct your own tempo changes, using the spacebar as your baton. So your office chair isn't quite a podium and your studio isn't quite Carnegie Hall? So what! You can still rule over every last detail of your tempo using TempoTap.

1. Click the HyperScribe Tool ![icon].

2. From the View menu, choose Studio View. The TempoTap staff appears above the instrument staves, as shown in Figure 4.9.

3. In the TempoTap staff, click the measure you would like to begin conducting. A green cursor appears to the left of the selected measure.

4. Tap the tempo on the spacebar or any note on your MIDI keyboard.

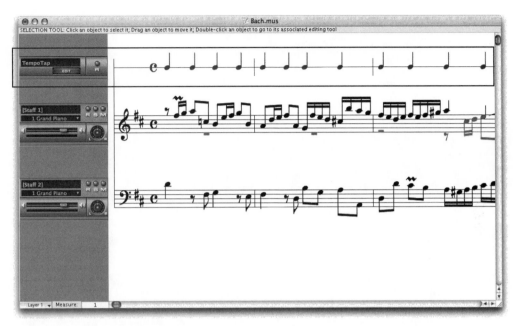

Figure 4.9 The TempoTap staff appears above the top staff in Studio View.

5. When you are done, click the score with your mouse. The Last Recorded Tempo dialog box appears, as shown in Figure 4.10.

Figure 4.10 After a TempoTap session, Finale displays the tempo reached by its conclusion.

6. Click OK. Your tempo changes have been applied to the score. Repeat these steps if necessary. The Last Recorded Tempo value applies to the subsequent measures until it reaches additional tempo-change data.

5 Managing Your Instrumentalists

If only I could really tell you how to do that. Perhaps I might suggest not writing for violists, or tubists...certainly not trombonists! But elitist or unruly behavior aside, practical solutions other than alcoholic beverages can temper the inevitable psychological turmoil. Ensuring the proper transposition, clef, and notation style is a good start, not to mention a playable range and less-than-notey page turns.

But, by *instrumentalists,* I am also referring to the staves in your Finale document, which are slightly more predictable. Yes, composing with Finale means setting up your staves properly, considering the score order, grouping, and individual staff attributes. Accomplishing these tasks with as little effort as possible is important because if you are lucky enough for some virtuoso like Pamelia Kurstin to swing by for a surprise appearance, you don't need Finale getting in the way as you introduce your theremin staff.

In fact, no aspect of the general score framework need ever get in the way. And, being one of the formulaic aspects of music notation, there are specific ways to handle these issues in Finale. So, while no single method could ever completely abolish the many distracting and unholy usages of a spit valve, we might somehow take comfort in Finale's relatively amiable attitude toward your instrumentation decisions.

Here's a summary of what you will learn in this chapter:

- Assembling the ranks (setting up new scores)
- Micromanaging (working with parts)
- Macromanaging (instrumentation tricks)

Assembling the Ranks

Preparing your musical canvas can be very easy in Finale. So easy, in fact, we needn't waste too many trees on it. The Document Setup Wizard is already described in the Finale help files, as well as in every third-party Finale resource of which I am aware. Ironically, it is perhaps the only part of Finale that is so extraordinarily intuitive that any basic description seems to contradict its reason for being—to make score setup really, really, easy.

In this section, I want to treat the Setup Wizard like a mechanic treats a golf cart on the back nine. Let's reach under the hood and disable the governor so we can get it moving over 10 mph.

Creating Custom Ensembles

If you write for a particular ensemble, such as your flute septet or your uniquely orchestrated high-school band, tell Finale about it to help make things speedier whenever you start a new project.

1. From the File menu, choose New > Document with Setup Wizard. If you see an ensemble on the left that is similar to yours, select it.

2. Click Next. The Add or Delete Instruments page appears.

3. Add, delete, and/or reorder the instruments. I've set up an ensemble resembling a typical high-school band.

4. Click Save as New Ensemble to open the Save Ensemble dialog box.

5. Type the name of the ensemble (for example, "Fourth period band") and click OK. See Figure 5.1.

6. Next time you use the Setup Wizard, your ensemble option appears at the bottom of the Select an Ensemble list. See Figure 5.2.

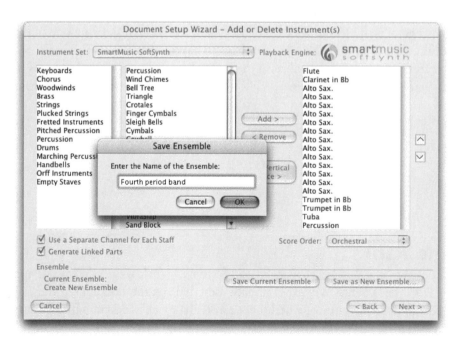

Figure 5.1 Define ensembles in the Setup Wizard to quickly begin new compositions uniquely tailored to your preferred instrumentation.

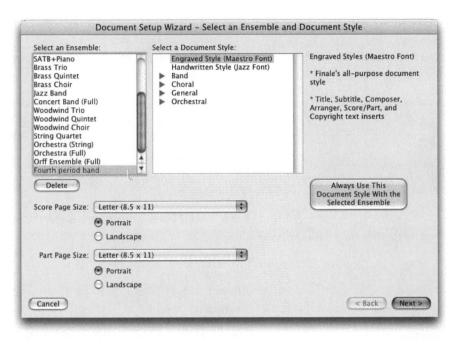

Figure 5.2 Choose your custom ensemble on the first screen of the Setup Wizard.

Ensembles are deceptively easy to comprehend. They are actually more powerful than you might think because you can combine them with a neat package of libraries, metatools, and document settings, also known as a Document Styles.

Super Templates: Document Styles

There is no sense reinventing the wheel, or even bothering to change wheels when the one you have already works beautifully. While defining a custom ensemble allows you to reuse the same instrumentation again and again, Document Styles allow you to reuse, well, just about everything else, including

- Metatools (!)

- Libraries (articulation and expression definitions)

- All document settings

You can transfer libraries and document settings between documents already in progress (by saving and loading a library via the File menu), so including them in your new documents is a matter of convenience. But, you *cannot* transfer metatools between documents. If you want to use all of your cleverly defined keyboard shortcuts to change tools and enter markings, save that document (or any document with the desired metatool assignments) as a Document Style.

To save a file as a Document Style, simply save it to the Finale/Document Styles folder (no need to delete the music). Then, when you begin a new document, choose it on the first screen of the Setup Wizard.

To demonstrate the power of Document Styles, create one from a document in progress:

1. From the File menu, choose Open. Navigate to the Finale/Sample Files folder and open Beethoven.mus. Now assign a tool metatool and an articulation metatool.

2. Select the Articulation Tool ⬛. Press Shift+F4. Laptop users, also press the Fn key when assigning metatools to the F keys. (Press Option+Ctrl+F, choose the Articulation Tool, and click OK.)

3. Press F4 (Ctrl+F) to choose the Articulation Tool.

4. Press Shift +Z to open the Articulation Selection dialog box.

5. Double-click ⬛ to return to the score. Hold down Z and click a note to ensure the ⬛ appears. Now save the file as a Document Style.

6. From the File menu, choose Save As, and go to the Finale/Document Styles folder.

7. Windows users, from the Save as Type drop-down menu, choose Finale Template File (*.ftm). Macintosh users will save the file as a standard .mus file.

8. Name the file Doc Styles Test and click Save. Now begin a high school–band score using these metatool assignments.

9. From the File menu, choose New > Document with Setup Wizard. The first screen of the Document Setup Wizard appears.

10. Choose the desired ensemble (Fourth period band, in this case), and then choose the Document Style you saved earlier, Doc Styles Test. See Figure 5.3.

11. Finish the Setup Wizard. You can leave the rest of the settings as is. The new document might take a moment to load.

12. Enter a couple notes.

13. Press F4 (Ctrl+F) to select the Articulation Tool.

14. Press Z key and click one of the notes you entered. A ⬛ appears.

Long-of-tooth Finale users may ask, "But can't I just define and save my desired metatools and libraries in my default file or my favorite template?" Good question. Yes, you can, but as you work on projects, you may decide to change your workflow, define new metatools, or alter document settings. Besides, you might want to apply them to a different ensemble. You don't need to spend valuable time constantly editing the default file (or template) to meet your needs. If you're lost, don't worry; I will cover saving your own custom default files and templates soon.

I am covering Document Styles first because they are versatile and I want you to feel comfortable saving and using them. They allow new documents to remain up to date with your work habits as your unique Finale technique matures. Besides, you can save any number of Document Styles

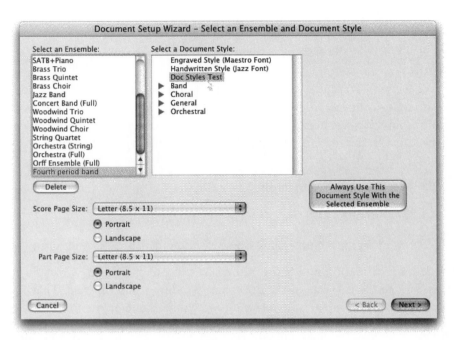

Figure 5.3 Mix and match any document style with any ensemble on the first screen of the Setup Wizard.

definitions, so you may eventually assemble a sprawling warehouse to choose from whenever you begin a project.

Templates

If you really don't need the customizability of Document Styles and instrumentation choices, you can always use a template. **Templates** are documents already configured for a particular instrument, ensemble, and/or style. When you open a template, Finale actually tears off a copy as an Untitled document, so the original template remains untouched and looks the same next time you open it.

Templates are great for composers who demand the exact same style, instrumentation, and page formatting all the time. For example, if you only write for Boomwhackers Percussion Tubes, you may never need to start any document using any device other than Finale's two Boomwhackers Percussion Tubes templates.

To open a template:

1. From the File menu, choose New > Document from Template.

2. Navigate to the desired template and double-click it to open it.

3. Complete the Score Information and Score Settings screens of the Setup Wizard.

Finale has some nice templates, including those you see in Figure 5.4.

Customizing Templates

A template you like will inevitably require some tweaking. If you are in the middle of your project and would like to reuse your metatools in future documents, why not save it as a Document Style? But, if your future projects need a specific type of page formatting and instrumentation, I recommend opening a fresh template, making the changes, and saving the file as a new template.

Let's open and customize one of Finale's templates:

1. From the File menu, choose New > Document from Template.

2. Open the Education folder and double-click Boomwhackers-R Tubes Grand Staff.

3. Complete the Score Information and Score Settings screens of the Setup Wizard. The template opens. Notice the title bar of the document window reads Untitled. That means this is a copy of the template; saving will not change the template itself.

4. Define metatools or choose the Page Layout Tool 🔲 and drag some systems around. (You can make any changes you want: add staves, define metatools, change the page layout.)

5. When you have made the desired changes, choose Save As from the File menu. (If you're working on a Mac, skip these steps and go to the following paragraph.)

6. From the Save as Type drop-down menu, choose Finale Template File (*.ftm).

7. Navigate to the Templates folder, name the file My Custom Template, and click Save. You can save templates in the Templates folder for convenience, or create a separate folder on your computer for templates. If you decide to create a separate templates folder, see "Assigning a Custom Templates Folder" later in this chapter.

Templates work a little bit differently on a Macintosh than on Windows. On a Macintosh, the act of choosing File > New > Document from Template indicates that the .mus file you choose will open as a new, untitled document.

To use your custom template on either platform, follow these steps:

1. From the File menu, choose New > Document from Template.

2. Double-click your My Custom Template file to open it.

3. Complete the Setup Wizard. Notice the file opens as a new Untitled document.

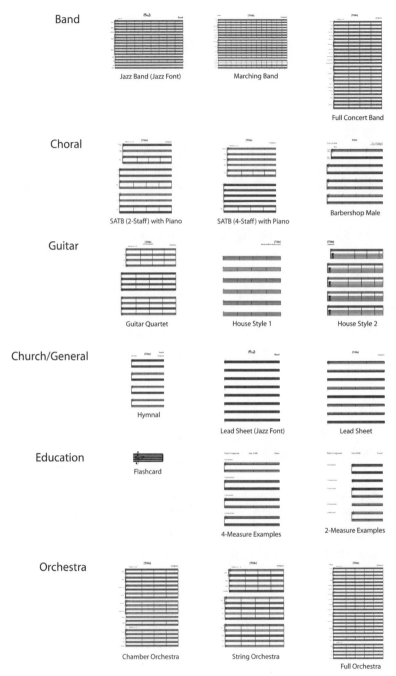

Band — Jazz Band (Jazz Font) — Marching Band — Full Concert Band

Choral — SATB (2-Staff) with Piano — SATB (4-Staff) with Piano — Barbershop Male

Guitar — Guitar Quartet — House Style 1 — House Style 2

Church/General — Hymnal — Lead Sheet (Jazz Font) — Lead Sheet

Education — Flashcard — 4-Measure Examples — 2-Measure Examples

Orchestra — Chamber Orchestra — String Orchestra — Full Orchestra

Figure 5.4 Finale includes many attractive templates. Wouldn't it be nice if you could preview them before you opened them? Here are a few.

Note: Remember, you can transfer all your custom expressions, articulations, chords, Smart Shapes, and even document settings across documents by saving and loading a library from the File menu. Your custom metatool assignments are the only major document attributes that are not transferrable.

Saving an Existing File as a Template

I brace for a flogging from my technical editor because this next topic is dangerous, but we are living on the edge here. If you already have a complicated network of specific articulation/expression definitions and metatools assigned in an existing document, save it as a Document Style or a template! But, delete all the extra stuff first.

1. From the File menu, choose Save As. Name the file Scratch and click Save.

2. Delete all the music.

3. Press Ctrl+A Backspace (Command+A Clear) and delete all the extra staves. (Shiver . . . be *sure* this is a scratch document.)

4. Now, save the file as a Document Style (to the Finale/Document Styles folder) or template (to the Finale/Templates folder. Begin new scores using this Document Style or template as you would normally.

Note: Do not—DO NOT—simply delete all the music in a score and begin composing a new project in the same document. Always save it as a Document Style or template and start fresh (without the unnecessary file residue).

Assigning a Custom Templates Folder

It is advisable to store all templates you use regularly outside the Finale folder in a special place. This way, when you upgrade, Finale will continue to identify your custom templates folder properly. To tell Finale to look to a specific folder for templates (other than the default Finale/Templates location), do the following:

1. Windows users, press Alt+E to open the Edit menu; then press G.

    Mac users, press Command+, (comma). The Program Options dialog box appears.

2. Choose Folders.

3. Next to Templates, click Browse (check Templates and click Select). Choose the desired folder and click OK (Choose). See Figure 5.5.

Figure 5.5 Use the Program Options to specify a custom templates folder.

Micromanaging

If your personality has a power-hungry, dictatorial, control-freak bent, you are perfectly positioned to utilize Finale to its fullest potential. You may be relieved to hear that it doesn't whine, protest, or file frivolous lawsuits. It will never strike, pull strings behind the scenes, or engage in all-out rebellion. As long as you stick to a few simple principles, no amount of abuse can possibly hurt Finale's feelings.

Of course, break one of these basic principles and Finale's personality may suddenly change. And when it does, you will curse the upturned nose of the Special Tools Tool 🔧, or shake your fist at the evil eye of the Articulation Tool 🎵. But, alas, the tools do not hear your screams. Finale was always just a combination of ones and zeroes, and it was only your composition that was touching and beautiful. You brought your creation into the world despite the cold arrangement of bits, not because of it.

We all compose with the same combination of ones and zeroes, and there is little reason to fear the incredible power that comes with it. How you employ your own tyrannical rule over Finale is up to you, but when the evil eye returns, it's nothing personal. You probably just didn't listen to something I said.

Let's talk about some of the inevitable instrumentation choices you will encounter and how to manage them appropriately, thus avoiding the wrath of the machine.

Adding, Removing, and Reordering Staves

Now you've done it. You've carefully chosen all your instruments in the Setup Wizard alongside your own custom Document Style, and now, not minutes after you began your project, you already need to add, delete, or reorder your staves. Unbelievable! Well, Finale figured as much, and fortunately there is something you can do about it.

To prepare for this section, do the following:

1. Open the file Mozart.mus in the Finale/Sample Files folder. (The sample files are also available at www.composingwithfinale.com.)

2. Choose the Page Layout Tool 🗋.

3. From the Page Layout menu, choose Optimize Staff Systems. The Staff System Optimization dialog box appears.

4. Choose Remove Staff System Optimization and click OK.

5. Press Ctrl+E (Command+E) to move to Scroll View.

Deleting a Staff

To delete a staff, do the following:

1. Select the Staff Tool 📊. Handles appear to the upper left of each staff; see Figure 5.6.

2. Click the Violin II staff handle (second from the top), and be sure no measures are selected. Measure selection trumps staff selection in this case. To select multiple staves, Shift+click additional handles.

3. Press the Delete key to delete and reposition (or right-click [Ctrl+click] a handle and choose Delete). Alternatively, press Shift+Delete to kill the staff without repositioning (or right-click [Ctrl+click] a handle and choose Delete).

Select the Staff

Delete

Delete and Reposition

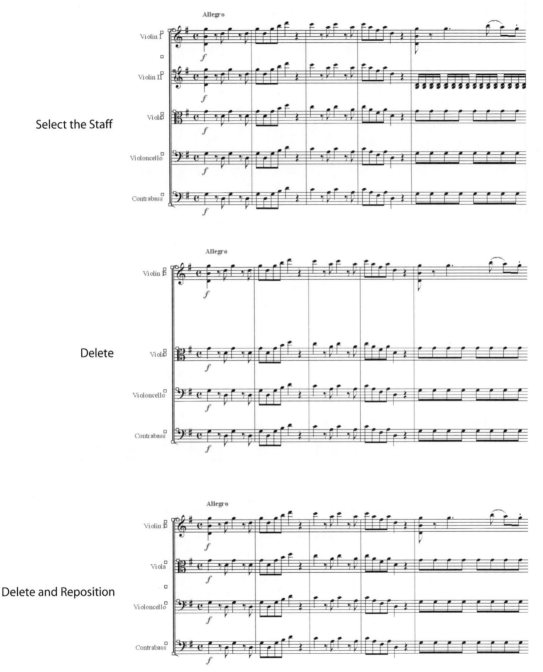

Figure 5.6   Use the Delete or Delete and Reposition commands to delete staves.

Inserting a New Staff

If Mozart were alive today, he might decide his former works could use some additional rhythmic development. Let's add some Roto Toms to our current document.

1. Select the Staff Tool .

2. Click the handle of the Contrabass (bottom-most) staff. The inserted staff always appears above the one you select. If no staves are selected, the inserted staves appear at the bottom of the score.

3. From the Staff menu, choose New Staves (with Setup Wizard).

4. Choose the Marching Percussion category and then double-click Roto Toms.

5. Click Finish. The Roto Toms staff appears above the Contrabass staff, as shown in Figure 5.7.

Figure 5.7 Use the New Staves (with Setup Wizard) command under the Staff menu to insert new staves.

Reordering Staves

The Roto Toms staff actually belongs at the bottom of the score, so let's move it there. Changing the order of staves in the score is one of those things you can easily do as long as you know what you're doing.

1.   Select the Staff Tool ▦.

2.   From the Staff menu, make sure Auto Sort Staves is checked.

3.   Click the handle on the Roto Toms staff and drag it below the Contrabass staff; see Figure 5.8. Don't worry about the exact spacing.

4.   From the Staff menu, choose Respace Staves to bring up the Respace Staves dialog box.

5.   Make any desired spacing changes and click OK.

Instrument Doubling

Now that you can add, remove, reorder, and respace instrument staves at will vertically, what happens when it's time for your versatile sax player to shred on her flute? Let's talk about how to switch instruments horizontally.

The basics are simple:

1.   Select the Staff Tool ▦.

2.   Select the region of measures destined to be performed by the alternate instrument.

3.   Right-click (Ctrl+click) the highlighted region, and choose the alternate instrument. (If you don't see it, skip to the set of steps that follow). You have just applied a Staff Style. A blue bar appears above the selected measures, indicating a Staff Style has been applied. See Figure 5.9.

You might be interested in doubling some strange instrument like English Horn. If the instrument you need is not in Finale's default list of Staff Styles, do the following:

1.   Select the Staff Tool ▦.

2.   From the Staff menu, choose Define Staff Styles. The Staff Styles dialog box appears.

3.   Click New.

4.   Click in the Available Styles text box and enter the name of the instrument.

5.   Assign the proper instrument transposition, clef, and other attributes here. If you are unsure of the specific staff settings, start the Document Setup Wizard and create a new document with the desired staff. Then, double-click the staff with the Staff Tool to open

Figure 5.8 Drag staff handles and then choose Respace Staves to reorder staves.

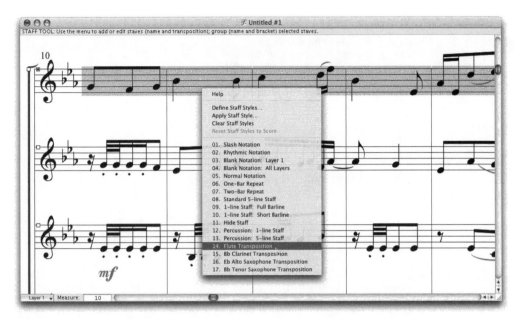

Figure 5.9 Apply a Staff Style to assign a region of measures to a different instrument.

the Staff Attributes dialog box. These settings are basically the same as those of the Staff Styles dialog box, and can be used as a reference. See Figure 5.10.

Tip: You can take a screenshot of the Staff Attributes dialog box to review it alongside the Staff Styles dialog box, as shown in Figure 5.10. To save a screenshot to the Desktop, press Alt+Print Screen, open Paint (or another graphics editor), and press Ctrl+V (Shift+Ctrl+4+ spacebar and click the dialog box).

---

6. When you have assigned the staff settings, click OK.

7. Select the region of measures destined to be performed by the alternate instrument.

8. Right-click (Ctrl+click) the highlighted region, and choose the alternate instrument to apply your new Staff Style.

To transfer existing Staff Styles between documents, save and load a Staff Style library (via the File menu).

Composing and Multiple-Part Staves

If you must make things as difficult as possible, your score will contain too many staves to fit on the page vertically. You can create multiple-part staves, like "Flutes 1 & 2," to fit all the staves

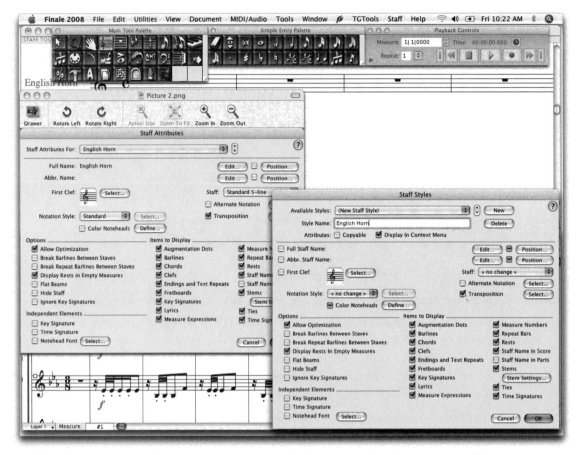

Figure 5.10 If you don't know the proper settings for a new Staff Style, add the staff to a new document with the Setup Wizard and use it as a reference.

on the page. If both flute parts play the exact same music, you haven't made things as difficult as possible, and can skip this section (and would combine the two flute parts anyway). But, since you are composing a piece that demands multiple lines on virtually every staff throughout, here is some advice:

- Consider composing on separate staves and combining them later. The distraction of dealing with the extra notation concerns may prove counterproductive to the creative process. See "Combining Parts" later in this chapter.

- Always use layers for multiple independent lines on a single staff. (Do not use the Voices feature of Speedy Entry unless you really know what you are doing. Layers are especially helpful if you intend to extract a multi-part staff into two separate parts later.

- To work with individual layers (especially copy/paste), from the Document menu, choose Show Active Layer Only.

- While using the caret in Simple Entry, you can begin entering a new layer at any point by using the change layer keyboard shortcuts: Alt+Shift+*layer* # (Command+Option+*layer* #).

- For specific standards regarding proper stemming, double stops, and other notation standards, refer to a good notation book. *Music Engraving Today* by Steven Powell or *Music Notation: A Manual of Modern Practice* by Gardner Read are both good resources.

Tip: You can use the Vertical Collision Remover plug-in to automatically respace staves to avoid collisions of notes and markings between staves. From the Plug-ins menu, choose Scoring and Arranging > Vertical Collision Remover.

Combining Parts

If you have already composed two similar parts into two separate staves and now wish to combine them into a multi-part staff, you must do so by copying and pasting; unfortunately, there isn't a clever utility that makes this automatic.

Splitting one multi-part staff into two separate staves can be done automatically using the TGTools Process Extracted Parts plug-in. But, it is more likely you composed into separate staves and are now interested in combining the content from two staves into a single staff for reasons of practicality (to fit all the staves on the page of the conductor's score, for instance).

We are going to isolate the two parts, identify passages that are not in unison, copy those passages into a different layer, and then copy across to the other staff.

1. From the File menu, choose Save As.

2. Name the file Scratch and click Save. Whenever attempting something like combining staves, it's always a good idea to create a sandbox in case disaster strikes. If everything works out, you can just as easily make it your working copy.

3. To isolate your two staves, you might create a Staff Set including just the two and then zoom in. (See Chapter 2, "Getting the Best Angle," for details.) I created a simple example in Figure 5.11. For this example, we merge the lower **source** staff into the upper **target** staff.

4. Pres Esc a couple times to choose the Selection Tool.

5. Click to the left of the source staff to highlight the entire staff.

6. From the Edit menu, choose Move/Copy Layers. The Move/Copy Layers dialog box appears, as shown in Figure 5.12.

Figure 5.11   Isolate the two staves you would like to combine using Staff Sets and then zoom in for easy viewing.

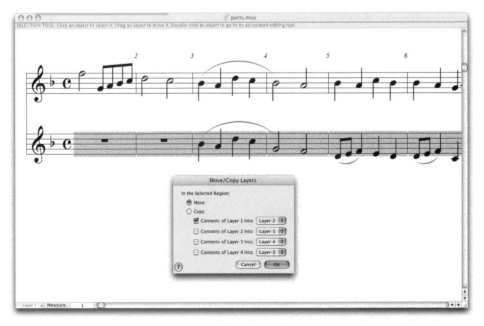

Figure 5.12   Select the entire source staff and use the Move/Copy Layers dialog box to move the content to Layer 2.

7. With the Move radio button selected, check Contents of Layer 1 Into Layer 2.

8. Click OK. All notes in the source staff are red, indicating they are now in Layer 2. Now, you need to combine the measures that are different, which is the case in measures 4-6.

9. Move to Layer 2 by choosing Layer 2 from the Layer Select buttons (drop-down menu) in the lower-left corner of the document window, or press the Layer 2 keyboard shortcut: Alt+Shift+2 (Command+Option+2).

10. From the Document menu, choose Show Active Layer Only. Notes in the target staff disappear. You must check this command for the source staff notes to be pasted without overwriting the notes in Layer 1.

11. Select the unique measures from the source staff (in this case measures 4-6) and drag them up to the target staff. See Figure 5.13.

12. From the Document menu, choose Show Active Layer Only. Notes in Layer 1 appear; see Figure 5.14.

13. When all of the desired music has been transferred into the target staff, you can delete the source staff using the Staff Tool.

Figure 5.13   Copy the unique content to the target staff with Show Active Layer Only selected.

Figure 5.14 Turn Show Active Layer Only off to display both voices.

Note: You can assign each voice in a multi-part staff to a separate linked part. See "Part Voicing" in the Finale user manual for details.

Play This, Don't Play That

Multi-part staves require you to specify which parts should play what music using specialized markings such as *a2*, *div.*, and the like. You need to add these as expressions, but Finale doesn't include these in the default expression library. Let's take this opportunity to add them ourselves:

1. Choose the Expression Tool ![icon].

2. Double-click where you want to add one of these markings. The Expression Selection dialog box opens.

3. Choose the Technique Text category and click the Create Technique Text button.

4. Type a2.

5. Click OK.

6. Select the a2 expression slot. Now, assign it to a metatool key.

7. Hold down Shift and type A. The a2 expression is now assigned to the A key.

8.   Click OK.

9.   Repeat steps 3-5 for other required markings like *solo* or *tutti*.

10.   Double click an expression to enter it into the score. To use the a2 expression, hold down A and click the score. To save time, assign all your frequently used expressions to metatools.

Range Checking

Being nice to your instrumentalists means handing them parts that they have a fighting chance of playing properly. Printing a score without checking the range is like printing a book without running spell check.

1.   From the Plug-ins 🖋 menu, choose Scoring and Arranging > Check Range. The Check Range dialog box appears, as shown in Figure 5.15.

Figure 5.15   Forgetting to check the range in a Finale document is like forgetting to run spell check in a word-processer document.

2.   Choose the desired skill level of your ensemble (Advanced, Intermediate, or Beginner) and click Check. If Finale finds any notes out of range, you see the Note Out of Range dialog box.

3.   If it finds an out-of-range note, Finale suggests a note within the appropriate range and gives you the option to change the notes automatically. Do not just run through and click change (obviously). Double-check to be sure the plug-in isn't reporting cue notes, which are likely to be out of range. Then, review Finale's suggested note to be sure it's in the desired octave.

Page Turns

If you aren't famous, there is a chance your performers aren't taking your original composition as seriously as you are. This is a very real and practical consideration for a maturing composer. If you found a nasty error on the first page of this book, I would expect you to second guess the second page. To prevent this, I have the benefit of an arsenal of editors who will scrutinize every word of this for spelling, grammar, and technical accuracy. You probably do not have that benefit. And, you are writing in a language far more complicated. So, it is extra important for your work to be completely free from all of the unnecessary mistakes that amateur composers make. One of those mistakes is overlooking page turns.

Fortunately, Finale makes this somewhat easy. But, it isn't compatible with Linked Parts, so make it one of the last things you do before printing the final version. (By the way, if you are famous, just have your engraver worry about the page turns.)

1. From the File menu, choose Extract Parts.

2. Check the part(s) you want to extract.

3. Leave Open Extracted Part checked to tell Finale to open the part automatically.

4. Click OK. The part opens.

5. From the Plug-ins 🖋 menu, choose Scoring and Arranging > Smart Page Turns. The Smart Page Turns dialog box appears, as shown in Figure 5.16. The default settings are usually okay. See the Finale user manual for details.

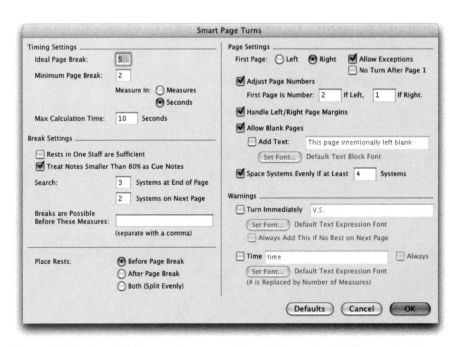

Figure 5.16 Acceptable page turns are extremely important. When reviewing your work, run the Smart Page Turns plug-in before you print.

6.   Click OK to begin analyzing the score.

7.   Review the results.

You can make additional changes to the measure layout by selecting measures and using the up and down arrows. And, you can make more detailed adjustments by reading and understanding the "Measure Layout," "Page Layout," and "Music Spacing" sections of the Finale user manual. Something as ubiquitous as "adjusting the whole music layout to accommodate page turns" is not always as easy as just running a plug-in, but this should give you a good start.

Macromanaging

If it's difficult to see the forest through the trees, Finale's forest is lush with impressive oaks, towering pines, and exotic palms. And, although all are suitable for climbing, sometimes it makes sense to take a step back and weigh the trouble of scaling to the top with the advantages of changing the forest altogether. Sometimes finding the low-hanging fruit requires actions that seem a bit dramatic, but some are really less risky than you might think.

The following are large-scale score-editing procedures dedicated to sidestepping the need to dig in and fiddle with the armada of specific staff settings. Just like your music sometimes requires you to step back and think about the big picture, when it comes to handling Finale, it always pays to consider changing the forest rather dealing with an uncooperative tree.

Note: It must be stressed: Before doing anything crazy, *always* save your document as a scratch copy.

A Brave New World

Don't be afraid to copy music across documents. In fact, you might even consider your music the core and your document interchangeable beneath it. Finale's Document Setup Wizard does such an excellent job of defining new instrument staves that transferring your music to a new document is often far easier than changing individual staff attributes. This is yet another reason to leave the page-layout concerns (which are not particularly transferrable) for last in the editing process.

I mentioned this technique in Chapter 4, "Listen," under "Applying Garritan Sounds to Existing Scores," but it is so incredibly useful that its practice warrants further discussion.

This technique is vital if you ever

- Scan a piece of music and need to apply the music to new, properly configured staves.

- Import a MIDI file and need to apply the music to new, properly configured staves.

- Import a MusicXML file and need to apply the music to new, properly configured staves.

- Import any other type of file and need to apply the music to new, properly configured staves.

- Want to overhaul the instrumentation of a document for any reason (for example, convert a brass quartet to a string quartet).

- Want to use metatools assigned in a different document or Document Style.

- Want to use instrument staves already configured for Garritan (VST/UA) playback.

- Want to use instrument staves already assigned to unique MIDI channels.

- Want to apply music to clean new instrument staves for any reason not listed here.

Let's practice by instantly applying the music from one of Finale's sample files to a completely new ensemble. Open the file Mozart.mus.

1. Press Ctrl+E (Command+E) to move to Scroll View. Notice the five staves. Let's apply this music to a new score setup as a brass quintet.

2. Go to the Edit menu. If Edit Filter is checked, uncheck it.

3. Choose the Selection Tool. Press Ctrl+A (Command+A) to select all.

4. Press Ctrl+C (Command+C) to copy. All the music is now copied to the clipboard.

5. From the File menu, choose New > Document with Setup Wizard. The first screen of the Document Setup Wizard appears.

6. Under Select an Ensemble, choose Garritan Brass Quintet. See Figure 5.17. We might as well use the Garritan sounds while we're at it.

7. Click Next, Next, Next, and Finish to complete the Setup Wizard. The new empty document appears and Finale loads the GPO sounds.

8. Press Ctrl+A (Command+A) to select all.

9. Press Ctrl+V (Command+V) or, from the Edit menu, choose Paste. The music appears. Now let's change the transposition slightly so it's in a possible range.

10. Right+click (Ctrl+click) a staff and choose Key Signature > Edit Key Signature. The Key Signature dialog box appears.

11. To the right of the preview window, click the down arrow four times to choose the key of E flat.

12. Under Transposition Options, for Transpose Notes, click the drop-down menu and choose Down.

13. Click OK. See Figure 5.18 and note the instrumentation. You probably want to also delete the extra measures at the end.

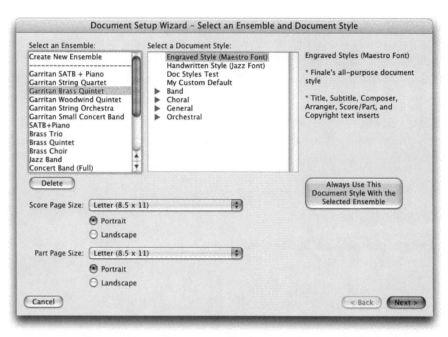

Figure 5.17 Set up new scores with the Setup Wizard to assign your new instrumentation.

Figure 5.18 Copy and paste music into a new document to easily update the instrumentation.

You have just instantly orchestrated this Mozart excerpt for brass quintet. Alright, so maybe it will need some tweaking (trumpets have difficulty with double stops), but you get the idea. This is a powerful technique with many possible implementations.

Note: Copying and pasting into a new document started with the Setup Wizard is always recommended whenever you import a scanned document.

The Ultimate Fake Book

Have a bunch of lead sheets to hand out but uncertain of the exact ensemble to prepare for (depending on who shows up)? You can prepare a lead sheet for instant access to a variety of different instrument transpositions using linked parts.

This kind of flexibility is nice for a lot of reasons. For example, you can change the key to accommodate a particular vocalist's range, then print out the parts before the rehearsal. This is also beneficial if you actually read off of your laptop monitor. "Alright, let's try it in B..." <sound of a couple buttons being pressed>, "3, and ...."

1. Open your lead sheet document.

2. Choose the Staff Tool ▦.

3. From the Staff menu, choose New Staves (with Setup Wizard). The Staff Setup Wizard appears.

4. Add the desired instruments and click Finish.

5. In the Edit menu, make sure Use Filter is unchecked.

6. Click to the left of the top staff (the one with music) to select the entire staff.

7. Press Ctrl+C (Command+C) to copy.

8. Click the first measure of the subsequent staff.

9. Press Ctrl+Alt+V (Ctrl+Command+V). The Paste Multiple dialog box appears.

10. After Paste Vertically, choose To the Bottom of the Score as shown in Figure 5.19. Then click OK.

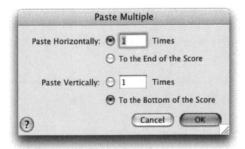

Figure 5.19 Paste vertically to the bottom of the score to populate all the instrument staves with the music.

11. From the Document menu, choose Manage Parts. The Manage Parts dialog box appears.

12. Click Generate Parts. Finale generates a part for each staff.

13.   Click OK. You return to the score. Notice any notes out of range. To transpose down an octave, select a staff and press 8. Press 9 to transpose up an octave. (Click to the left of a staff to select it through the last measure.)

14.   To navigate through the parts, press Ctrl+Alt+> (Command+Option+>).

15.   Print whatever parts you need depending on the ensemble de jour. You can also change the key on the spot to accommodate your new-found Russian throat singer.

Multiple Movements

If you need to append multiple movements of a score one after another, use the ScoreMerger utility shown in Figure 5.20. There is no alternative unless you have devoted your life to the study of Finale. Even then, it's never worth the effort. Even with ScoreMerger, be sure to ask, "Do I really need to do this?" If the answer is "Yes," go for it. Otherwise, go compose something.

To access ScoreMerger, from the File menu, choose ScoreMerger. For more information, click the Help button (? icon). Then, scroll to the bottom and click To Combine Files with ScoreMerger. The user manual describes this utility flawlessly.

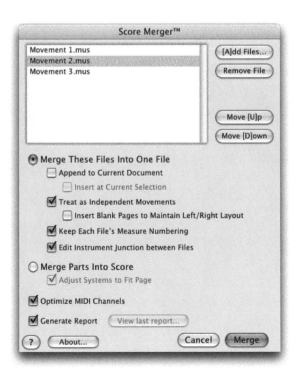

Figure 5.20 ScoreMerger makes combining files feasible—but only do this if you really need to.

6 Arranging and Rearranging

Most, if not all, composers are really arranging and rearranging all the time, adapting to the consequences of every new subtle nuance, epiphany, or agreeable accident. Maybe you nudge the coffee table in your living room ever so slightly whenever you walk by until it's just right. Or, perhaps you draft a complex diagram to reveal the perfect combination of aesthetics and utility around your new bronze Snoopy sculpture. Maybe it is ultimately decided that the sculpture stays, a new house shall be built around it, and the coffee table is best used for kindling. In other words, putting together the pieces—from a glimmer in the eye to the raising of the baton—is really what a composer does. What those pieces are, and the methods used, should be at the artist's discretion because they are actually all a part of the composition itself.

If the content of this chapter seems a bit light considering the title, it is. This whole book is about arranging and rearranging. On a personal note, I have often thought a good arranger is under-appreciated. I tend to think every unique innovation is an expression of one's self regardless of deceptive and unflattering terminology. As listeners, why dwell infinitely on what already exists when we could open ourselves to appreciate the wonderful uniqueness in even the slightest adaptations? After all, even every live performance is actually its own unique interpretation. But, on our side of the coin, as dedicated innovators, why rely on someone else's work unless we're sure it will inspire more than confine? If Einstein was right, and "the secret to creativity is knowing how to hide your sources," maybe the great arrangers just didn't get the memo. Or, maybe we underestimate those veiled, selfless artists who recognize when a composition is simply not finished.

But I digress. And now back to this innovation, which will certainly be unfinished at its printing and has been inspired by so many wonderful influences I hardly dare call it my own (that might be tough to get through).

Chapter 3, "Moving Stuff Around," and Chapter 5, "Managing Your Instrumentalists," relate directly to arranging techniques: copying music and instrumentation. In this chapter, we will discuss some of Finale's arranger utilities, so you don't work harder than you need to. If you need to move your two-ton antique davenport across the room, these are your ropes and pulleys.

Here's a summary of what you will learn in this chapter:

- Exploding and imploding
- Layers

Pyrotechnics and Finale: Exploding and Imploding

Scott Yoho, long-time MakeMusic middle manager (and rockin' lead singer and guitarist of The Auto Body Experience), would sometimes refer to the result of a nefarious bug as "glass shards flying from your computer screen." And, while this unfortunate behavior may resemble the sound of a disgruntled Finale user talking to a customer-support representative, I assure you I have never witnessed its literal manifestation.

Nonetheless, **exploding** is definitely an important function of Finale, and done in a controlled environment it presents little risk of permanent bodily harm. You will be using this feature to easily distribute stacks of chords into different staves. And, if you ever need the opposite, Finale also allows you to easily increase the staff density as well, **imploding** music from several staves into one.

In any case, both of these features are explosive in the sense that they are powerful and can save you plenty of time.

Exploding

Redistributing music to different staves is a very useful procedure. It basically allows you to separate stacks of notes from one staff into several staves as shown in Figure 6.1.

Notice the contents of the top staff before explosion. It has no layers and is composed completely of chords with ties joining the longer durations. For this example, I set the smallest note value to a quarter note in the quantization settings and then recorded in HyperScribe. I ignored the ties during my recording and added them manually after the fact. This type of homophonic, hymn-like music is a bundle of potential energy perfectly suited for explosion.

To explode the example in Figure 6.1, follow these steps:

1. Select the top staff.

2. From the Utilities menu, choose Explode Music. The Explode Music dialog box appears, as shown in Figure 6.2.

3. For this example, I chose Place Music Into Existing Staves, starting with the Trumpet 1 staff. Since all the music needed to go directly into the subsequent staves, this setting works wonderfully.

4. Click OK. The music is redistributed into a clean, playable arrangement for a brass quartet.

Maybe your creation isn't as perfectly suited for explosion as my example. For example, if your music is made of multiple voices (with completely independent rhythms, for instance), explosion

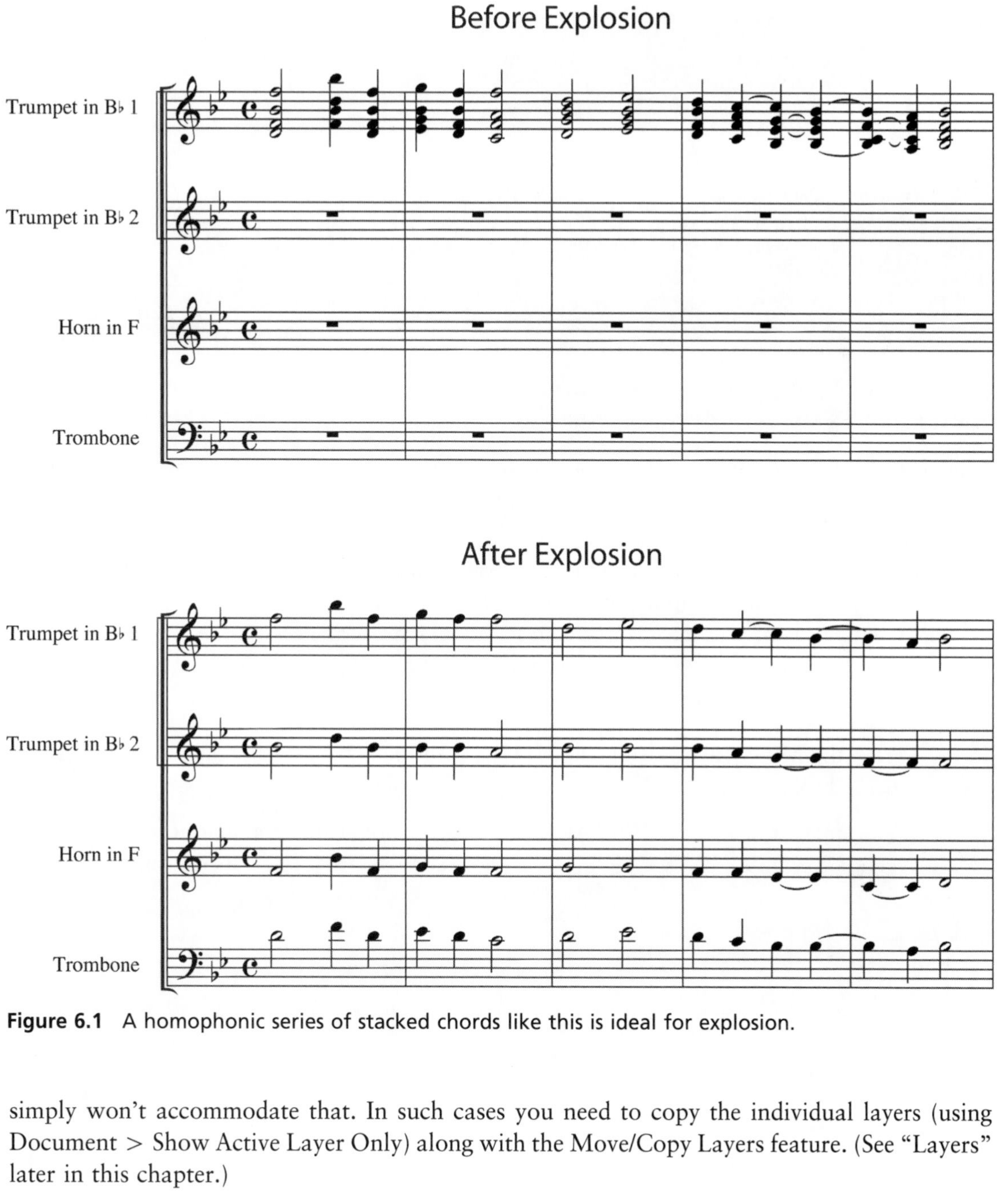

Before Explosion

After Explosion

Figure 6.1 A homophonic series of stacked chords like this is ideal for explosion.

simply won't accommodate that. In such cases you need to copy the individual layers (using Document > Show Active Layer Only) along with the Move/Copy Layers feature. (See "Layers" later in this chapter.)

However, our example does include some independent rhythms indicated with ties (see measures 4-5), which should be combined into half notes. Finale can accommodate this sort of thing easily, which I cover next.

Figure 6.2   The Explode Music dialog box allows you to choose how you want the notes distributed.

Retranscribing

If you are planning to enter or record into a single staff and then explode, you can add ties manually before or after exploding for longer durations, as I did in Figure 6.1. (Or, if your keyboard skills permit, you can record them in your HyperScribe session.) You should change those tied notes in measures 4-5 of the Trumpet 2 and Horn staves to half notes, and you can convert them automatically by retranscribing.

1. From the MIDI/Audio menu, choose Quantization Settings. The Quantization Settings dialog box appears.

2. Set a smallest note value. This example's smallest note value is a quarter note, so choose the quarter note icon; see Figure 6.3. These settings are just a general thing to check

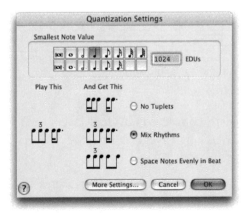

Figure 6.3   To combine common tied notes after entering and exploding, check the quantization settings to verify the smallest note value.

before retranscribing to make sure you don't convert a bunch of your carefully crafted sixteenth-note runs into quarter-note chunks.

3.   Click OK.

4.   Select the region.

5.   From the MIDI/Audio menu, choose Retranscribe. In our example, the tied quarter notes join into half notes, leaving the other music untouched. See Figure 6.4.

When you retranscribe to join tied notes, you may need to apply different quantization settings to different regions. For example, if your rhapsody suddenly changes meters and tempo, your smallest note value could easily change from an eighth note to a half note. In other words, just be careful that you don't make a habit of trusting the Retranscribe command (even if it does seem to always work properly with the default quantization settings).

Caution: Retranscribing deletes note-attached items like articulations and slurs.

Note: Before you retranscribe, check both the Quantization Settings dialog box and the More Quantization Settings dialog box to make sure the settings are correct. These include things like whether you want Finale to look for tuplets and allow dotted eighths in compound meters.

Exploding into Specific Staves

What if the target staves you want to explode to aren't directly beneath the source staff? What if they are distributed throughout your score, and not even in the right order? If this is the case, you could manually copy the results into the desired staves, but there is a much geekier way. Define a Staff Set that includes the target staves and then explode.

A Staff Set not only allows you to isolate target staves, but also allows you to explode to them in any order. Remember, the order of staves in a Staff Set is completely independent from regular (non-Staff Set) Scroll View and from Page or Studio View. This provides a nice sandbox to play in.

Let's take a woodwind quintet excerpt and explode it into discontiguous staves, and in an order different than the score order. See Figure 6.5.

Here's how it's done:

1.   Move to Scroll View and choose the Staff Tool 🎼.

2.   From the Staff menu, make sure Auto Sort Staves is checked.

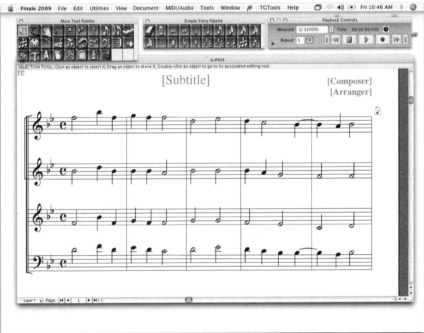

Figure 6.4 Retranscribe to apply the shortest duration specified in the Quantization Settings dialog box.

Before

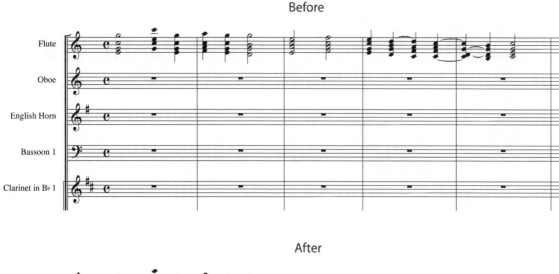

After

Figure 6.5 Use Staff Sets to explode into any staves and in any order. Here, I explode notes from the Flute staff into the Oboe, Clarinet, and Bassoon staves, in that order, and skip the English Horn staff.

3. Hold down Shift and select the handles of the desired target staves. For our example, select the Flute, Oboe, Bassoon, and Clarinet 1 staves, skipping the English Horn staff.

4. Hold down Ctrl, go to the View menu, and choose Program Staff Set > Staff Set 1. (Hold down Option, go to the View menu, and choose Program Staff Set > Staff Set 1.) See Figure 6.6. Finale displays the Staff Set and eliminates the other staves from view.

5. Use the staff handles to drag the staves into the desired order. For this example, the lowest note should go into the Bassoon staff, so drag the Bassoon below the Clarinet staff. See Figure 6.7.

6. Once the staves are in order, highlight the source staff.

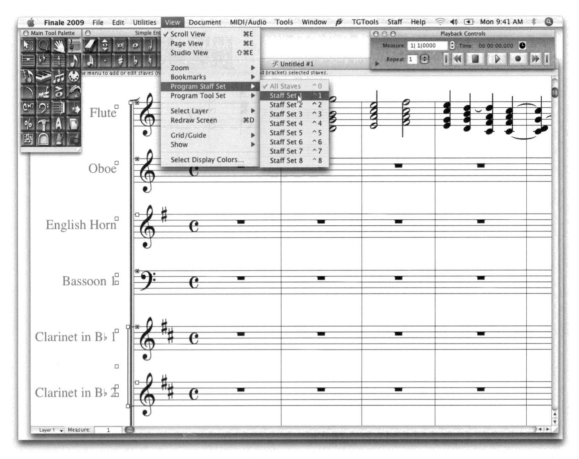

Figure 6.6   Create a Staff Set including the desired target staves.

7.   From the Utilities menu, choose Explode Music. For this example, I've configured the Explode Music dialog box as shown in Figure 6.8.

8.   Click OK to distribute the music into the subsequent staves; see Figure 6.9.

9.   Drag the Bassoon staff back to the desired position if you want. Exact positioning isn't important here, as it doesn't apply to any view other than this Staff Set.

10. From the View menu, choose Select Staff Set > All Staves. The full score reveals your results, as shown in Figure 6.10.

Now you can forget about the Staff Set, program a new one over it, or use it again if a different part of your score requires the same procedure. From the working score's perspective, Staff Sets can be kind of like productive dreams: You wake up and suddenly discover the solution to a nagging problem and aren't quite sure how you got there.

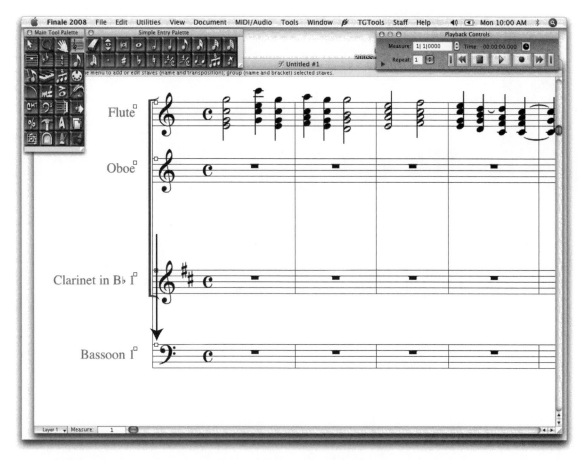

Figure 6.7 Rearrange your staves within a Staff Set to explode in any order.

Imploding

Imploding, as you can probably guess, is exploding in reverse. It allows you to combine music from multiple staves into one. However, unlike explosion, Finale implodes all visible layers, and overlapping note durations are truncated. It is possible to create a crowded mess of a staff if you aren't careful.

Let's implode the retranscribed results of our brass quartet to see what kind of results we get:

1. Select all measures you would like to implode. For our example, press Ctrl+A (Command+A) to select all.

2. From the Utilities menu, choose Implode Music. The Implode Music dialog box appears. For now, choose Top Staff of Selection to move everything into the Trumpet 1 staff. See Figure 6.11.

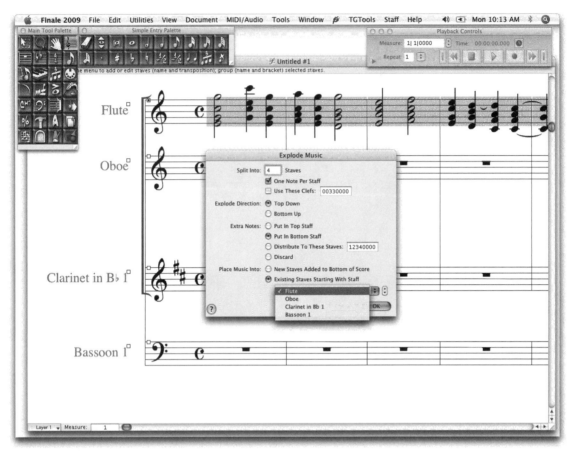

Figure 6.8 Choose the target staves in the Explode Music dialog box. Notice Finale recognizes the current staff order.

3. Click Quantization Settings to change the smallest note duration. Implode Music retranscribes automatically based on your quantization settings.

4. Click OK. Finale implodes all the music into the top staff of our selection. See Figure 6.12.

This example has only one layer, but if there were more, they would be included in the target staff. Notice Finale changes half notes in measure 5 to quarter notes. If you would like to mix rhythms in your implosion results, move the original material into a different layer. See "Layers" later in this chapter. (To ignore all layers other than the active one while imploding, from the Document menu, choose Show Active Layer Only.)

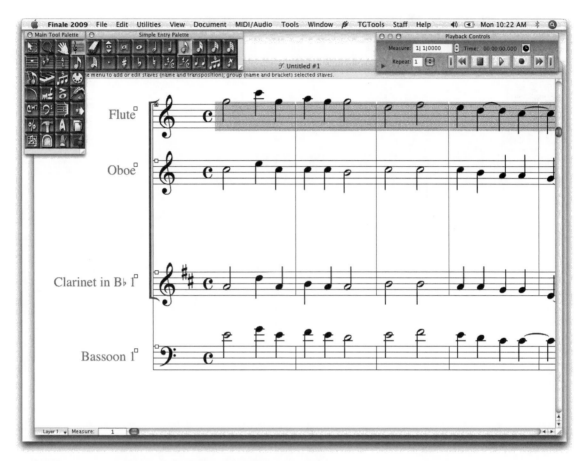

Figure 6.9 Finale explodes into the specified staff order.

You might think this would be great for piano reductions. While you can use it for that, try the Piano Reduction plug-in first.

Piano Reductions

Before you use Finale's robust copying and implosion functions to craft your piano reduction, just apply the plug-in. This is another one of those tools that can give you more time for composing.

From the File menu, choose Open and navigate to Finale's Sample Files folder. Open Tchaikovsky .mus (also available at www.composingwithfinale.com).

The results of the Piano Reduction plug-in depend on your quantization settings, so consider quantization prior to creating your piano reduction. An eighth-note duration is the obvious

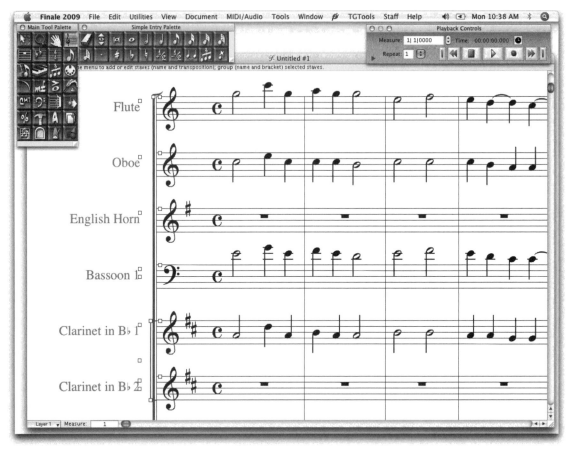

Figure 6.10 The full score staff spacing and order are completely autonomous from the Staff Set we've been working with.

choice for this piece, so in the following steps, you will select an eighth note for the smallest note value before applying the plug-in.

1. Press Ctrl+E (Command+E) for Scroll View and zoom to 125%.

2. From the MIDI/Audio menu, choose Quantization Settings to open the Quantization Settings dialog box.

3. For Smallest Note Value, select the eighth-note option ♪.

4. Click OK.

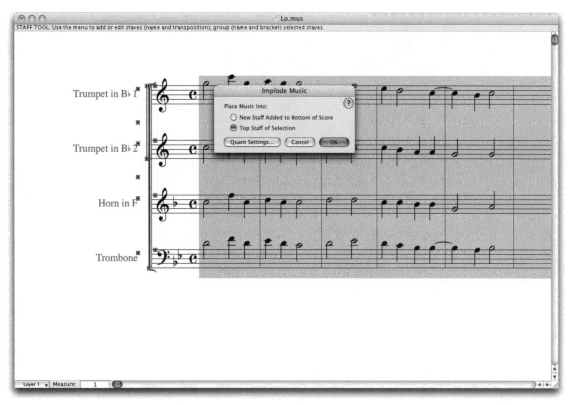

Figure 6.11 The Implode Music dialog box allows you to implode into the top staff or a new staff.

5.   From the Plug-in menu, choose Scoring and Arranging > Piano Reduction. The Piano Reduction plug-in appears, as shown in Figure 6.13.

6.   Ctrl+click (Command+click) to select the desired staves. For this example choose all of them.

7.   Click OK. Finale does some heavy processing and then generates your piano reduction below the bottom staff. Notice the extra dynamic markings in the first measure in Figure 6.14.

8.   Press Esc a couple times to choose the Selection Tool.

9.   Click the extra expressions and press Delete to remove them. You need to look through and tweak Finale's reduction, but the plug-in does a good job and is definitely the recommended way to create (or at least begin) piano reductions.

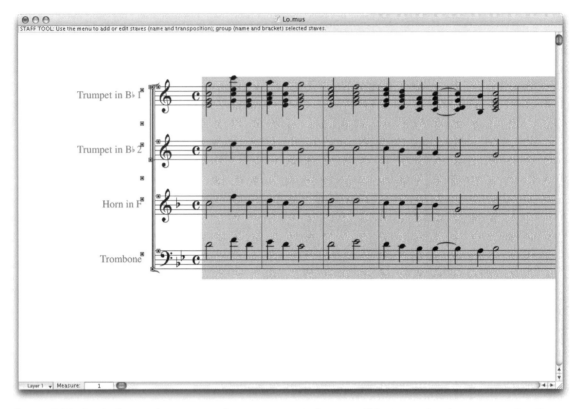

Figure 6.12 Implosion results accommodate as many attacks as possible, truncating longer note durations.

Layers

Each **layer** is a unique set of notes virtually independent of all the other layers (aside from a few positioning features and the like). Layer 1 is entirely sufficient for many types of scores. For example, a brass quintet seldom, if ever, requires a second layer because each instrument is monophonic and no more than one instrument appears on a staff.

Layers are common in keyboard music, SATB choral scores (see Figure 6.15), and conductor's scores with multiple-part instrument staves.

Note: The number of affective layers you introduce into your composition, no matter how uniformly trite and tragic, is in no way associated with the number of Finale layers employed. Although the melding of independent voices may be intended to speak to listeners at multiple levels, the practice itself cannot contribute to the accessibility of your composition any more than it can contribute to the intellectual depth of your audience.

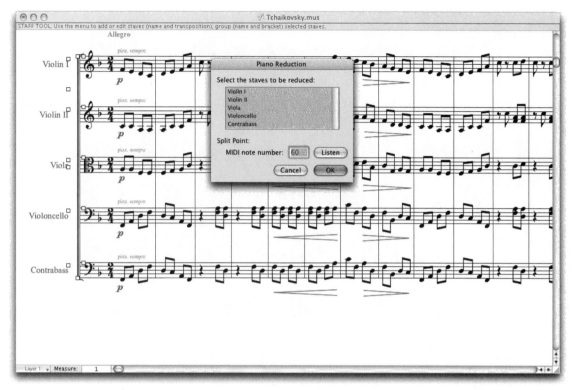

Figure 6.13   Use the Piano Reduction plug-in to create piano reductions.

While using layers, remember the following:

- The active layer is listed in the lower-left corner of your document window. It's sometimes easy to forget which layer is active, so get used to referring to this indicator.

- Always use Layer 1 first, and then add layers consecutively (2, 3, 4) as necessary.

- Layer 1 should be notated higher on the staff than Layer 2 (for proper stemming).

- To work with individual layers, from the Document menu, choose Show Active Layer Only.

- To transfer notes from one layer to another, from the Edit menu, choose Move/Copy Layers.

- To adjust the appearance of layers (stem direction, floating rest position, and so on), from the Document menu, choose Document Options > Layers.

In Chapter 3 (under "Clearing, Copying, or Changing Specific Voices/Layers"), you read how to copy individual layers from one place to another without overwriting other layers. As your documents become more complicated (and your Finale sophistication matures), you may find

Figure 6.14   Finale's Piano Reduction plug-in includes some extras and requires some cleanup, but it's a good start.

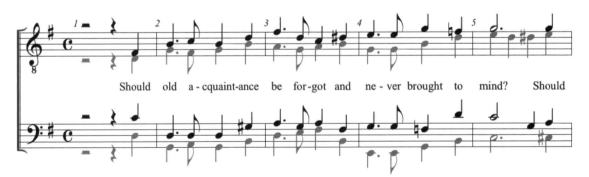

Figure 6.15   Composing scores with multiple voices on a staff generally requires the ability to move and copy layers.

yourself staring blankly at staves adorned with a potpourri of colors (black, red, green, and maybe even blue). Compositions in progress require a quick and easy way to modify these layers—notably, the ability to transfer them from one layer to another. To do so you use Finale's Move/Copy Layers feature.

Moving Layers

Consider a simple scenario requiring a layer transfer. The example used here is the Bach.mus file located in the Finale/Sample Files folder (or at www.composingwithfinale.com).

In Figure 6.16, measure 5 of the top staff, Bach has written the right hand in Layer 1. When he decides to place high harmony above the string of eighth notes, he must first move the existing content to Layer 2 to achieve the proper stem direction. If I had hopped into a time machine and

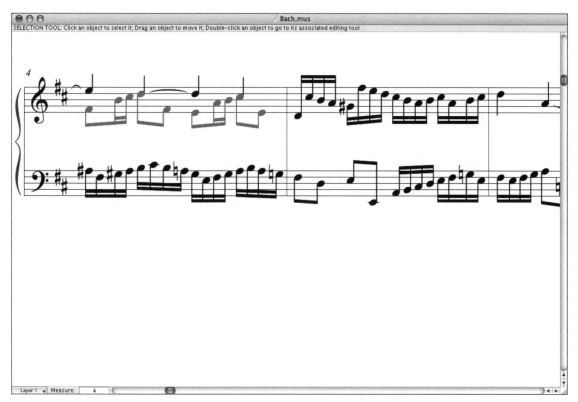

Figure 6.16 Composing scores with multiple voices on a staff generally requires the ability to move and copy layers.

were seated next to him, I would probably shake uncontrollably considering my proximity to greatness, but hopefully would manage the following steps:

1. Select measure 5 in the top staff.

2. From the Edit menu, choose Move/Copy Layers. The Move/Copy Layers dialog box appears.

3. Choose the Move radio button and then select Move Contents of Layer 1 Into Layer 2, as shown in Figure 6.17.

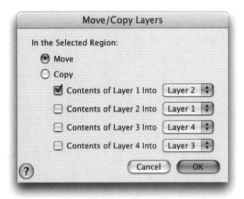

Figure 6.17   The Move/Copy Layers dialog box allows you to move and copy layers.

4. Click OK. All notes in Layer 1 change to red, indicating they are now in Layer 2. The images in this book are grayscale, so you'll just have to take my word for it.

5. Now Johann can enter the high harmony in Layer 1, as shown in Figure 6.18.

The preceding steps illustrate one example requiring the Move/Copy Layers feature, but a great number of similar situations require this.

Note that as an alternative to moving layers, you can copy to a different layer to duplicate the existing notes—great for composing contrapuntal sections.

Tip: Create a dummy staff to temporarily house music while composing scores with multiple layers, copying and pasting back and forth to the working staves as necessary.

Dealing with Extra Rests

Plenty of rest may be required to restore your constitution after an arduous day making music. But when using multiple layers, too many rests may actually discourage an otherwise sprightly

Figure 6.18 Move layers to accommodate counterpoint to be added above or below existing notes.

Figure 6.19 Finale offers several ways to join rests in multiple layers.

state. In other words, if you have begun your harpsichord sonata and notice extra rests, one above another when you require only one (see Figure 6.19), you have a few options:

- Select the region. Then, with the full version of TGTools (www.tgtools.de), go to TGTools > Parts > Join Rests in Multiple Layers.

- In Speedy Entry, after entering a rest, press * (Shift+8) to move it to the default center position. When you do this for both layers, the rests overlap.

- In Simple Entry, after entering a rest (or while it is selected), press H to hide it. Ctrl+drag (Option+drag) the other rest into place or use the arrow keys to nudge it to the center position.

7 The Composer's Wild Kingdom

Before moving into the techniques tailored for specific types of projects, I will conclude this tome with a menagerie of other composer necessities. As I mentioned at the beginning, no book could possibly assemble every composer's pet specimen of Finale utility. It is a wild kingdom of incomprehensible variety. And, while I may be qualified enough to tame a parakeet, there are far greater beasts whose close proximity is ill advised. (I have taken the liberty to steer you clear of the worst of those already.)

I suggest not straying too far from the yellow brick road (unless you *save* first), but I do encourage exploiting all the exotic scenery you can from a safe distance. After reading this book and the entire Finale user manual (or another comprehensive Finale resource), I sincerely hope and expect you will find yourself bushwhacking through the lion-, tiger-, and bear-infested forests with impunity.

This chapter continues to confront situations common to composers who dabble in tonality and tend to write metrically (using time signatures, for example). Dealing with pitches and meters is the bread and butter for many, and adjusting these aspects with ease is important, especially if your work transforms into as many diverse incarnations as mine on its way to the orchestra (or remote corners of a hard drive). Finally, because Finale can't claim a stranglehold on all of life's problems, you also learn how to integrate other music applications into your creative technological sphere, hopefully, without creating more of said problems.

Here's a summary of what you will learn in this chapter:

- Transposing

- Doing the math: durations and meters

- Composing with Finale and friends: digital audio workstations (DAWs)

Transposing

Transposing is both a utilitarian procedure, necessary to transfer music into an appropriate key or range, and a creative one, allowing you to manipulate pitches within a key as part of the creative process. Both are a required tool in the composer's arsenal, so we will delve into both. Let's discuss the creative stuff first.

Transposing Diatonically Within the Key Signature

The world of music making has few constants, but repetition and the major/minor scale are both persistent staples. Fortunately, in this medium, transposition can be an excellent creative tool that brings the basic tonal editing options extremely close to your fingertips. The ability to transpose is especially important when you are developing a motif, creating a theme, or just experimenting with tonal ideas.

Transposition Shortcuts

To explore basic transposition functions, open the file Bach.mus in the Finale/Sample Files folder (also available at www.composingwithfinale.com). If you have reprogrammed your transposition metatools, these steps will not work (but if you have done that, you have a sufficient grasp of these steps anyway, and can skip them).

1. Press Esc a couple times to choose the Selection Tool.

2. Select a region of music. Now we will transpose this music diatonically.

3. Press 6 a few times. Finale transposes *down a step* each time you press 6.

4. Press 7 a few times. Finale transposes *up a step* each time you press 7.

5. Press 8 a couple times. Finale transposes *down an octave* each time you press 8.

6. Press 9 a couple times. Finale transposes *up an octave* each time you press 9.

Tip: To transpose with tools that support measure selection other than the Selection Tool, press Ctrl+n (Command+n). n stands in for 6, 7, 8 or 9.

I don't mean to yell, but these transposition shortcuts are very powerful. Don't ever bother going into the Transposition dialog box to transpose up a fourth: Just press 7 three times! Between octave and diatonic shortcuts, most of your transposition needs should be met.

Like all metatools, you can program these. Just press Shift+n (6, 7, 8, or 9) to open the Transposition dialog box, where you can assign an interval to that number.

Chromatic Transposition and Parallel Harmony

To transpose chromatically, or retain the original pitches to add a strand of parallel harmony, right-click (Ctrl+click) the highlighted measures and select Transpose to display the Transposition dialog box shown in Figure 7.1. Here, I configured Finale to transpose down a sixth, leaving the original notes in place.

To transpose a diminished fifth or augmented fourth, click the Chromatically radio button and then choose your selection from the Interval drop-down list.

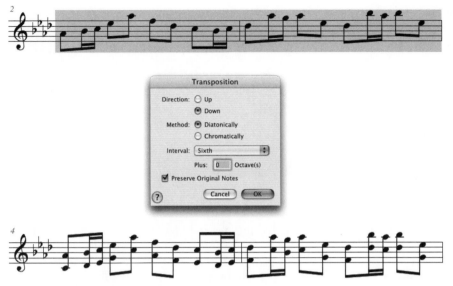

Figure 7.1   Parallel sixths are pretty.

Tip: To alter a section's pitches to create an inversion, a retrograde, or a similar manipulation, use the Canonic Utilities plug-in. Highlight the region and, from the Plug-ins menu, choose Scoring and Arranging > Canonic Utilities.

Changing the Instrument Transposition

As mentioned in Chapter 5, "Managing Your Instrumentalists," transposing instruments is completely automatic in Finale. To set music for a different instrument transposition, simply add a new instrument staff with the Setup Wizard and copy the music into the new staff. Doing this is easier than messing with individual staff attributes, and is completely safe.

Follow these steps to change the instrument transposition:

1.   Choose the Staff Tool ![icon].

2.   Select the handle of the staff you would like to transpose.

3.   From the Staff menu, choose New Staves (with Setup Wizard).

4.   Add the desired instrument and click Finish. The new staff appears above the one you selected.

5.   In the Edit menu, ensure Use Filter in unchecked.

6.   Click to the left of the source (original) staff to select the entire staff.

7. Drag to the new staff. When the black border appears at the beginning of measure 1, release. Finale copies your music into the new staff, adjusting the notes into the proper transposition. If the pitches are the same, in the Document menu, uncheck Display in Concert Pitch.

8. To delete the original staff, right-click (Ctrl+click) the handle and choose Delete and Reposition.

Changing the Key

If your music requires a change to the concert key signature, it's easiest to use a context menu.

1. Press Esc a couple times to choose the Selection Tool.

2. Right-click (Ctrl+click) the first measure of the desired key change and choose Key Signature.

3. Click the desired key, as shown in Figure 7.2. No need to select the region; key-signature changes always apply to all staves (unless a staff is set to Independent Key Signature in the Staff Attributes).

Figure 7.2 Context menus are the bee's knees.

When you change the key with a context menu, Finale changes the key for all measures up to the next key-signature change, or to the end of the score. If Finale transposes the pitches in the opposite direction (up instead of down or vise versa), choose Edit Key Signature from the context menu to open the Key Signature dialog box, where you can specify the transposition direction.

Right Notes, Wrong Key Signature

You have just finished a beautifully accurate HyperScribe session. After the entry frame disappears you notice the score is littered with accidentals. Don't worry, you don't need to re-record; just change the key signature to match the music. The following steps apply whenever you've found yourself in the wrong key as you write:

1.   Click the Key Signature Tool ▓.

2.   Double-click the measure that requires the key change. The Key Signature dialog box appears.

3.   Choose the desired key signature. How do you know in what key it should be? When the tonal center isn't obvious, a bit of music-theory training comes in handy. But, you can just choose whichever key cancels out the most accidentals without creating new ones.

4.   Choose the Hold Notes to Original Pitches radio button. Be sure Enharmonically is chosen in the adjacent drop-down menu.

5.   Click OK. Finale changes the key signature, leaving the pitches intact, as shown in Figure 7.3. Notice the first note in the second measure of the left. Finale automatically changes the staff position of the D flat to its enharmonic equivalent (C sharp).

What Key to Use: Finding the Range

Maybe you have a favorite key. I do. It's E flat major or maybe its relative, C minor. I gravitate toward three flats because the triads seem smooth, rich, and natural between one another in that key, and not at all for technical reasons (although its quality on an equal-tempered piano probably has something to do with it). In any case, E flat major happens to be an excellent key for brass—great range, easy key signatures all around, and some other intangible quality. Since I especially enjoy writing for brass, it is fortunate I am not a slave to B major or something. Imagine the painful loneliness of the dirge trapped in A sharp minor by necessity, never removed from its high-school file cabinet. I'm sure it is as beautiful as sunrise on the dunes of Neptune.

Regardless of your perfectly appropriate key, your music is inherently limited to the range of your instruments. If you let the overall range slip your mind in the throes of rampant inspiration, you may need to give yourself a reality check to ensure that an existing key will accommodate your creation. In Chapter 5 you learned how to ensure your music is within the proper range for each instrument, but now I'd like you to consider you are in the midst of the creative process. I

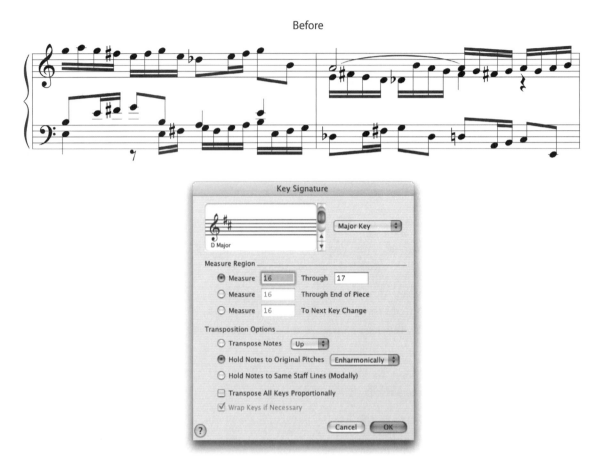

Before

After Key Change (Holding Notes to Original Pitches)

Figure 7.3 When you've composed in the wrong key signature, change the key, holding notes to their original pitches.

want you to be aware of the overall vertical breadth of your music even if you don't know the exact instrumentation. Allowing some leeway at the upper and lower extremities gives you more options as you continue your composition, such as the difficulty level and possible keys. You can instantly check the highest and lowest notes in any region using the Find Range plug-in.

To use the Find Range plug-in, follow these steps:

1.   Select a region.

2.   From the Plug-ins 🖋 menu, choose Scoring and Arranging > Find Range. The Range dialog box appears, as shown in Figure 7.4.

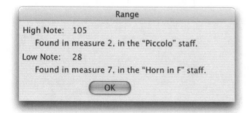

Figure 7.4   Check the highest and lowest notes in a region with the Find Range plug-in.

Tip: If these numbers seem cryptic, refer to "MIDI Note to Pitch Table" in the Finale user manual.

Now that we've discussed the most common ways to manage pitch on a regional scale, let's delve into its sibling, rhythm.

Doing the Math: Durations and Meters

They say mathematics and music go hand in hand, that aptitude in calculus often translates to virtuosic prowess. After all, Peter Tchaikovsky was a mathematician, Albert Einstein was a violinist, and even Federal Reserve Chairman Alan Greenspan is a Juilliard-educated clarinetist. As a life choice, I can't understand how someone who understands numbers would actually go into music. But, mysteries of the human mind aside, whether or not algorithms are a natural part of your thought process, Finale's ability to manipulate rhythms is extremely powerful, and a vital tool during the creative process.

Changing the Time Signature

This section will look familiar. If your music requires a time-signature change, it's easiest to use a context menu.

1.   Press Esc a couple times to choose the Selection Tool.

2.   Right-click (Ctrl+click) the first measure of the desired meter change.

3.   Choose Time Signature and select the desired time signature, as shown in Figure 7.5. No need to select the region—time-signature changes always apply to all staves (unless a staff is set to Independent Time Signature in the Staff Attributes).

Figure 7.5 Context menus are still the bee's knees.

When you change the meter with a context menu, Finale changes the time signature for all measures up to the next time-signature change, or to the end of the score.

When you change the time signature, Finale automatically **rebars** the music. This means that the barlines are redistributed among the existing music to fit within the framework of the new meter (for example, beat 4 of the first measure becomes beat 1 of the second). Usually, the time signature you are composing into is so apparent that it is set prior to entering the notes, which I recommend.

Changing Durations and Meters

While composing, I often discover that my time signature is completely off. For example, a piece I wrote in 4/4 should be written in 2/4 or 2/2. If the denominator is the same duration, often a simple time-signature change is all that is required. But a few extra steps are required when you need to change from (for example) 3/8 to 3/4. A change like this requires doubling all the note durations, changing the time signature, and changing the tempo. See Figure 7.6.

Here's how it's done:

1.   Press Esc a couple times to choose the Selection Tool.

Before

After Doubling Durations and Changing the Time Signature

Figure 7.6 If you've composed in the wrong meter, no problem: Just change the durations, time signature, and tempo accordingly.

2.   Select the region of measures you need to change. We will change this entire piece from 3/8 to 3/4.

3.   Adjust your pickup measure, if you have one.

4.   From the Document menu, choose Pickup Measure.

5.   In the Pickup Measure dialog box, choose the required pickup (in this case, a quarter note). Click OK.

6.   From the Utilities menu, choose Change > Note Durations. The Change Note Durations dialog box appears.

7.   Choose Change All Note Durations By, then click the drop-down menu and select 200%, as shown in Figure 7.7. For our example we must double all the durations. If we were moving to 3/2, we would triple them.

Figure 7.7   Alter all note durations in a region in the Change Note Durations dialog box.

8.   Check Rebar Music and click OK. Your settings double the note durations and each former measure's worth of music occupies two, as shown in Figure 7.8.

9.   Move the barlines and change the time signature. Choose the Selection Tool, and highlight all measures in the region. If there is a pickup measure, *do not* select it. (We'll deal with that later.)

10.   Choose the Time Signature Tool and double-click the selected region. The Time Signature dialog box appears.

11.   Use the scrollbars to select the desired time signature, and be sure Rebar Music is checked, as shown in Figure 7.9.

12.   Click OK to distribute the music into the appropriate measures.

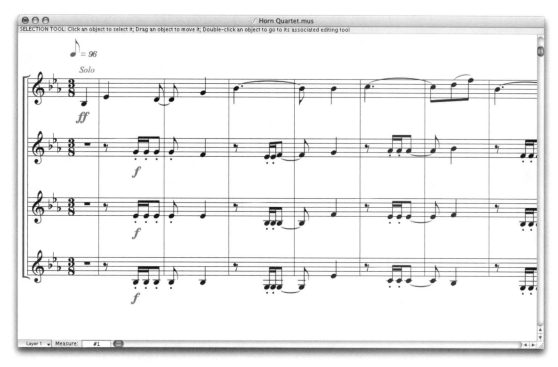

Figure 7.8 Doubled note durations take up twice as many measures.

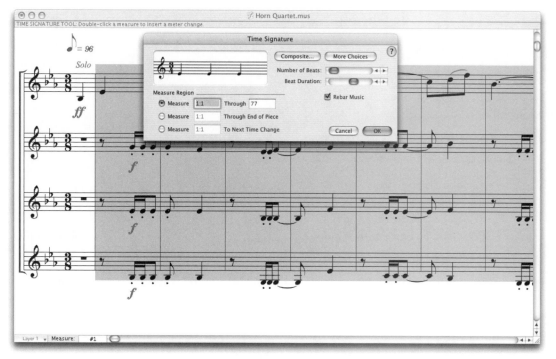

Figure 7.9 Set the desired time signature in the Time Signature dialog box.

13.   Right-click (Ctrl+click) the pickup measure and choose 3/4. Now we change the tempo marking. Since our durations are twice as long, we double the tempo.

14.   With the Selection Tool, double-click the expression. For our example, change the eighth note to a quarter note (quarter note = "q"), then change the playback attributes to playback at quarter = 96. See Figure 7.10. For more details regarding editing expressions, see "Expressions" in the Finale user manual.

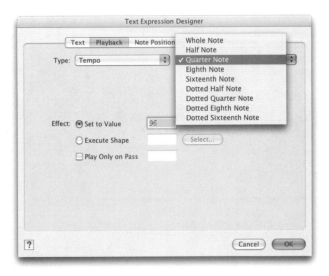

Figure 7.10 Edit expressions.

15.   Click OK to distribute the music into the appropriate measures. For this example, you need to retranscribe measure 5.

16.   Select the music, choose MIDI/Audio > Retranscribe, double-check the quantization settings, and click OK.

17.   Re-enter the slurs. The possibility of losing note-attached Smart Shapes is an inherent side effect of the procedure.

Our piece now looks like the "After" example in Figure 7.6. The same basic procedure applies for any similar change, including transfer to a smaller note duration (3/4 to 3/8, for example).

When I run into this problem I remember how fantastic it is to compose at the computer. So much can be sketched into the document before deciding even basic things like the time signature. It's just one of the many fun ways you can adjust the notation framework to accommodate your creation rather than the other way around.

Complex Meters and Beaming

Complex time signatures and their corresponding beaming (see Figure 7.11) can be virtually painless after learning a few basic principles.

Figure 7.11   Applying complex time signatures and the desired beaming subdivisions needn't get in the way of your rhythmic genius.

Finale includes several common complex meters in the time-signature context menu already. For example, to assign 7/8 time, choose the Time Signature Tool, right-click (Ctrl+click) a measure or selected region, and choose one of the 7/8 options: (2+2+3) or (3+2+2). Figure 7.11 illustrates these two options in the first two measures. Measure 3, however, illustrates a beaming pattern of 2+3+2, an option unavailable in Finale's default context menu, so let's define and add that one ourselves. The following applies for any such complex time signature:

1. Choose the Time Signature Tool 🎼.

2. Double-click the measure (or a region) to open the Time Signature dialog box.

3. Click Composite to open the Composite Time Signature dialog box.

4. In the first Beat Groups box, enter the beaming subdivision pattern. Our example is 2+3+2, as shown in Figure 7.12. The preview above will display the beaming.

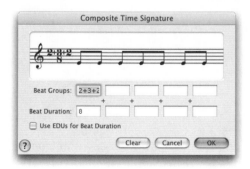

Figure 7.12   Enter 2+3+2 in the *first box*, like this.

5.   Enter the denominator in the first Beat Duration box (in this case, 8 for eighth note).

6.   Click OK and then OK to return to the score.

See? Complex meters really aren't that complex. If you are getting carried away, taking rhythm to its experimental limits, advanced time signatures (covered next) need to be truly ingrained in your workflow.

Tip: To display 7/8 instead of 2+3+2, in the Time Signature dialog box, set the regular time signature to 7/8. Then, click Options (More Choices). Check Use Different Time Signature for Display, then click Composite to define the beat groups.

Time-Signature Metatools

I know I sound like a broken record bringing up metatools again. You may need to use the same two or three obscure time signatures over, and over, and over again. If this is the case, you absolutely must assign time-signature metatools!

Follow along to assign a time-signature metatool:

1.   Select the Time Signature Tool ▓.

2.   Press Shift+*n* (0–9). For now, press Shift+1 to open the Time Signature dialog box.

3.   Use the scroll bars to the right of the preview to assign your time signature. Or, click Composite to create a complex key signature with a specific beaming pattern (described earlier in this chapter).

Note: For compound time signatures, like 6/8, be sure to indicate the full beat duration in the denominator. (For example, in 6/8, this is usually a dotted quarter note.)

---

4.   Click OK.

5.   Highlight a region of measures, press the 1 key, and double-click the region you highlighted. (Or, just press 1 and double-click to apply it to a single measure.)

Composing with Finale and Friends

I've always been amused by the story about the rookie computer user who sits down in front of the monitor, presses the CD-ROM eject button, and places his coffee cup in the CD tray. As a tech-savvy composer it is important to learn the capabilities of a wide variety of tools to see how they fit with your unique creative requirements, however unorthodox those requirements may be. But it is also vital to understand a tool's intended usage to take advantage of it most effectively. The Finale installation DVD does work well as a coaster, but it's so much more than that.

I have no idea where Finale fits best into your process, but if you are trying to brew a pot of coffee with it, you have probably made some incorrect assumptions about what Finale actually is. Finale is a scorewriter if it is anything at all, and decades of intellectual energy have been focused on the singular task of allowing you to easily notate and print sheet music. At the same time, decades of effort have also focused on other tools useful to composers, most notably, **digital audio workstations** (**DAWs**).

DAWs are very popular compositional tools and, since they usually include MIDI-sequencing capabilities, allow you to do some of the same things Finale does:

- Record from a MIDI keyboard or other external MIDI device.

- Play back using high-quality synthesizers or sample libraries.

- Edit pitch, rhythm, and every other aspect of the music.

Note: MIDI stands for Musical Instrument Digital Interface. A MIDI file is the digital incarnation of notes on a staff—a set of instructions to be performed by a computer or electronic instrument. MIDI files don't include any visual information (dynamic markings, slurs, and the like) because computers take things a bit more literally than humans and pick nits like requiring the exact volume, pitch, and duration. Still, they work wonderfully as a sketch framework while composing until the familiar visual abstractions can later be introduced as text/markings/shapes in Finale.

Digital Performer, ProTools, Cubase, Sonar, Logic, and ACID are all examples of DAWs. This book is about composing in Finale, so it doesn't seem very smart to encourage composing in a DAW. But this book isn't ultimately about Finale—it is about releasing creative energy. I have found that using both Finale and a DAW together during composition is a fantastic way to remove a great number of hindrances. If the shortest distance between two points is a straight line, one point is your inspiration, and the other your finished composition, I am willing to bet that both a DAW and Finale fall somewhere on that line (once you've learned how to use them).

All DAWs share these important features:

- Convenient viewing and editing options. DAWs include easily accessible and editable MIDI data in several viewing environments. See Figure 7.13.

- Integration of MIDI sequences and audio recordings. Finale allows a single audio track to accompany your document, which works great for a simple addition like a solo vocal line. If you plan to work with several audio tracks and MIDI sequences simultaneously, however, a DAW is required.

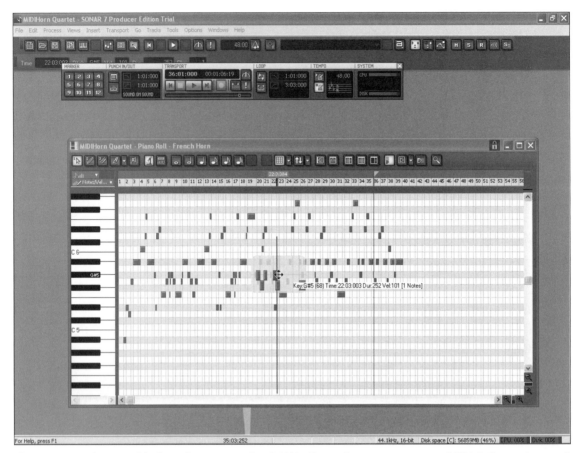

Figure 7.13 The graphical environment of a DAW allows for easy access to MIDI information and includes powerful, intuitive editing functions.

■ Advanced audio-processing capabilities. Finale offers the basic mixer controls (volume, pan, instrument, and even reverb), but DAWs include all the functions of a traditional recording studio in addition to powerful plug-ins that can tweak even the most nuanced aspects of the performance.

You can use a DAW for the initial entry to be transferred to Finale. Or, after completing the composition, you can import the music into a DAW to include audio tracks or apply advanced processing. Integrating a DAW's capabilities is just part of everyday life for many amateur and professional composers. And while I can't detail all the wonderful capabilities of each DAW, I encourage you to check them out. It will take time to learn how to use one. You will curse the mountains of tools and options just like you did when you learned Finale. You may even have to go out and buy a book for guidance....

"Intelligence is like four-wheel drive," says Garrison Keillor, "it just enables you to get stuck in more remote places."

Those remote places are where all the really fun stuff happens.

Often, a MIDI file is the mode of transfer between Finale and a DAW (or MIDI sequencer). After outlining the basic sketch, I start importing MIDI excerpts into Finale. A common misconception holds that a cutoff point is required when the score is transferred from a DAW into Finale. This is a myth. You can continue composing with your DAW, importing MIDI, and copying the imported MIDI file results into your working Finale score. Then you can save a MIDI file from Finale, import it into your DAW, edit it, and return it to Finale. In other words, there is virtually no limit to the ways you can use these two products in tandem.

Keep a few important things in mind when transferring your compositions across programs with MIDI files:

- All text and markings will be lost when a MIDI file is exported from Finale. This includes articulations, expressions, slurs, and other Smart Shapes. If you plan to re-import the music later, you must re-enter these elements.

- Finale includes Human Playback data while saving MIDI files. Since Human Playback's interpretation has some randomness, no two MIDI files will be precisely the same unless you turn Human Playback off in the Playback Settings dialog box (Playback Controls). Alternatively, you can use the Apply Human Playback plug-in to introduce hard Human Playback MIDI data to your document.

- Remember that MIDI files have no actual sounds. A MIDI file is simply a set of instructions that indicate which notes to play when, at what volume, and so forth. The sounds depend on the synthesizer used, so if you move a MIDI file across programs or (especially) computers, the synthesized instruments may sound quite a bit different.

Here is one example of how you might approach the usage of MIDI files: By limiting your composition's first sketches to fit within the scope of a MIDI file (pitches, durations, and rhythms with no markings), you can compose using any program that includes MIDI-sequencing capabilities. Your composition could cycle through several different programs for specific types of editing before being returned to Finale and marked up accordingly.

Caution: We live in a dangerous world with a massive number of options that allow us to involuntarily destroy our compositions as often as they allow us to improve them. If a technology exists that can help us, it is our obligation to embrace its full potential—along with all the implications—if we are to achieve our own potential and the intended nature of our creation. Play with fire, but understand it, and have a big bucket of water nearby.

To take advantage of the universal flexibility of MIDI files, let's learn how to import and export them.

Importing from a DAW or MIDI Sequencer

All MIDI sequencers and DAWs that include MIDI sequencers allow you to save as a MIDI file. As you edit the MIDI data in a MIDI sequencer, remember that Finale can interpret the pitches, durations, and rhythms and translates them into notation. Other aspects, such as pitch bends (glissandi), play back in Finale, but need manual editing to notate properly.

When you plan to transfer a sequenced file into Finale, note the following:

■   Always quantize to the granularity required in the Finale document (dividing each measure evenly into the smallest common duration). Without considering quantization, your results will be interesting, but likely won't resemble readable notation.

■   If your sequence includes triplets, be sure the durations are perfect (the beat split into thirds). Alternatively, you can tell Finale to ignore triplets during import and fix them later.

■   You can define dynamic level by setting **key velocity** (MIDI attack volume) as you compose your MIDI file. After you import the MIDI file into Finale, use the Auto-Dynamic Placement plug-in to assign dynamics to your defined key velocities. (See "Assigning Dynamic Markings in a MIDI Sequencer" later in this chapter.)

■   If different sections of the sequence require different quantization settings during import, import the file multiple times (using the required Finale quantization settings) and combine the sections by copying between Finale documents. Or, save each section as a separate MIDI file to be imported separately and combined.

■   With Human Playback turned on, Finale applies its own MIDI data when you initiate playback based on the markings you have added (hairpins, dynamic markings) and ignores MIDI data (Controller 7 Volume, for instance) defined deliberately in a sequencer. If you find that the MIDI data you defined prior to importing is not coming through in Finale, either turn Human Playback off, or adjust the Human Playback Preferences dialog box accordingly.

Saving and Opening a MIDI File

Let's import a file composed in Sonar:

1.   In Sonar, from the File menu, choose Save As. The Save As dialog box appears.

2.   Name the file. Click the Save as Type drop-down menu and choose MIDI Format 1. See Figure 7.14. This process is the same in most other products. If not, check the documentation for information on saving as a MIDI file in Format 1 (or Type 1).

3.   Choose a folder for the MIDI file and click Save.

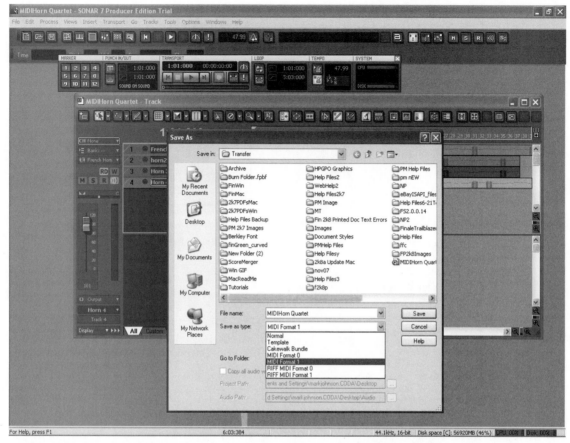

Figure 7.14   Saving as a Format/Type 1 MIDI file will look something like this.

4.   Open Finale.

5.   From the File menu, choose Open. The Open dialog box appears.

6.   Navigate to the folder housing the MIDI file you just saved.

7.   After Files of Type, choose MIDI File [*.mid] (from the Enable pop-up menu, choose Standard MIDI File). See Figure 7.15.

8.   Double-click the MIDI file. The Import MIDI File Options dialog box appears, as shown in Figure 7.16.

9.   If each instrument is set to a different channel in the MIDI file, choose Channels Become Staves.

10. Click the Quant Settings button to change the smallest note value to the same smallest duration quantized in the MIDI file.

Figure 7.15   Specify you want to open a MIDI file in the Open dialog box.

Figure 7.16   The default options in the Import MIDI File Options are usually okay.

Tip: If you get double noteheads in the imported file, choose a smaller note value in the quantization settings. If you get unwanted, meaningless tuplet definitions, try a larger note value.

---

11.   Click OK. The MIDI File Status dialog box appears and the file opens.

If you are opening a MIDI file from an unknown source, you may need to adjust the MIDI import and quantization settings to accommodate the many ways the MIDI file could have been set up. (For example, are the voices saved in different tracks or channels and what are the best quantization settings?) See "MIDI Files" in the Finale user manual for more info.

Orchestrating Your Imported MIDI File

Your work is not done after importing the MIDI file. Now you need to either copy the results into your working score or create a new document with the required instrumentation. Let's assume you have just imported your full composition and need to apply the imported tracks to the appropriate staves.

Finale does not adequately configure the page formatting or staff information, so you need to orchestrate by beginning a new score with the Setup Wizard. If you are reading this book cover to cover, these steps will look familiar.

1. Press Esc a couple times to choose the Selection Tool.

2. Press Ctrl+A (Command+A) to select all.

3. Press Ctrl+C (Command+C) to copy.

4. From the File menu, choose New > Document with Setup Wizard.

5. Complete the Setup Wizard, choosing the desired Document Style and instrument staves. Be sure the staves are in the appropriate order (same as the imported MIDI file). On the second screen, be sure Use a Separate Channel for Each Staff is checked. All the other settings will be overwritten (aside from the title, composer, etc.), so don't worry about them.

6. After the new score appears, press Ctrl+A (Command+A) to select all.

7. From the Edit menu, make sure Use Filer in unchecked.

8. From the Edit menu, choose Paste. The music populates your new score.

If you are importing compositions for the first time, you should consider the above steps a necessary part of importing MIDI files. Alternatively, you could insert the music from the imported MIDI file into your favorite template. For more information on saving Document Styles and templates, refer to Chapter 5.

Exporting to a Sequencer

If you have completed your composition and tried using VST/AU instrument libraries with Human Playback, but still are not satisfied with the playback quality, save it as a MIDI file and open it in a DAW or MIDI sequencer. I could tell you all about Finale's powerful MIDI-editing capabilities, but if you're really picky, you probably need to produce a performance-quality demo. If you're doing that, I recommend investing in a real DAW and in the time it takes to learn how to use one.

Follow these steps to export a MIDI file from Finale:

1. From the File menu, choose Save As.

2. From the Save as Type drop-down menu, choose MIDI File [*.mid] (for Format, choose Standard MIDI File). See Figure 7.17.

Figure 7.17   Choose to save as a MIDI file in the Save As dialog box.

3. Choose a location and click Save. The Export MIDI File Options dialog box appears, as shown in Figure 7.18.

4. Choose the desired format (usually Format 1) and click OK.

5. Open your MIDI sequencer or DAW.

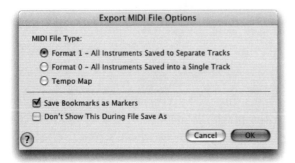

Figure 7.18   Choose the desired MIDI file format in the Export MIDI File Options dialog box.

6.   From the File menu, choose Open.

7.   Click the Files of Type drop-down menu and choose MIDI File. (Click the Enable drop-down menu and choose Standard MIDI File.)

8.   Navigate to the MIDI file you just saved and double-click to open it.

You might need to reassign the instruments after importing the MIDI file, particularly if you are using a non-General MIDI sound bank and/or a different synthesizer.

Assigning Dynamic Markings in a MIDI Sequencer

Finale's Auto-Dynamic Placement plug-in allows you to analyze your music's key velocities and insert dynamic markings accordingly. This includes the key-velocity data recorded from a HyperScribe session (how hard you struck the keys), but also the key velocities deliberately defined while composing in your MIDI sequencer. By anticipating the use of the Auto-Dynamic Placement plug-in, you can define key velocities that you know Finale will interpret as a specific dynamic level when you run the Auto-Dynamic Placement plug-in.

To do this, we must define the appropriate key velocities in our MIDI sequencer, save and import the MIDI file into Finale, modify the Auto-Dynamic Placement plug-in to match Finale's default expression key velocities (using a particularly unintuitive piece of Finale's interface), and apply the Auto Dynamic Placement plug-in. Piece of cake . . . .

Caution: Really, this works only if you follow my exact instructions. After you get through it once you can benefit from this over and over.

---

1.   Open your composition in a MIDI sequencer. We will use Sonar for this example.

2.   Assign key-velocity data to your MIDI sequence according to the required dynamic level. Use Table 7.1 as a reference. I recommend using the smallest value for each range (***mp*** = 62, for example) to align these settings with Finale's expression playback data.

3.   To review and change the key velocity in Sonar, right-click the notes in the Piano Roll, as shown in Figure 7.19.

4.   From the File menu, choose Save As, choose MIDI (Format 1) for Type, and click Save.

5.   In Finale, from the File menu, choose Open. For Files of Type, choose MIDI File [*.MID]. (From the Enable pop-up menu, choose Standard MIDI File.)

6.   Open the MIDI file you just saved.

Table 7.1 Key Velocities and Dynamic Equivalents*

Dynamic Marking	Key-Velocity Range
ppp	23–35
pp	36–48
p	49–61
mp	62–74
mf	75–87
f	88–100
ff	101–113
fff	114–126

*Only when following these instructions.

7. Select all and copy to a new document with the desired orchestration (see "Orchestrating Your Imported MIDI File" earlier in this chapter).

8. Highlight the region you want to apply dynamics to. For this example, we'll select measures 31–35.

9. From the Plug-ins 🎵 menu, choose Expressions > Auto-Dynamic Placement. The Auto-Dynamic Placement plug-in appears (see Figure 7.20).

10. Enter 12 for Min Velocity Change Between Dynamics.

11. Click the Dynamic Marking pop-up menu and choose pppp.

12. Enter 23 for Minimum Velocity.

13. Click the Dynamic Marking pop-up menu and choose ppp.

14. Enter 36 for Minimum Velocity. Continue assigning the dynamic levels as shown in Table 7.2.

15. Highlight the region you want to apply dynamics to. For this example, select measures 31–35.

16. From the Plug-ins 🎵 menu, choose Expressions > Auto-Dynamic Placement. Finale adds the dynamic markings based on the specified key velocities. See Figure 7.21.

Yes, the steps are wonky and we all wish every part of Finale held up to the usual high standard. The fact of the matter is that these steps work and allow you to essentially define dynamics in

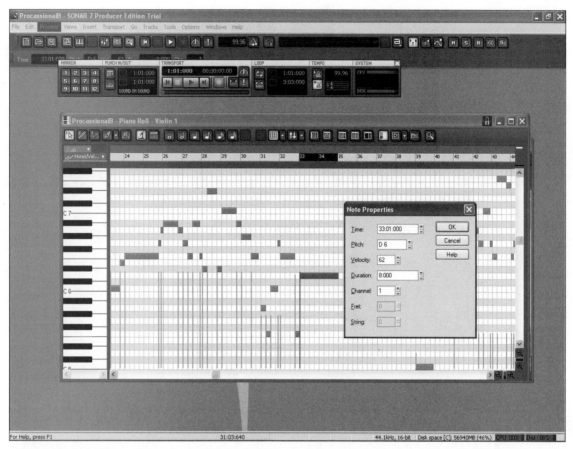

Figure 7.19   The key velocity (Velocity) for beat 1 of measure 33 in the Violin is 62, which gives a *mp* dynamic marking later (after adjusting the Auto-Dynamic Placement plug-in settings).

your DAW/MIDI sequencer. Also, the engineering time that could have been spent fixing this was instead probably used to add some other feature you really couldn't live without. Take the wonkiness with a grain of salt; those engineers at MakeMusic have their work cut out for them.

Importing and Exporting MusicXML

MusicXML is an interchangeable file format that represents western music notation from the 17th century onward. You can open files saved in MusicXML format in 90 different music applications including scorewriters, DAWs, OCR scanning programs, and a variety of other music software products. (See www.recordare.com/xml.html for details.) Your composition can benefit from an even wider variety of editing options. However, Finale is the crème de la crème of graphical score editors, so MusicXML benefits users of other programs the

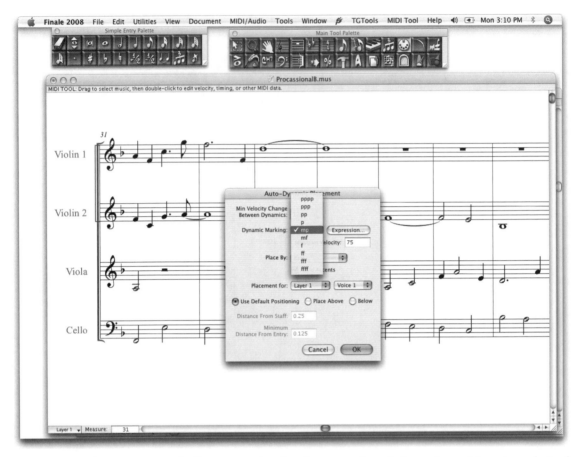

Figure 7.20 The Auto Dynamic Placement plug-in allows you to set dynamic markings to a desired range of key velocities (and doesn't work like you think it should).

most. (Can't notate it in your software? No problem. Save it as a MusicXML file and open it in Finale.)

Note: If you cannot notate a musical figure in Finale, design it in Adobe Illustrator (or another vector graphics editor) and import it into Finale as an EPS graphic. Sorry, no other scorewriter can beat Finale's power when it comes to graphical score editing. You might even export an EPS excerpt from Finale (with the Graphics Tool), edit it in Illustrator, and then import it back into Finale.

Of particular interest for Finale users, you can open MusicXML files in any Finale version natively back to Finale 2004 on Windows or Mac (and even back to Finale 2000 on Windows)

Table 7.2 Auto-Dynamic Placement Settings

Dynamic Marking Setting	Minimum Velocity Value*
pppp	23
ppp	36
pp	49
p	62
mp	75
mf	88
f	101
ff	114
fff	127
ffff**	127

*Actually refers to minimum key velocity of next-highest dynamic level.

**Key velocities between 12–22 translate to ffff.

with the help of the Dolet for Finale plug-in. (See www.recordare.com/finale/index.html.) This allows backward compatibility, a feature long requested by Finale users. If your colleague is living in the dark ages with Finale 2008 and needs to open your file, export it as a MusicXML file. Also, note that MusicXML files can be opened in a variety of music software products.

Exporting a MusicXML File

To export a MusicXML file:

1. From the File menu, choose MusicXML > Export. The Export MusicXML dialog box appears.

2. For Format/Files of Type, choose 1.1 (unless you intend to open the file in a program that only supports MusicXML format 1.0, such as Finale 2003 through Finale 2005 for Windows).

3. Choose a location and click Save.

That's it. Now open the file in your other MusicXML-compatible program. If that program happens to be Finale, continue with the following section.

Figure 7.21   Finale assigns dynamics based on the key velocities you assigned in your MIDI sequencer.

Importing a MusicXML File

You can import a MusicXML file many ways depending on your Finale version. If the following steps don't work, search the Finale user manual to learn how to import a MusicXML file with your version. The following steps do apply to all recent Finale versions.

1.   From the File menu, choose MusicXML > Import. The Import MusicXML dialog box appears.

2.   Double-click the desired MusicXML file. Finale imports and opens the MusicXML file.

8 Lead Sheets

The remainder of this book is a collection of advice for particular types of projects in tutorial form. You can focus on the chapters that relate to your compositions' format, but since there are many common elements, I encourage you to tackle them all. Most significantly, I will be offering a variety of methods regarding note entry, which is far too broad a category to discuss in its own section. Instead, each of these tutorials presents a unique situation and a different entry approach. Along the way, you will generate elements specific to the particulars: lead sheets, piano music, choral scores, guitar tab, and so on.

I'm not going to hold your hand quite as much as the *Finale Installation and Tutorials* manual does. This guide assumes you have completed those, learned enough to be dangerous, and now require some additional target practice. Also, don't expect these to be complete by any stretch of the imagination. No amount of training can match battle-hardened experience; besides, the possibilities you dream up are as predictable as the weather. Even so, we know the dew generally falls in the morning and seasons will inevitably change.

With that, you've woken up with a catchy tune in your head. You've got a general idea of the chord changes and even have some lyric ideas. A slight chill is in the air as you walk across the room and open the blinds. Yes, you've already composed the first few lines and have already fallen in love with it. But right now it's only a vague concept trapped somewhere beneath the bony recesses of your noggin. If you don't act fast you could lose it, and find yourself looking back during the long days wondering what might have been. It's time to launch Finale and document your creation.

Here's a summary of what you will learn in this chapter:

- Starting a new lead sheet
- Adding the melody
- Adding the chords
- Adding the lyrics

Starting a New Lead Sheet

The exact format of your new document is less important than generating a staff and beginning your sketch. Fortunately, Finale assumes that you might want to create a lead sheet and has one ready for you.

Opening a Lead-Sheet Template

To begin a new lead sheet:

1.   From the File menu, choose Launch Window.

2.   Click the Templates button. The Open/Open as Template dialog box appears.

3.   Open the General Templates folder shown in Figure 8.1.

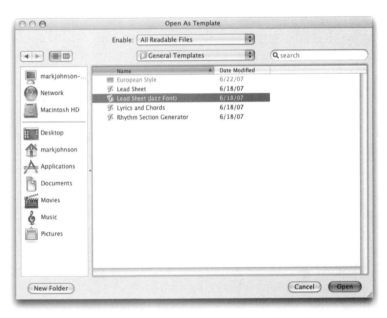

Figure 8.1   Finale includes lead-sheet templates that allow you to get started quickly.

4.   Double-click Lead Sheet (Jazz Font). The Jazz Font displays your music with a handwritten feel. Alternatively, you can choose the Lead Sheet option to use the regular Maestro font. The Score Information screen of the Document Setup Wizard appears, as shown in Figure 8.2. Enter any information you can.

5.   Click Next. The Score Settings screen appears, as shown in Figure 8.3. Again, just enter what you can. For this example, assume the key of C will work and set the time signature to the unabbreviated 4/4.

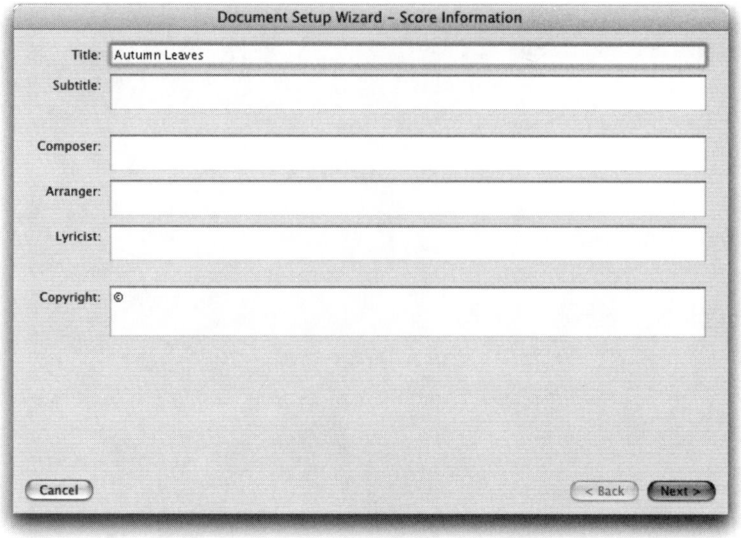

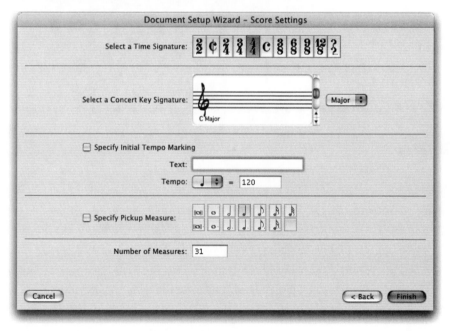

Figure 8.2   Enter what you can on the Score Information screen. Or, just click Next.

Figure 8.3   Enter what you can on the Score Settings screen. Or, just click Finish.

6.   Click Finish to open the new document based on your settings; see Figure 8.4.

Notice the unique characteristics of a lead sheet provided by the template. A left barline is on each system and the clef and time signature appear at the beginning of the first system only.

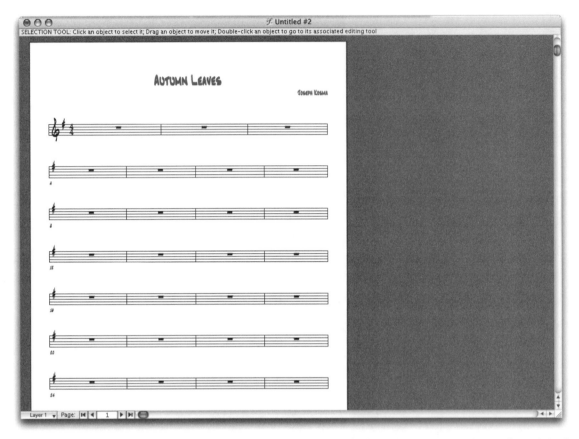

Figure 8.4 The template appears as a new, untitled document based on your settings. The original template is unchanged.

See Figure 8.4. These are reasons to use the Lead Sheet template rather than the regular Document Setup Wizard. (On the other hand, if you want to eliminate the left barline and add the clef and time signature on every system, begin with the Document Setup Wizard instead.)

Since you are in the process of composing, you will likely not know the answers to every question asked in the Setup Wizard, which is fine. You can change every setting in the Setup Wizard later. In fact, now that our score has been created, we already need to change a few things.

Setting Up Your Score After Completing the Setup Wizard

What terrible planning! You mean you didn't have every score element planned before you finished the Setup Wizard? That's almost like cooking without a complete recipe or driving down a road you haven't inspected thoroughly with satellite imagery! What if there is a pothole!?

Here are some changes you might have to make.

Adding a Pickup Measure

You just realized there should be a three-beat pickup measure in place of measure 1, but forgot to specify that in the Setup Wizard. No worries:

1. From the Document menu, choose Pickup Measure. The Pickup Measure dialog box appears.

2. Choose the dotted half note icon to specify a three-beat pickup; see Figure 8.5.

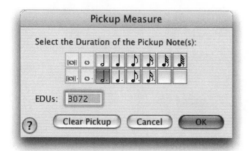

Figure 8.5 Specify the duration of the pickup measure in the Pickup Measure dialog box.

3. Click OK to return to the score.

The first measure looks the same, but is actually a pickup measure and eliminated from the measure numbering. When you begin entering notes, three beats will fill this measure.

Updating the Title, Composer, and Other Score Information

The title, composer, arranger, and other information you entered (or didn't enter) on the Setup Wizard's Score Information screen can be added or changed at any time. To do so, use the File Info dialog box.

1. From the File menu, choose File Info to open the File Info dialog box, shown in Figure 8.6.

2. Make the necessary changes and click OK. You return to the score with the edits applied.

Note: The title, composer, lyricist, and other text blocks that appear on the first page of your score are actually text inserts, and they are defined in the File Info dialog box.

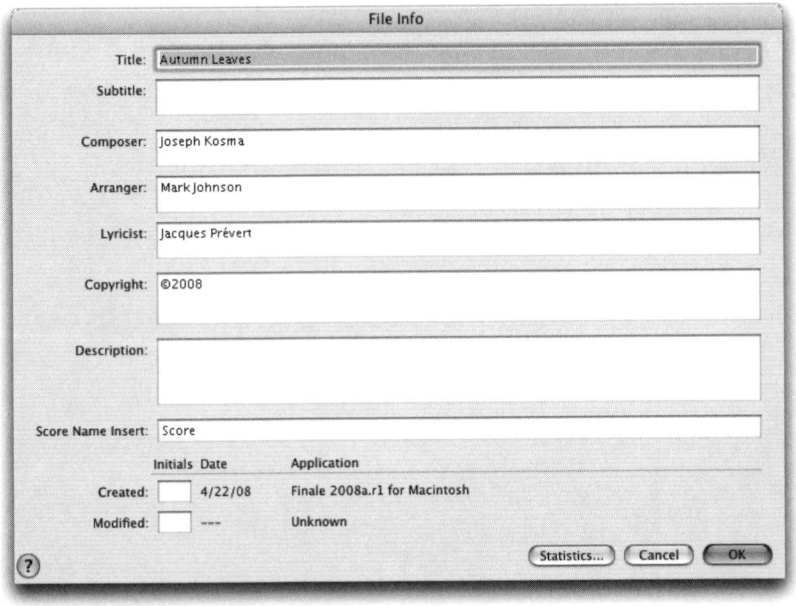

Figure 8.6 Edit the title, subtitle, composer, lyricist, arranger, and other score information in the File Info dialog box.

Changing the Key Signature

The key of E minor will work much better. Again, not a problem:

1. Press Esc a couple times to ensure the Selection Tool is selected.

2. Right-click (Ctrl+click) the first measure (now the pickup measure) to display the context menu.

3. Choose Key Signature > E Major.

Finale adds a sharp to the key signature. The key signature in Finale's Lead Sheet template appears at the beginning of every system. Some lead-sheet formats include the key signature on the first system only.

Adding or Changing the Tempo Marking

We didn't specify a tempo marking in the Setup Wizard. If we had, Finale would have placed it above the first measure as an expression. You can just as easily add a tempo marking/ metronome marking at any time and above any measure with the Create Tempo Marking plug-in. If a tempo ever needs to be changed, just delete it and add a new one with the plug-in.

Follow these steps to add a tempo marking:

1. Press Esc a couple times to ensure the Selection Tool is chosen.

2. Click the first measure to select it.

3. From the Plug-ins 🐷 menu, choose Expressions > Create Tempo Marking. The Create Tempo Marking dialog box appears.

4. Enter the desired text and specify a metronome marking. For this tune, we need a Medium Swing tempo. See Figure 8.7.

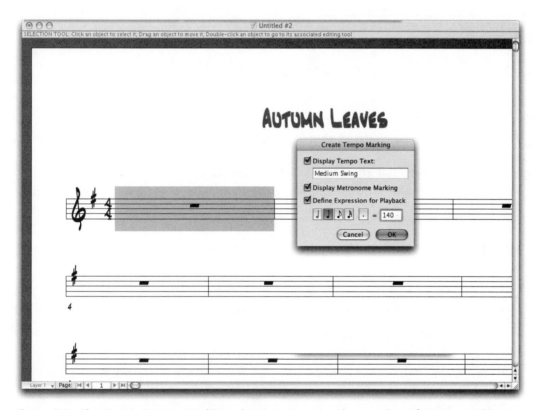

Figure 8.7 The Create Tempo Marking plug-in automates the creation of tempo markings.

5. Click OK to place the tempo marking above the measure you selected.

Now change the font so it matches the other text on the page.

1. Double-click the tempo marking. The Expression Selection dialog box appears. Medium Swing is highlighted.

2. Click the Move To drop-down menu, choose Tempo Marks, and click OK.

3. Click Edit. The Expression Designer appears.

4. Check Use Tempo Marks Category Fonts. The expression is now in the Jazz font.

5. Click OK, then Select. The tempo marking is now updated to match the Tempo Marks' category font, as shown in Figure 8.8.

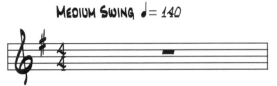

Figure 8.8   You can change the font of tempo markings with the Expression Designer.

Yes, you can edit any aspect of an expression in the Expression Designer, but generating a new one with the plug-in is so easy that you should consider it first.

Placing the Key Signature on the First Staff System Only

This isn't an option in the Setup Wizard, but it is a possible requirement for your lead-sheet format.

To place the key signature on the first system only, follow these steps:

1. From the Document menu, choose Document Options. The Document Options dialog box appears.

2. Choose the Key Signature category from the list on the left. The Document Options – Key Signatures dialog box appears, as shown in Figure 8.9.

3. Check Display Key Signature Only on First Staff System.

4. Click OK.

Adding the Melody

Ah yes... entering the actual notes and stuff. I'd like to say you will be able to follow my exact instructions and then soar like an eagle—a fluent Finale typist entering 1,000 notes a second at your slightest passing whim. That will not happen. As I strap you into the hang glider, I make no assurances you'll get a feel for it when you're airborne. I'll be realistic. This might take a bit of getting used to.

The problem with entry isn't that it's a particularly difficult interface; the problem is finding which entry method works best for you. Do you like to press buttons or are you the point-and-click type? Are you drawn to the dark inner secrets of Finale's Transcription Mode, or a slave to your MIDI guitar? I can't claim to know these things (thankfully), and I certainly can't begin to suspect the outrageous ideas you have in mind for your composition.

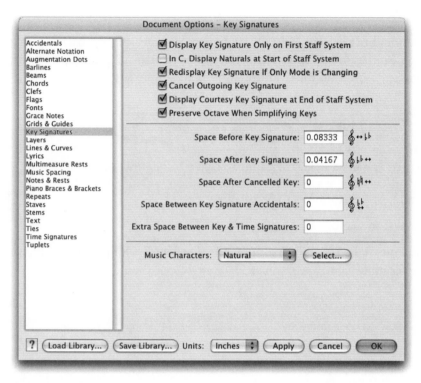

Figure 8.9 Check Display Key Signature Only on First Staff System to reveal the key signature exclusively on the initial staff system.

When you fly off the ledge, I wish you well, and expect you'll be somewhat prepared to avoid disaster on the way down. Yes, the wind may bite and you might lose some altitude as you figure it all out. Just stay calm. Things will work out. If they don't, you probably won't feel a thing anyway.

In this section you will learn how to harness some of the Simple Entry Tool's hidden power by means of the Simple Entry Caret.

Tip: Laptop users, choose the Laptop Shortcut Table to use keyboard shortcuts designed for laptop users. Simple menu > Simple Entry Options > Edit Keyboard Shortcuts. You find this command in the Keyboard Shortcut Set drop-down menu.

Note: If you haven't completed the Finale 2009 Entry Exercises, do so now. Navigate to the Finale 2009/Tutorials folder and open EntryExercise.mus. Follow the instructions. This is the most effective way for me to introduce the power of Simple Entry. Once you complete the Simple Entry exercises, you are ready for these steps.

Entering Measures 1-8

We will enter the tune "Autumn Leaves" (see Figure 8.10) to demonstrate one approach to using the Simple Entry Caret. You can treat the Simple Entry Caret like a cursor in a word processor, although your notes are loaded with a bit more information than simple letters.

Figure 8.10   You can easily enter the main theme of "Autumn Leaves" using the Simple Entry Caret.

1.   Press Ctrl+E (Command+E) to move to Scroll View.

2.   Press Ctrl++ (plus) (Command++) to zoom in a bit.

3.   Choose the Simple Entry Tool 🎵 and press numpad 5 (or Alt+5 [Option+5]) to change the caret to a quarter note (laptop users, just 5). Your screen should now look like Figure 8.11.

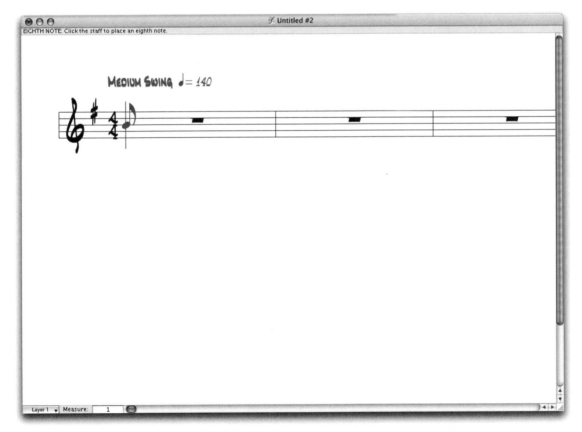

Figure 8.11   I prefer Scroll View at 200% for a legible viewing environment while entering.

4. Our first note is bottom-line E. Press Shift and then the down arrow key once to move the crosshair down an octave and type E to enter the note. You can use the letter keys (A through G) to specify pitch. Finale adds the pitch closest to the position of the caret (which is why we needed to move the caret down one step). See Figure 8.12.

Figure 8.12   Press Alt (Option) and then the note duration to change the duration of the pitch you have just entered.

Note: In Simple Entry, you can always use your MIDI keyboard to specify pitch. Extra notes appear magically sometimes because you dabble at your keyboard with the Simple Entry Tool selected. If this happens, press Ctrl+Z (Command+Z) to undo the mayhem and remember to select a different tool for dabbling. Press Esc twice to hide the caret and deselect any selected notes. Press Esc once more to switch to the Selection Tool.

---

5. Press F, G, and then C.

6. Press Alt+7 (Option+7). The quarter note in measure 2 changes to a whole note. It's important to remember that you can always change the duration easily immediately after entering the note.

7. Press T. As shown in Figure 8.13, a tie appears on the whole note.

Figure 8.13   Press T to add a tie.

8. Press Enter. A third-space C appears. Pressing Enter adds the pitch and duration displayed on the caret.

9. Press Shift+down arrow once to move the caret down an octave. (Shift+up arrow moves the caret up an octave.)

10. Press D, E, F, numpad 6. The caret changes to a half note.

11.   Press B, B, T, numpad 5, B. (Pressing Enter is the same as pressing the pitch letter again.)

12.   Finish measures 4-7 (which are similar to the previous steps). See Figure 8.14 for a reference. For the notes in measure 6, remember to press the + key after entering a note to raise it by a half step.

Figure 8.14   The caret is an effective way to enter music because you can specify each pitch and duration before or after entering the note. If you can get a feel for the keystrokes, this is very powerful.

Tip: Remember, all Simple Entry keyboard shortcuts are listed conveniently under the Simple menu (in the Simple Edit Commands and Simple Navigation Commands submenus.)

---

13.   As you enter, consider copy/paste opportunities that can make your life easier. Press Esc a couple times to choose the Selection Tool.

14.   Press Ctrl+E (Command+E) to move to Page View. This view can be nice when you need to see multiple systems simultaneously in scores with fewer staves. Right-click+ drag (Command+Option+click+drag) the score so you can see the first measure.

15.   Highlight the pickup measure and drag+copy the region to the last three beats of measure 8, as shown in Figure 8.15.

Note: Automatic Music Spacing adjusts the measure layout as you enter, which explains the three wide measures in the second system of Figure 8.15.

Entering Repeats

I'm going to consider repeats part of the melody. After all, a repeated section is just a shortcut that allows us to save ink, space, and the time it would take to enter the notes again. In this piece, measures 1-8 are repeated with a three-measure first ending at measure 6. Then, the second ending must be marked at measure 9. Luckily, Finale's interface for repeat entry is excellent thanks to some more brilliant design work by Kami (excuse the shameless wife promotion).

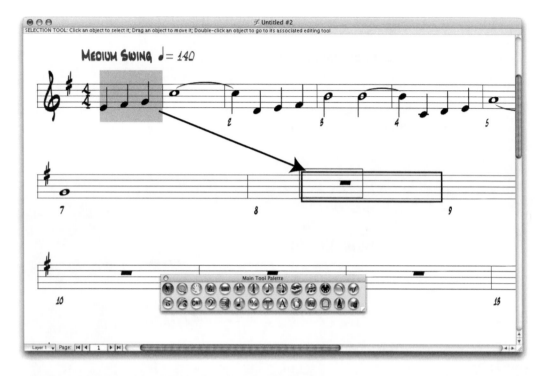

Figure 8.15 Copying and pasting can save you time as you enter.

We'll start with the first ending:

1.   Press Esc a couple times to ensure the Selection Tool is selected.

2.   Highlight measures 6-8.

3.   Right-click (Ctrl+click) the highlighted region, and choose Repeats > Create First and Second Ending, as shown in Figure 8.16. The first and second endings appear.

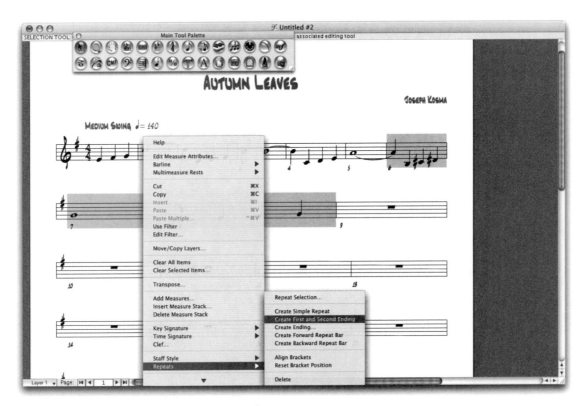

Figure 8.16   Use context menus to easily define repeats.

4.   Right-click (Ctrl+click) measure 1 and choose Repeats > Create Forward Repeat Bar. Finale places a repeat bar on measure 1, as shown in Figure 8.17.

That's it! You could also use the Repeat Tool along with the Repeat menu and context menus as an alternative to the Selection Tool's context menu, but it takes a few more clicks and you lose the satisfaction of knowing you accomplished this in the most efficient and geeky way possible.

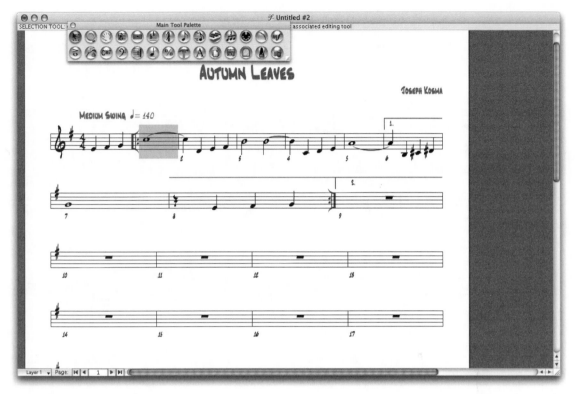

Figure 8.17   Repeat bars and endings are defined for playback automatically when entered.

Note: To easily define more complicated repeats (e.g., D.S. repeats) and create codas on a separate system, use the Create Coda System plug-in (Plug-ins menu > Measures > Create Coda System).

Entering Measures 9-26

The remainder of the piece is also easy to type (see Figure 8.18). We'll enter the rest of the music with the caret and then do some basic measure-layout formatting.

We will continue using the Simple Entry Caret. I am going to list the steps with brevity, which will (hopefully) allow you to get a feel for using the Simple Entry Caret in practice…

1.   Press Ctrl/Command-E to move back to Scroll View.

2.   Press Ctrl+1 (Command+1) to move to 100%.

Autumn Leaves

Joseph Kosma

Figure 8.18 After these steps, your score will look like this.

3.   Choose the Simple Entry Tool .

4.   Hold down Ctrl (Option) and click the last note in measure 8 to select it. You can also use this technique and drag up or down to change the pitch without affecting its rhythm, or to select a note to modify it.

5.   Press the right-arrow key to activate the caret on the first beat of measure 9.

6.   Press numpad 5 (laptop users, 5) to select a quarter note duration (or, if you don't have a number keypad, Ctrl+Alt+Shift+5 [Command+Option+Shift+5]).

Note: Laptop users, you can always substitute numpad duration keystrokes with Ctrl+ Alt+Shift+# (Command+Option+Shift+#).

---

7. Type the following:

A

Shift+T (for a reverse tie)

F

A

G

numpad 7

E

T

numpad 5

Enter

Your score should now look like Figure 8.19.

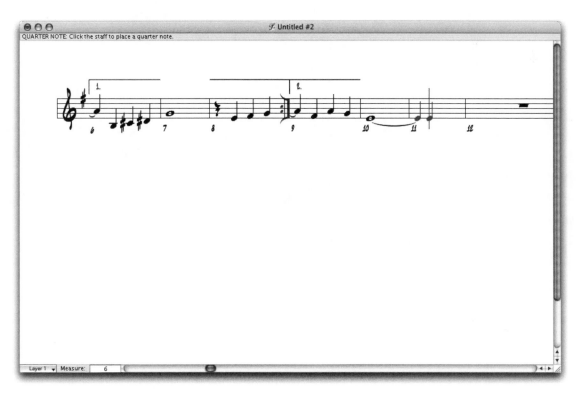

Figure 8.19 Typing in notes can be quick and easy once you get the hang of it.

8. Type the following (all numbers on the numpad), going top to bottom and then left to right, or refer to Figure 8.20:

Enter	A	5
R (for rest)	T	up arrow
D	5	C
+	Enter	6
E	down arrow	B
F	D	B
down arrow	Shift+up arrow	T
B	D	B
up arrow	C	. (dot)
6	7	5
F	B	down arrow
T	T	E
5	5	6
Enter	Enter	A
Enter	Enter	. (dot)
E	R	5
F	A	G
7	+	6
G	B	F
T	C	5
5	C	G
Enter	A	Shift+down arrow
Enter	A	B
F	6	7
G	F	E
7	. (dot)	

Figure 8.20 For each note, type the upper keystrokes to enter and modify, then type the lower keystrokes prepare for the next entry.

9. When you have finished entering the notes, press Esc a couple times to choose the Selection Tool.

10. Click measure 27 (the first empty measure after the music).

11. Press Shift+End (or the right-arrow key four times).

12. Right-click (Ctrl+click) the highlighted region and choose Delete Measure Stack (or press Delete) to remove the extra measures.

13. Press Ctrl+E (Command+E) to move to Page View. From the View menu, choose Zoom > Fit In Window to display the full page. See Figure 8.21.

14. From the Utilities menu, choose Fit Measures. The Fit Measures dialog box appears.

15. After Lock Layout With, enter 4 (if is not already there), and click OK. Four measures are on a system (except the last system, which has three). It should look like Figure 8.18.

Of course, the preceding steps are just one way to enter the notes. In fact, you may devise your own method, even within the confines of the Simple Entry Caret (changing rhythmic durations after entering the note, for instance). I encourage you to experiment with Simple Entry, paying special attention to many powerful keyboard shortcuts. You learn more about Simple Entry in Chapter 13, "Instrumental Ensembles."

Tip: Don't like Finale's Simple Entry keyboard shortcuts? Redefine them. To do so, from the Simple menu, choose Simple Entry Options and click Edit Keyboard Shortcuts.

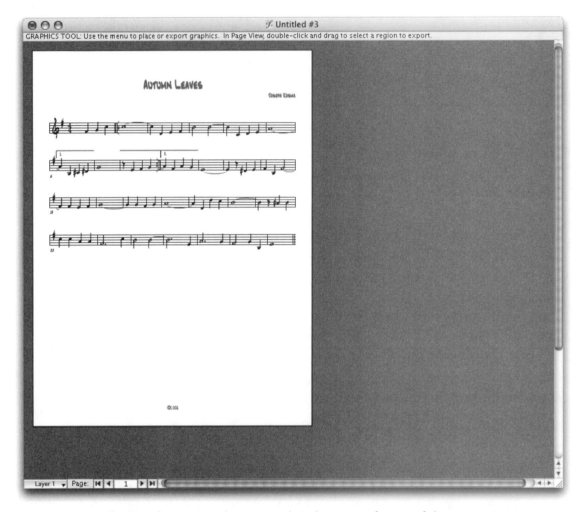

Figure 8.21 We'll adjust the measure layout to take advantage of some of that extra space.

Adding the Chord Symbols

The next item on our lead-sheet list is chords. The procedure for entering chord symbols is more straightforward than for entering notes.

1. Press Ctrl+E (Command+E) and navigate back to measure 1.

2. Press Ctrl+1 (Command+1) to move to 100%.

3. Choose the Chord Tool ![chord tool icon].

4. Select Type Into Score from the Chord menu.

5. Click the whole note in measure 1. A blinking cursor appears above the whole note.

6.   Type a-7 and press the spacebar. The blinking cursor now appears above measure 2. Finale translates your text into an A minor 7 chord symbol; see Figure 8.22. You could also type am7, using m instead of − (minus sign) to indicate minor.

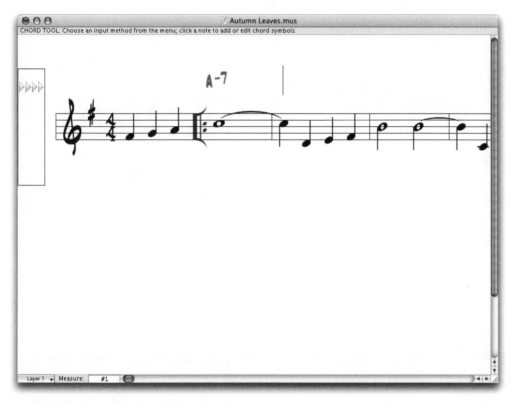

Figure 8.22 Basic chord symbols are easy. Just type the closest equivalent.

7.   Type d7 and press the spacebar four times. The cursor appears above the first beat in measure 3. Now we need to enter a G major 7.

8.   When you are uncertain of the correct suffix, type the root, and then :0 (colon zero). In this case, type g:0 and press the spacebar. The Chord Suffix Selection dialog box appears, as shown in Figure 8.23.

9.   Double click the Maj7 suffix (in slot 13). Now that you know this suffix is in slot 13, you can use that number in the future instead of typing 0. (Note you could also type Maj7 to add this suffix.)

10.   For practice, type g:13 and press the spacebar. Finale enters a Gmaj7 chord suffix. Press Ctrl+Z (Command+Z) to undo.

11.   Click the first note of measure 4.

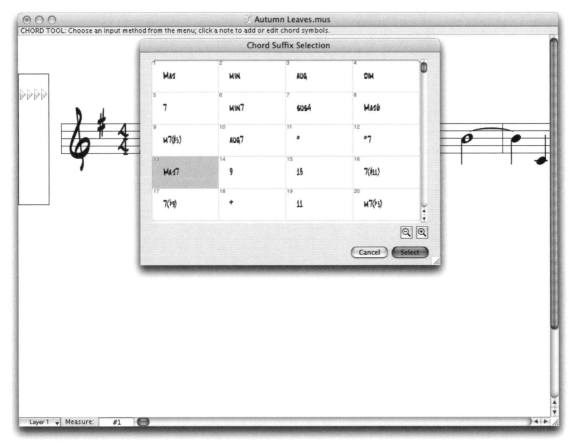

Figure 8.23 Type the root, enter :0, and press the spacebar to choose the suffix from a list.

12. Enter the remaining chord symbols shown in Figure 8.24. If you run into trouble, note the tips in the following bullets.

13. When you've finished entering the chords, press Ctrl+E (Command+E) to move to Page View.

  - Use # (Shift+3) to indicate a sharp. (Use a b to indicate a flat.)

  - In measure 7, type a - (hyphen) for the minor suffix.

  - The minor seven flat five suffix, -7(♭5), is near the bottom of the list (#82).

  - The D7 chord in measure 23 is on beat 3. Since there is no note on beat 3, add two half notes in Layer 2, hide them (H key), then attach the D7 chord symbol to the second half note. See Figure 8.25. Layer 2 must be the active layer while attaching chord symbols to notes in Layer 2. Return to Layer 1 and continue entering.

Figure 8.24 Type the root, enter :0, and press the spacebar to choose the suffix from a list.

Figure 8.25 Use hidden rests in Layer 2 to add chord changes over held notes.

Notice the chord symbols in the second and third systems collide with the repeat brackets. Let's fix that.

1. Click the second system to display the positioning triangles to the left of that system.

2. Drag the third positioning triangle up until the chord symbols do not collide with the repeat ending brackets. See Figure 8.26. The third positioning triangle applies to that system only.

Figure 8.26 Use the positioning triangles to adjust the chord baselines.

3. Repeat for the third system.

Note: The first positioning triangle applies to all chords in all staves for the whole document. The second positioning triangle applies to all chords in that staff only (for the whole document). The third applies to that staff in that system only (as we saw). You'll never need the fourth one (I haven't, anyway). These work the same for lyrics and expressions.

Adding the Lyrics

A single line of lyrics will not give you many problems in Finale. However, the first thing you notice in your lead sheet is the tight space between the chord symbols and the staves above.

Respacing the Systems to Make Room for Lyrics

To fit the lyrics between the systems, space them out a bit first:

1. Choose the Page Layout Tool ▣.

2. From the Page Layout menu, choose Space Systems Evenly. The Space Systems Evenly dialog box appears.

3. Choose Space Systems Evenly on Current Part or Score > All Pages. See Figure 8.27.

4. Click OK to respace the systems to fill the page. Now there is enough room for the lyrics.

Typing the Lyrics into the Score

We will use the same method adding lyrics that we did for adding chords: Type Into Score.

1. Click the Lyrics Tool ▣ and move to Page View if you aren't there already.

2. Press Ctrl+0 (Command+0).

3. Type 150 and click OK. Drag the music so measure 1 is visible.

4. Click the first note of the pickup measure. A blinking cursor appears below the staff.

5. Type The fall-ing leaves. Press the spacebar twice.

6. Type drift by the win-dow. Press the spacebar twice.

7. Type The aut-umn leaves. Press the spacebar twice.

8. Type of red and gold. Press Esc to choose the Selection Tool. (Word extensions and hyphens appear after switching tools.) Compare your document to Figure 8.28.

9. Click the whole note in measure 1. Leaves is highlighted.

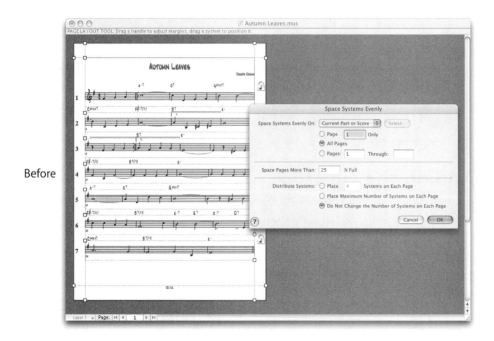

Before

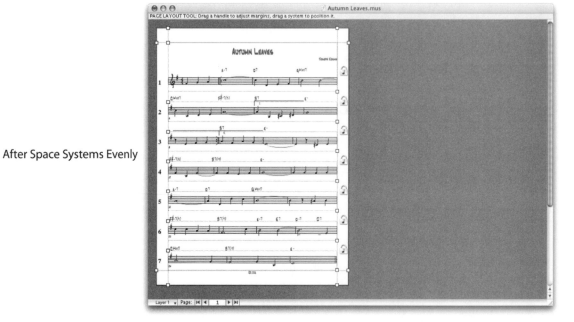

After Space Systems Evenly

Figure 8.27 Use Space Systems Evenly to easily redistribute the system spacing to fill the page.

Figure 8.28 Type your lyrics into the score like a word processor; Finale adds the hyphens and word extensions automatically.

10. Press the down arrow to move to verse 2. The blinking cursor appears below Leaves.

11. Type lips, spacebar, spacebar, the sum-mer kiss-es, spacebar, spacebar, the sun-burned hands.

12. Press the spacebar seven times so the cursor appears on beat 2 of measure 8. This is the last measure of the first ending, so we need to enter the pickup.

13. Type I see your. Press the spacebar twice.

14. Type I used to hold. Press Esc to bring up the word extensions and hyphens. Notice the word extension in the second verse extends well into measure 6. This is not right.

15. Double-click the word extension to display its handle. Click and drag the handle back to the barline as shown in Figure 8.29.

Figure 8.29 Click and drag overextended word extensions.

Note: The Break Smart Word Extensions (Measure Attributes) measure setting automatically applies to measures when you add repeat endings. If you ever have trouble breaking word extensions, highlight the measure and double-click it with the Measure Tool. Check Break Smart Word Extensions and click OK. Now your manual edits will stick.

---

16.   Press Esc to remove the word extension's handles and review the exact positioning.

17.   Select the Lyric Tool. From the Lyrics menu, check Type Into Score. That bugger gets unchecked when you edit word extensions. Your score should look like Figure 8.30.

18.   Click beat 3 of measure 11. Press the up arrow to be sure you are in verse 1.

19.   Finish the entering the lyrics yourself. When you're done, the page should look like Figure 8.31.

Congrats! You finished creating a real lead sheet and it doesn't even look half bad. It's not something you'd send to the presses, but your combo might put up with it. Most importantly, you've learned the basics for taking your idea and setting it in stone, or at least the digital equivalent. How many tunes like "Autumn Leaves" have been dreamed up and never notated? I guess we'll never know. But, hopefully you're one step closer to holding on to your next great idea.

And because I love hidden tracks, I'm going to squeeze in some bonus material down here. There isn't room in this book to slaughter everything, so here are some condensed tricks that pertain to this example. First, notice some extra space in the last system? I suppose we might as well add a cautionary pickup in case the group wants to play it again.

1.   Double-click the Measure Tool 📄. Finale tags a measure onto the end, creating a new page.

2.   Press Esc to choose the Selection Tool.

3.   Move to page 2, click the last measure, and press the up arrow. Four measures are now on the last system.

Figure 8.30   Verses complicate lyrics a bit, but after that it's often smooth sailing.

4.   Highlight the pickup measure and drag to the last three beats of the last measure.

5.   Click the Repeat Tool 📊.

6.   Double-click measure 26 (the second-to-last measure). The Repeat Selection dialog box appears.

7.   Double-click the Fine marking {FINE} and click OK. Drag Fine over measure 26. Now adjust the final barline to appear at the end of measure 26.

8.   Click the Measure Tool 📊.

9.   Double-click measure 26. The Measure Attributes dialog box appears.

10.   In the Barline row, click the final barline and click OK. Now let's rid ourselves of the pesky automatic final barline.

11.   From the Document menu, choose Document Options > Barlines.

Figure 8.31 When you're done it should look something like this.

12. Uncheck Final Barline at End of Piece and click OK. The final barline disappears.

13. Choose the Smart Shape Tool 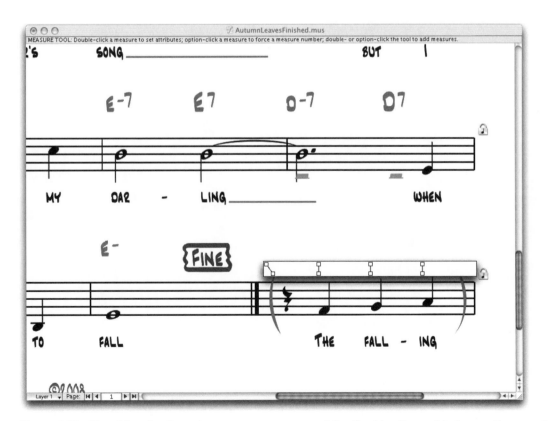.

14. Click the Slur Tool in the Smart Shape Palette.

15. From the Smart Shape menu, check Attach to Measures.

16. Click above the beginning of the measure and drag below the staff. When the slur looks like a parentheses, release the mouse button. Do the same for the end of the measure.

17. From the Smart Shape menu, check Attach to Notes (to restore the usual behavior).

18. If you want to move the rest to the right a little bit, choose the Measure Tool. Click the lower barline handle on the last barline. The Beat Chart handles appear above measure 27.

19. Drag the handle for beat 1 to the right, as shown in Figure 8.32.

Figure 8.32 To add a play-it-again measure we removed the final barline, added parentheses as Smart Shape slurs, and edited the beat chart.

Note: Some people think using Smart Shapes for large parentheses is a hack solution. Ways to spend a little extra time making these look prettier include creating shape expressions (drawing them with the Shape Designer), creating text expressions (using font characters), or creating articulations (duplicating existing parentheses articulations, and increasing the font size).

Tip: Oh, and just one more thing: If you're in Windows, select all and apply the MiBAC Jazz Rhythm Section Generator (Plug-ins > Scoring and Arranging > MiBAC Jazz Rhythm Section Generator). Now you can listen to this with rhythm piano, a drum set, and walking bass. Oh, man, that's just so freaking cool.

9 Piano Scores

As far as musical innovations are concerned, the invention of the pianoforte with touch-sensitive dynamic functionality, sustain-pedal support, and an expansive range arguably ushered in a golden age of creativity and expression. Never before had an individual been given simultaneous power over so many aspects of the music. How hard should I strike each key? When should I depress the damper? Or, much later, with what implement should I reach into the piano and pluck the strings manually? Despite this new tool's complexity, composers delighted in exploiting the bounty of options to their fullest, and virtuosos spent lifetimes mastering them.

While our instrument also includes a bounty of options, I sincerely hope you will not spend a lifetime mastering them. That old phrase "the first 10 years are the hardest" doesn't have to carry over into software, and your decision to read this book is a good indication that it doesn't apply to you. But, whether you are using Finale, SCORE, or ink and vellum, if you have notated virtuosic keyboard music, you are well aware of the challenges. Ever since wily pianists began pushing those limits, surly engravers have been shaking their fists in enraged bemusement, blotting their scores in tears. With that in mind, let us dip a toe into the world of keyboard music and see what bites.

Here's a summary of what you will learn in this chapter:

- Starting a new piano score
- Notating a piano piece
- More keyboard figures

Starting a New Piano Score

A couple centuries ago, if you happened to be a tortured virtuoso with impaired hearing pining over an impossible love, having the technical skills to cut a quill pen to your liking would be very important…especially if you intended to use it to scribble one of the most dark, mysterious, and beautiful piano compositions in history. Today, your name is Ludwig van Beethoven, and what will become Sonata No. 14 in C-sharp minor is being casually noodled on your piano. See Figure 9.1. Today's Beethovens who are blessed with such inspiration might be well served to have experience entering multiple layers, triplets, and cross-staff notes. If that doesn't seem as romantic as shaving a quill, I'd like to think it's just a matter of perspective.

Sonata, Op. 27, No. 2

Figure 9.1 We will use Beethoven's "Moonlight" Sonata to demonstrate several practical piano notation techniques.

In this chapter we will discuss these and other techniques important for piano compositions.

To prepare for this chapter, make sure your measurement units are set to inches. From the Edit menu, choose Measurement Units > Inches (from the Finale 2009 menu, choose Preferences > Measurement Units > Inches).

Beginning with the Setup Wizard

Earlier I mentioned that the Setup Wizard is so intuitive that any thorough explanation actually detracts from its usefulness (and wastes trees). Now I challenge you to begin a new piano score using the Setup Wizard (File > New > Document with Setup Wizard) without my help. All you need to know is the following:

- You do not need to change anything on the first screen. (In the future, choose your own document style.)

- The title is "Sonata, Op. 27, No. 2."

- The subtitle is "Sonata quasi una Fantasia."

- The composer is Ludwig van Beethoven.

- It is in cut time.

- It is in C-sharp minor (four sharps).

- The tempo indication should be Adagio sostenuto $\flat^9 = {}^9 66$.

Everything else can be specified after completing the Setup Wizard. When you complete the Setup Wizard, your score should look like Figure 9.2.

Adding Expressive Text

First we need to add a long strand of expressive text beneath the tempo marking, making it crystal clear that without a damper pedal, this entire piece must be played very delicately.

1. Choose the Expression Tool ![icon].

2. Double-click above the first measure to open the Expression Selection dialog box.

3. Click the Expressive Text category on the left. The preview window updates to show only expressive text markings.

4. Click Create Expressive Text to open the Expression Designer dialog box.

5. Type Si deve suonare tutto questo pezzo delicatissimamente e senza sordino. (See Figure 9.3.)

Figure 9.2 The Setup Wizard allows you to get started quickly. If you don't like how the score looks, don't worry—you can change anything on the page later.

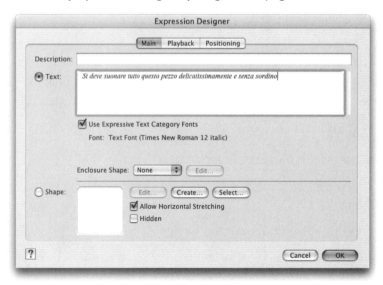

Figure 9.3 When you create a new expression, Finale applies the text style and font specified for the category (in this case, the Expressive Text category).

Tip: Click Edit Categories in the Expression Selection dialog box to change the font, size, style, or positioning of all expressions in any category.

---

6.   Click OK > Select. Finale adds the expressive text above the first measure.

7.   Click the expression's handle and drag it beneath the tempo marking. See Figure 9.4.

Figure 9.4   Expressive text is positioned relative to the beat.

Tweaking the Title and Page Layout

I have never really liked the way Finale positions the title, composer, or top system. A rogue score marking on the upper left needs to be deleted. Let's take a moment to dispatch these nuisances before we tackle the music.

1.   Choose the Text Tool .

2. Click the Score text block in the upper left of the page.

3. Press Delete. Do the same for the Arranger text to the right.

4. Right-click (Ctrl+click) the title and choose Edit Frame Attributes. The Frame Attributes dialog box appears. (You could just drag or nudge the title, but it's good to get in the habit of using precise measurements, because eyeing it will always come up a bit short.)

5. To the right of Vertical: Top (Header), replace 0 with 0.3.

6. Click OK. Nothing happens. The title moves up (.3 inches from the top page margin).

7. Repeat steps 4–6 for the subtitle. Use −.05 to move it beneath the top page margin.

We have some space to move the top system up a bit. The easiest way to do this is to decrease the distance between the staff and the top system's top margin. After this, the subsequent systems will move toward the top of the page, respectively.

1. Choose the Page Layout Tool 🔳.

2. Right-click (Ctrl+click) the top-left handle on the top system and choose Edit Margins. See Figure 9.5.

3. In the Edit System Margins dialog box, find the text box to the right of Top and replace 1.2222 with 1.

4. Click Apply. The system and all subsequent systems move toward the top of the page. Now we have some extra room on the page. (Our expressive text and tempo marking are attached to the first measure, so they move along with the system.) Now, we can maximize page usage even more by shrinking the left page margin.

5. Right-click (Ctrl+click) the left handle on the top page edge and choose Edit Margins.

6. Next to Left, replace 1 with .75 and click Apply. The margin moves to the left .25 inches. See Figure 9.6.

When you have adjusted the page formatting and title/composer positioning to match your precise specifications, save the file as a Document Style for use later. That way you won't need to make these changes every time you start your new piano composition. Remember, to save a Document Style, simply save to the Finale/Document Styles folder. Next time you use the Setup Wizard, this Document Style will be available on the first screen.

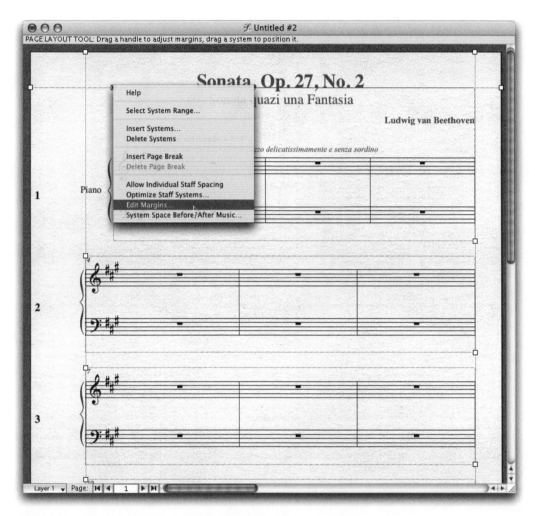

Figure 9.5   The Page Layout context menu offers easy access to system and page-margin values.

Notating a Piano Piece

HyperScribe offers the keyboard-savvy composer a quick and effective means to get notes on the page. By speeding up or slowing down the click track or using the foot pedal to tap the beats, real-time recording with a keyboard seems like the ideal option for notating keyboard music. Ironically, it is usually not. Why? Because keyboard music often includes multiple independent voices on each staff, cross-staff notes, divisi, ornaments, grace notes, and a whole bunch of other figures that HyperScribe simply cannot interpret properly. While the human ear may be capable of instantly isolating each independent voice in a complex passage of florid counterpoint, Finale is not. (Incidentally, when artificial intelligence does reach that point, you will likely have bigger problems to worry about.)

Figure 9.6   On the left is Finale's default and on the right is my personal preference. Your preferences will probably differ, but whatever they are, you can use the previous steps to help perfect them.

In this section, therefore, rather than using HyperScribe's real-time entry, we will cheat a little and use step-time entry, which allows us to hand-craft the notation with a bit more precision as we progress. Step-time entry is especially advisable while entering music with multiple voices and tuplets, which, in our example, occurs simultaneously.

Step-time allows us to specify the pitch using a MIDI keyboard, and is available in either Simple or Speedy Entry. Let's begin by entering the first six measures of eighth-note tuplets using Simple Entry.

Note: If you do not have a MIDI keyboard, you can always specify the pitches using your computer keyboard. See "Adding the Melody" in Chapter 8, "Lead Sheets," for details.

---

1.   Press Ctrl+E (Command+E) to move to Page View if you aren't there already.

2.   Choose the Simple Entry Tool ![icon]. The Simple Entry Caret appears at the beginning of measure 1.

3.   Press 4 in the numpad to change the duration to an eighth note. Or you can choose Ctrl+Alt+Shift+4 (Command+Alt+Shift+4).

4.   Press 9 to select the Simple Entry Tuplet Tool. Now both the Eighth Note Tool and the Simple Entry Tuplet Tool are selected in the Simple Entry Palette.

5. Play the first measure on your MIDI keyboard. Finale will enter the triplets automatically as you play. See Figure 9.7.

Figure 9.7   Finale automatically creates triplet definitions as you enter.

6. Continue entering triplets for the first six measures, as shown in Figure 9.8.

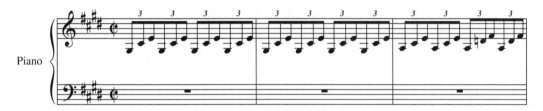

Piano

Figure 9.8   Yes, the beaming is all wrong. We'll fix that next.

Changing the Beamed Groups

We are in cut time, which usually means beaming is organized in half-note groups. Finale beams six notes together instead of just three. To fix this, follow these steps:

1. Choose the Time Signature Tool [icon].

2. Right-click (Ctrl+click) the first measure and choose 2/2 (Beamed as 4/4). The beams now-group three eighth notes instead of six, but the time signature has changed to the non-abbreviated 2/2.

3. Double-click the first measure to open the Time Signature dialog box.

4. Click Options (More Choices) to expand the dialog box.

5. Check Abbreviate and click OK (see Figure 9.9). The time signature is now displayed as ¢. Note that you can also define beat groups manually in the Time Signature dialog box by clicking Composite (see "Composite Time Signatures" in the Finale user manual).

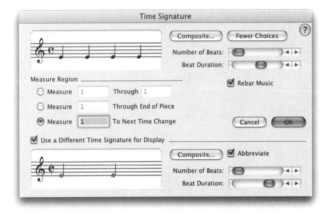

Figure 9.9   Use the Time Signature dialog box to change the appearance of the time signature and edit the beat grouping.

Applying Cross-Staff Notation

Cross-staff notation is a common characteristic of keyboard music, and one of those things that really got in the way for composers using early versions of Finale. These days, cross-staff notes generally don't cause much hassle. For this example, we need to move the first half of beat 1, measure 5, to the left hand.

1. Press Esc to select the Selection Tool.

2. Select the region including the first three notes of measure 5.

3. Press Alt+down arrow (Option+down arrow). Violà! The notes move to the lower staff. See Figure 9.10. To move notes from the left to the right staff, press Alt+up arrow

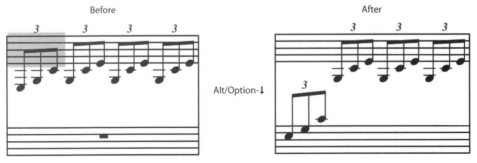

Figure 9.10   Highlight a region and press Alt+up arrow or Alt+down arrow (Option+up arrow or Option+down arrow) to create cross-staff notes.

(Option+up arrow) instead. Right now the tuplet number collides with the cross-staff notes.

4.   Click the Tuplet Tool ![tuplet tool] in the Main Tool Palette. (We don't need the Simple Entry Palette version right now.)

5.   Click+drag the tuplet's handle or press the up arrow key to nudge above the triplet beam.

Note: The notes still actually belong to the right-hand staff. You just applied the TGTools Cross Staff plug-in, which applied cross-staff functionality of the NoteMover Tool and a bunch of Special Tools actions. A big thanks to Mr. Tobias Giesen for this plug-in!

Adding the Melody

At measure 5, the melody enters on the last half of beat 2. Remember that to accommodate two separate voices on the same staff we need to use multiple layers.

Making Way for the Melody

Since we have already added the triplets in Layer 1, we need to move the notes in measures 5 and 6 to Layer 2, and then enter the first notes of the melody in Layer 1.

1.   Press Esc to choose the Selection Tool.

2.   Highlight measures 5–6 in the top staff.

3.   From the Edit menu, choose Move/Copy Layers. The Move/Copy Layers dialog box appears.

4.   Select the Move radio button and then check Contents of Layer 1 into Layer 2. See Figure 9.11.

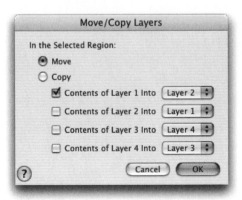

Figure 9.11   Move layers with the Move/Copy Layers dialog box.

5.   Click OK. The selected notes are now red, indicating you have moved them to Layer 2. Layer 1 is still selected.

Entering the Melody for Measures 5–6
To enter the melody for measures 5–6, do the following:

1.   Choose the Simple Entry Tool [♪].

2.   Ctrl+click (Option+click) measure 5 in the top staff to display the Simple Entry Caret.

3.   Press 6 in the numpad to select a half-note duration.

4.   Press 0 (zero) or Tab add a half rest above the staff.

5.   Ctrl+click (Option+click) and drag the half rest down to the middle staff line.

6.   Press the right arrow to activate the caret.

7.   Press 5 in the numpad, and press 0 (zero) or Tab to enter the quarter rest.

8.   Ctrl+click (Option+click) and drag the quarter rest down to the middle staff line. You can also change the default vertical placement of rests in Document Options—Layers.

9.   Press 4 in the numpad to select the eighth-note duration.

10. Play G sharp (as shown in Figure 9.12) and press the . (period) key.

11. Press numpad 3 and play G sharp again.

12. Press numpad 6 (to select a half note and play G sharp again) and press . (period).

13. Repeat steps 9 and 10 to enter the dotted eighth-sixteenth figure again at the end of measure 6.

Resolving Collisions
As the piano music you compose gets increasingly complex, you need to manually reposition individual notes more often. In our example, you'll notice the overlapping notes at the end of measure 6. Let's examine one way to resolve this type of collision.

1.   Press Esc to select the Selection Tool.

2.   Highlight measure 6, top staff.

3.   From the TGTools menu, choose Spacing > Make-Remove Space at End of Measure. The Make/Remove Space dialog box appears. If you don't have the full version of TGTools, download it from www.tgtools.de.

4.   In the text box, enter 10 and click Go. Finale adds 10 percent more space at the end of the measure.

Figure 9.12 When you enter notes in Layer 1 above Layer 2, the Layer 2 notes' stems flip automatically.

5.   Click the Measure Tool ▤. Two handles appear on every barline.

6.   Click the lower handle on the barline at the end of measure 6 to show the beat-chart handles.

7.   Click and drag the right-most beat-chart handle to move the sixteenth note into the new extra space; see Figure 9.13. Alternatively, you could use the Note Position Tool (in the Special Tools Palette) to move the sixteenth note horizontally.

TGTools includes several other utilities for managing spacing. When used in conjunction with the beat chart, Special Tools, and Speedy Entry (where you can drag notes horizontally), you can often easily manage even very crowded measures.

Music spacing and general collision avoidance is an ugly topic, and one of particular concern for engravers and copyists. Since our focus is composing, a perfectly spaced score is usually not an option. Here are some general tips to help keep your music legible without digging into the Special Tools too much.

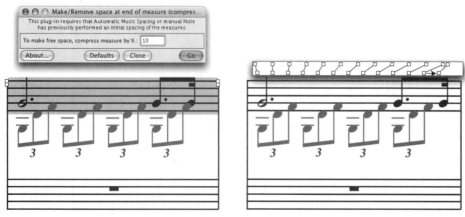

Figure 9.13 Use TGTools to add space at the end of a measure and use the Beat Chart or the Note Position Tool (Special Tools) to drag notes horizontally.

- Before manually editing the spacing, always apply Note Spacing to see if Finale can fix the problem automatically. Highlight the region and, from the Utilities menu, choose Music Spacing > Apply Note Spacing. Or, select a region with the Selection Tool and press 4.

- Note Spacing depends on your settings in Document Options—Music Spacing (Document > Document Options, and click Music Spacing). If you are running into a regular problem, review these settings to see if Finale can accommodate.

- Finale includes several Music Spacing libraries, including Loose, Medium, and Tight (Fibonacci is Finale's default). Load a Music Spacing library to experiment with your different spacing options. To do so, click Load Library in the Document Options dialog box (or, from the File menu, choose Load Library) and select the Music Spacing folder. After you've loaded the desired Music Spacing library, apply Note Spacing to a region to test the results.

- To increase or decrease the spacing of a specific measure, choose the Measure Tool and drag the top handle on a barline.

- When a measure simply won't fit on a system and all else fails, edit the measure layout. With the Selection Tool, highlight a measure and press the up arrow to move it to the previous system (or the down arrow to move it to the next).

Note: See Chapter 15, "Wrapping Up," for more information regarding music spacing, layout, and resizing.

Adding the Bass Notes

Simple Entry allows you to add multiple notes simultaneously:

1.   Choose the Simple Entry Tool .

2.   Ctrl+click (Option+click) the first measure of the bottom staff. The Simple Entry Caret appears.

3.   Pres 7 in the numpad. The caret changes to a whole note.

4.   Play both notes simultaneously. Both notes appear and the caret moves to measure 2; see Figure 9.14. If you are entering using your computer keyboard, enter the low C and then press 8 in the number row to add an interval of an octave.

Figure 9.14   Enter chords by playing multiple notes simultaneously in Simple Entry.

5.   Complete the first six measures in a similar way.

Adding the Slurs

To enter the slurs, do the following:

1.   Choose the Smart Shape Tool .

2.   Choose the Slur Tool in the Smart Shape Palette.

3.   To add a slur, simply double-click the first note and drag to the last note. Double-click the first note in measure 3, top staff; drag to the sixth note; then release the mouse button. See Figure 9.15.

Figure 9.15   Double-click and drag to enter the slurs.

4. Repeat step 3 for all the other slurs in the first six measures. When you add the slurs in measure 5 they will collide with the tuplet number.

5. Click the slur's handle and use the diamond positioning handles to change the slur's contour. See Figure 9.16.

Figure 9.16   Use the diamond positioning handles to adjust the slur contour.

Adding the Dynamics

Now we need to place some dynamic markings: a *pp* in measure 1 and again above measure 5 at the entrance of the melody. A *sempre* marking is beneath the first measure.

1. Choose the Expression Tool 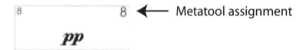.

2. Double-click in the middle of the top staff, above the first eighth note. The Expression Selection dialog box appears.

3. Click the Dynamics category. The dynamic expressions appear in the preview window. Note the metatool assignments to the upper right of each expression. See Figure 9.17.

    8   8 ⟵ Metatool assignment

    pp

Figure 9.17   We will use this metatool to enter the next *pp* marking.

Tip: New to Finale 2009: To change a metatool assignment for an expression, select the expression in the Expression Selection dialog, then hold down Shift and press the desired metatool key.

---

4. Double-click the *pp* expression. Finale adds the expression below the staff.

5. Use the left-most positioning triangle to drag the expression up a bit, as shown in Figure 9.18. (You can always simply drag an expression to move it independently.)

Figure 9.18 The left-most triangle applies the full score. The second applies to the whole staff. The third applies to that staff, that system only.

6. Hold down the 8 key and click the dotted eighth note in measure 5 of the top staff. The expression appears below the staff.

7. Click on the top staff of the second system to activate the positioning triangles and drag the third triangle above the staff. When the expression is positioned, release the mouse button. This change only applies to this staff and this system. Alternatively, you could simply drag the expression and it would continue to be positioned relative to the "full score" baseline.

    Now that we've added the dynamics, let's add the sempre marking to the right of the *pp* in measure 1.

8. Double-click directly above the second eighth note in measure 1 (on the staff). Choose the Expressive Text category, then double-click *sempre*.

9. Click the handle on *sempre* and drag the marking to the right of *pp*, as shown in Figure 9.19.

Tip: If you do not want an expression to be subject to regular baseline positioning changes, adjust that expression's Vertical Alignment setting in the Positioning tab of the Expression Designer dialog box. Or, adjust the Vertical Alignment setting in the Category Designer to apply the change to all expressions in that category.

Finishing Up

You have now learned enough to finish notating the first page of the score, as shown in Figure 9.20. Use the sample file included with Finale as a reference (Finale 2009/Sample Files/Beethoven.mus).

Here are some tips:

■ Go ahead and just enter all of the triplets in Layer 2.

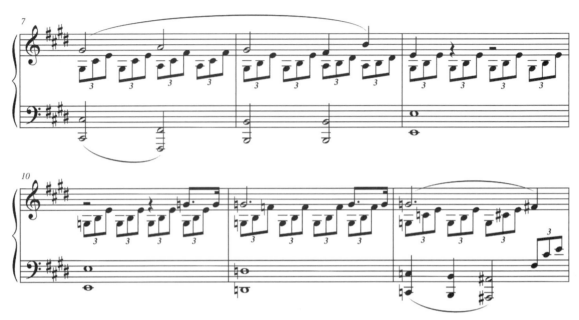

Figure 9.19 Drag expressions to their appropriate place relative to the baseline and any changes to the vertical positioning will apply to these expressions uniformly.

Figure 9.20 When you're done, measures 7 through 12 should look something like this.

- Don't worry about changing the stem direction. The stem direction will update automatically when you enter the other layer.

- Measure 10 includes naturals. If you enter these using a MIDI keyboard, the accidentals will be added automatically. If you are using your computer keyboard to enter, the + (plus) and − (minus) keys on the numpad can be used to increment a selected pitch up or down in half steps. (Laptop users, with the Simple Entry Laptop Set, use = and − to increment up and down by half steps.)

- In measures 10 and 11, use the TGTools Make/Remove Space at End of Measure plug-in to add extra space at the end of the measure. (Try 10 percent.) Then use the Beat Chart (Measure Tool) to move the sixteenth note to the right. (See "Resolving Collisions" earlier in this chapter.)

- In measure 12, enter the last eighth note triplet into the top staff and use the TGTools cross-staff plug-in to move the notes to the lower staff. Highlight the region and press Alt+down arrow (Option+down arrow).

Once you have finished entering this music there is still one major difference between your score and mine. See Figure 9.20. You haven't yet run Patterson Beams. As a composer who will not be tweaking every beam to engraver standards, I highly recommend always applying Patterson Beams before printing your sheet music. This utility seems to magically improve the appearance of your whole score.

1. Choose Document > Document Options > Beams.

2. Check Allow Primary Beam Within a Space.

3. Ensure Extend Beams Over Rests is unchecked.

4. Ensure Max Slope is a multiple of 6 (and 12 is okay). To view in EVPU, select it from the Units drop-down menu at the bottom of this dialog box.

5. Click OK.

6. Press Esc to choose the Selection Tool.

7. Press Ctrl+A (Command+A) to select all.

8. Choose Plug-ins (🔧) > Note, Beam, and Rest Editing > Patterson Plug-Ins Lite > Patterson Beams. The Patterson Beams dialog box appears.

9. Click OK.

More Keyboard Figures

This arrangement doesn't include fingerings, pedal indications, or an S slur, but all three could be appropriate here, so let's add them.

S Slurs

When a slur connects notes in different staves, use Finale's slur-editing handles to create the characteristic S-shaped contour.

1. Choose the Smart Shape Tool ![tool].

2. Make sure the Slur Tool is selected in the Smart Shape Palette.

3. Double-click the first eighth note in measure 13, drag to the last eighth note, and release the mouse button. The measure should now look like the left example in Figure 9.21.

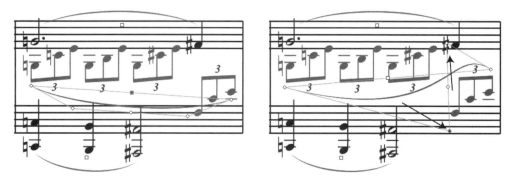

Figure 9.21 To create an S slur, use the diamond-shaped editing handles to adjust the contour.

4. Drag the diamond-shaped editing handles to adjust the contour of the slur (as shown in the right example of Figure 9.21).

Fingerings

Articulations, with positioning relative to the note, work well for fingerings as long as you use the right settings:

1. Choose the Articulations Tool ![tool]. Finale has already assigned the numbers 1–5 to the respective metatool keystrokes. Before we enter them, let's review some settings.

2. Click the first note in the top staff to open the Articulation Selection dialog box.

3. Click 1 and then click Edit to open the Articulation Designer.

4. Check Always Place Outside Staff.

5. Check Avoid Staff Lines (if it isn't checked already).

6. Click OK. Repeat steps 3 through 5 for articulations 2 through 5.

7. Click Select. Finale places a 1 above the staff.

8. Hold down the 2 key and click the second eighth note. Finale places a 2 above the staff.

9. Hold down the 3 key and click the third eighth note. Finale places a 3 above the staff. See Figure 9.22.

Figure 9.22 Enter articulations using metatools to quickly enter fingerings.

Piano Pedaling

To notate piano pedaling, we need to indicate when to depress the pedal and when to release it. You can indicate this many ways and all are added in Finale the same way. A couple appear in Figure 9.23.

Figure 9.23 Use the Custom Smart Shape Tool to add piano pedaling.

1. Choose the Smart Shape Tool ⬛.

2. Ctrl+click (Option+click) the Custom Line Tool ⬛ in the Smart Shape Palette. The Smart Line Selection dialog box appears.

3. Scroll down to select the desired figure. Several different line options are already available. Also the Ped * style is available here.

4. Click Select.

5. Double-click and drag to add the pedal indication.

10 Choral Scores

Back at St. Olaf (yes, it is a real college in Northfield, Minnesota), where we lived on a hill to be closer to God, choir was just a part of everyday life. The beautiful music, which seemed to burst from every corner of campus, was a legacy of the great choral champion F. Melius Christiansen. Each winter we donned our robes and sang "Beautiful Savior" in the great Christmas Festival tradition during which our athletic center was converted to a mesmerizing spectacle of voice and orchestra. As our ranks filled that enormous space with song, one really did feel part of something much greater. It was an opportunity I couldn't resist. Besides, choir was where all the really cute girls were.

Whatever motivates you to enter the arena of choral music, Finale is here to help bring your harmonious creations to life. Templates, lyric entry options, plug-ins, and other automatic features come together to provide fertile soil for all your needs while dealing with the integrated human instrument. Use Finale properly, and little can come between you and your SATB masterpiece. With a few special tricks it will practically write itself.

We'll pull out and dust off the HyperScribe Tool, Lyrics Tool, and Page Layout Tool for this one.

Here's a summary of what you will learn in this chapter:

- Starting a new SATB choral score

- Notating a choral piece with HyperScribe

- Setting words to music

- Adjusting the measure, staff, and system layout

Starting a New SATB Choral Score

The first thing to consider when you begin a new choral score is the system format (see Figure 10.1). If you are composing a hymn or homophonic piece, you might consider a closed score, which is basically a widely spaced grand staff. To begin a closed score, open the SATB (2-Staff) with Piano template in the Finale/Templates folder. (If you do not need the piano staves, just delete them.)

Figure 10.1 We will notate "Beautiful Savior" using HyperScribe.

Most choral scores require an **open-score** arrangement, which includes a separate staff for each voice. Open scores allow you to introduce divisi within a voice and are easier to read. Besides, if your creation doesn't require the extra staves, and you need to save paper, you can always implode the music into fewer staves later.

Tip: Misguided assumptions infringe on creativity more than Finale ever could. I challenge you to use this book's contents to create music true to your own passions, whatever they may be, even if you are determined to compose an "anti-art" cantata.

Again, we will use the Setup Wizard, because it's just so nifty (File > New > Document with Setup Wizard). Set up the score using the following information:

- On the first screen, choose the Choral (Engraver Font) Document Style. When you choose this Document Style, dynamics and expressive markings appear above the staff automatically.

- On the second screen, choose the Chorus and then add the Soprano, Alto, Tenor, and Bass staves.

- The title is "Beautiful Savior."

- In the Composer text box, enter Silesian folk tune.

- The Arranger is F. Melius Christiansen.

- The lyricist is Münster Gesanbuch, 1677.

- It is in 4/4 time.

- It is in D major (two sharps).

Tip: Ùse the Chãractêr Map tö add the silly umlauts ænd øther international çharacters. Click Start > Programs > Accessories > System Tools > Character Map (System Preferences > International). Click the Input Menu tab and select Check Character Palette and Show Input Tab in Menu Bar. Click the flag in the OS X Title Bar and choose Show Character Palette.

Everything else can be adjusted after completing the Setup Wizard. When you complete the Setup Wizard, your score should look like Figure 10.2.

If you do require a piano reduction, you don't need to bother adding the piano part yet. You can use the Piano Reduction plug-in to add it automatically after finishing your composition.

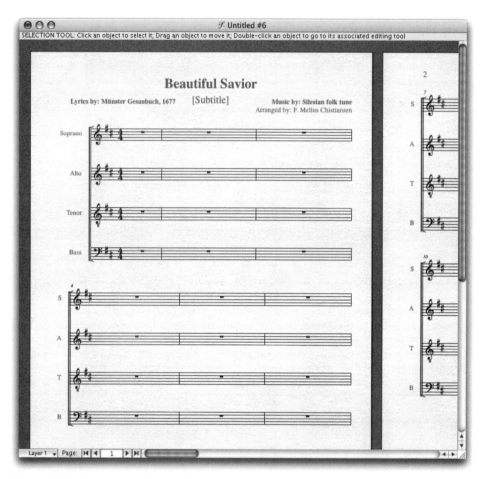

Figure 10.2   The Setup Wizard allows you to get started quickly. If you don't like how the score looks, don't worry, you can change anything on the page later.

Notating a Choral Piece with HyperScribe

We will be notating the hymn-like section of this arrangement, which includes the final 19 measures. To do so, we will use Finale's real-time entry method, HyperScribe. Don't worry, you don't need to be a pianist to take advantage of HyperScribe. *Hyper* refers to the speed with which you can cleanly enter music, not the tempo at which you must record. In this section, you will enter one voice at a time in a moderate tempo along with a click track, so whether you are a prodigy or a one-fingered wonder, you will be able to play this music.

Note: If your composition includes more complicated homophonic passages, the basic principles in this section will still apply.

Refer to the "Installation and MIDI Setup" chapter of the *Finale Installation and Tutorials* manual for instructions on setting up your MIDI keyboard. If you do not have a hard copy, you can find this topic in Finale's HTML help system (Help > User Manual > Finale Tutorials [Help > Finale Tutorials]).

If you do not have a MIDI keyboard, I recommend using this example to practice Simple or Speedy Entry using techniques you learned in Chapters 7, "The Composer's Wild Kingdom," and 8, "Lead Sheets" (and the *Finale Installation and Tutorials* and/or Simple Entry Exercises. mus file). You will need to use both Layers 1 and 2 for the tenor and bass staves. When you've entered the notes, skip ahead in this chapter to "Setting Words to Music (Adding Lyrics)."

Setting Up HyperScribe

Let's start by setting up HyperScribe's metronome click and quantization settings. We want to record at a forgiving tempo and with a forgiving quantization. Basically, we want Finale to do as much work for us as possible, so the note still goes in the right place even if we make a small mistake.

1. Click the HyperScribe Tool .

2. Choose HyperScribe > Beat Source > Playback and/or Click. If it is already checked, choose it anyway to open the Playback and/or Click dialog box.

3. Choose the Use This Tempo radio button.

4. Set the tempo to 96 if it isn't already.

5. In the Beat Equals section, click the quarter-note icon to set each beat to a quarter-note duration.

6. Set Start Signal for Recording to None (Record Immediately). The Playback and/or Click dialog box should look like Figure 10.3.

Figure 10.3   Use the Playback and/or Click dialog box to specify the speed of HyperScribe's metronome click.

7. Click OK. Now make sure you are using an acceptable quantization setting.

8. From the MIDI/Audio menu, choose Quantization Settings. The Quantization Settings dialog box appears.

9. For Smallest Note Value, enter the smallest note duration in the section you are about to record. In our example (look back to Figure 10.1), the smallest note duration is an eighth note, so click the eighth-note icon.

10. We will not be recording any tuplets, so choose the No Tuplets radio button. The Quantization Settings dialog box should now look like Figure 10.4.

11. Click OK to return to the score. You are now ready to start recording.

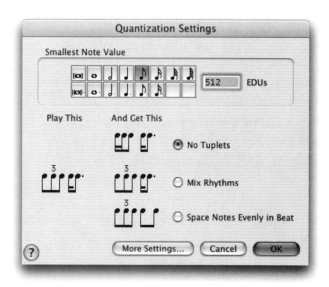

Figure 10.4 Change the Smallest Note Value setting to the smallest duration you intend to record.

Note: You can change the Smallest Note Value setting any time to accommodate the section you are recording. For example, to record the first 15 measures of the Soprano staff, you could set Smallest Note Value to a quarter note. Then, you might visit the Playback and/or Click dialog box to indicate a faster recording tempo given the greater margin of error offered by the quarter-note quantization.

Adding the Melody

Recording with HyperScribe is simple. Click a measure, wait for the two-measure count off, and play the music along with the metronome click. When you are done recording, click the score to end the HyperScribe Session. For this example, record the melody shown in Figure 10.5. Click the score when you are done. If you make a mistake, just click at any measure to begin recording again and HyperScribe will overwrite the existing content.

Figure 10.5   Record this melody using HyperScribe.

Tip: If you would like to increase or decrease the speed of the metronome click, from the HyperScribe menu, choose Beat Source > Playback and/or Click, and enter a different tempo for Use This Tempo.

Now that the melody has been entered, let's remove all those extra measures:

1. Press Esc to choose the Selection Tool.

2. Double-click measure 20 to select the full measure stack.

3. Press Shift+End. Alternatively, you could Shift+click the last measure.

4. Press Delete to remove the extra measures.

At this point you may be wondering what to do about the extra Alto staff in the first few systems and how to manage the number of measures per system. Don't worry, we will remove the extra Alto staff and adjust the measure and system layout after we've entered the music. I recommend leaving the measure and system layout alone until all the music has been entered. Concerning yourself with these issues distracts from the task at hand if you are composing, and can be done with greater focus and speed while wrapping up the project.

Adding the Harmony

You can add the harmony the same way you added the melody:

1. Click the HyperScribe Tool ▧.

2. Click measure 1 in the Tenor staff, wait two measures, and record the vocal line shown in Figure 10.6. (We will come back to the Alto staff later).

Figure 10.6   Finale plays the existing music as you record as long as Play Staves While Recording is checked in the Playback and/or Click dialog box.

3. Click the score when you are done.

    As before, if you make a mistake, just click at any measure to begin recording again and HyperScribe will overwrite the existing content. Notice Finale enters an E flat on the first half note in measure 10. Let's flip this enharmonic to a D sharp.

4. Choose the Simple Entry Tool 🎵.

5. Press Ctrl (Option) and click the E flat.

6. Press the \ (backslash) key to flip the note to a D sharp. Finale automatically adds a natural to the D on beat 4.

Adding a Secondary Voice with HyperScribe

This piece includes two independent vocal lines on both the tenor and bass staves. Therefore we need to take care not to overwrite the music we just entered. Here's how to enter the second tenor line:

1. Click the HyperScribe Tool 📚.

2. Choose Layer 2 [1 2 3 4 Layer 2 ▾] from the layer-selection buttons in the lower-left corner of the document window.

3. Click measure 1 in the Tenor staff, wait two measures, and record the vocal line shown in Figure 10.7. Click the score when you are done. As before, if you make a mistake, just click at any measure to begin recording again and HyperScribe will overwrite the existing content.

Now let's enter the baritone and bass lines into the Bass staff. Use the same method we used for the Tenor staff. Be sure to select Layer 1 to record the baritone line, then record the bass line in Layer 2. Use Figure 10.8 as a guide.

This time Finale notated the accidental properly in measure 7.

Figure 10.7 Choose a different layer record a different vocal line on the same staff.

Figure 10.8 Use both Layers 1 and 2 for the Bass staff as well.

Fixing the Rests

In both the Tenor and Bass staff, Finale creates two quarter rests on the last beat of the last measure automatically, one for each layer. To set rests to appear at the same vertical position (appear as a single rest):

1. From the Document menu, choose Document Options and select Layers.

2. Uncheck Adjust Floating Rests By _ Steps.

3. At the top, click the Settings For drop-down menu and choose Layer 2.

4. Uncheck Adjust Floating Rests By _ Steps again.

Beginning Divisi Mid-Measure

This piece happens to be filled with several little goodies that demonstrate some of the regular stumbling blocks composers face. In measure 17 of the Soprano staff, the voice splits into divisi on beat 3. Finale always automatically enters from the beginning of the measure. So, one might ask, how do I begin entering the second voice at beat 3? For this situation, you need to enter a hidden "placeholder" half rest before entering the Layer 2 notes...

1. Click the Simple Entry Tool ![icon].

2. Choose Layer 2 from the layer-selection buttons (pop-up menu) in the lower-left corner of the document window.

3. Press 6 in the numpad to select a half note (or click the Half Note Tool in the Simple Entry Palette).

4. Click to enter a half note at the beginning of measure 17 in the Soprano staff.

5. Press R to change the note to a rest.

6. Press H to hide the rest. Finale flips down the stems in Layer 1 accordingly.

7. Click the fourth line D to enter the half note. The existing half note's stem flips up accordingly.

Note: You can use these steps to add the divisi notes in the last three measures of the Alto staff as well (look ahead to Figure 10.25) after finishing this chapter.

Adding the Sostenuto Marking

The piece is marked Sostenuto, and we also want to set the tempo to audition playback properly.

1. Select the Expression Tool ![icon]. Double click measure 1.

2. Choose the Tempo Marks category and then click Create Tempo Mark. The Expression Designer appears.

3. Type Sostenuto.

4. Choose the Playback tab.

5. Under Type, choose Tempo, and specify a quarter note (if it isn't selected already). Then, after Set to Value, enter 80.

6. Click OK then Select. Sostenuto appears above measure 1.

7. Click the handle on this expression and drag it up a bit. We will be adding a dynamic marking between it and the staff next.

8. Click the Play button in the Playback Controls to listen to the arrangement. To adjust Human Playback's interpretation, from the MIDI/Audio Menu, choose Human Playback and select a style.

Adding the Dynamics

We certainly wouldn't want a sheepish performance, so let's add a *f* marking above the beginning of the first measure in each staff. If you are viewing your score in Page View, it will look a little disheveled at the moment. If it bothers you, move to Scroll View.

1. Choose the Expression Tool **mf**. Let's use one of Finale's new tricks to quickly enter all three of these at once.

2. Hold down the 4 key, click+drag over measure 1 in all staves, then release the mouse button. Finale adds four *f* markings above the beginning of measure 1.

3. Press the down arrow about 10 times to move the expressions closer to the staff (so they no longer collide with the Sostenuto marking). See Figure 10.9.

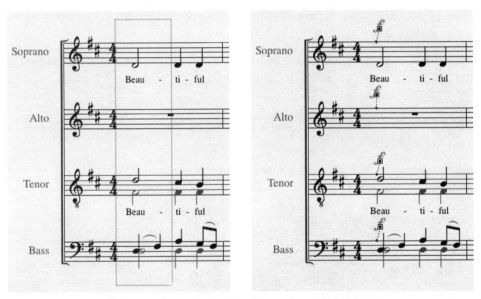

Figure 10.9 Use drag-apply to quickly add dynamics to multiple staves.

Tip: When unwanted artifacts appear, press Ctrl+D (Command+D) to redraw the screen.

---

4. Hold down the 5 key and click+drag over beat 2 of measure 15 for the Tenor and Bass staves. Finale adds *mf* above the Tenor and Bass staves.

5. Add a *ff* marking at beat 3 of measure 17 in all staves. The metatool for *ff* is 3. Upon entering an expression, you can always click the handle to drag it into place as needed.

There is an extra forte marking on measure 1 of the Alto staff, but we will be hiding that staff later, so you can leave it be. The fortissimo in measure 17 of the Alto staff will receive notes soon.

Adding a Tempo Alteration

This piece gives us an opportunity to discover the new power of expressions. The Finale 2009 upgrade fixed dreadful problems regarding expression entry. Tempo alterations are also expressions, but since they are in a different category, their positioning settings are separate. Tempo alterations usually appear above the top staff in a system (like our Sostenuto marking).

Let's create a senza rit. tempo alteration expression and add it above the top staff of measure 18. Even though this text actually means "without slowing down," we should treat it like a tempo alteration because, among other things, it's a lovely example of irony.

1. Choose the Expression Tool ![icon].

2. Double-click anywhere in measure 18. The Expression Selection dialog box appears.

3. Choose the Tempo Alterations category. Our expression isn't in the list, so let's create one.

4. Click Create Tempo Alteration to open the Expression Designer dialog box, as shown in Figure 10.10.

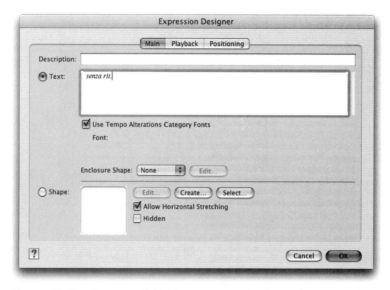

Figure 10.10 Category definitions automatically apply to expressions you create.

5. Type senza rit. (including the period) and Finale applies the Tempo Alterations category font and style.

6. Click OK, then Select. Finale adds the senza rit. expression above the top staff. Drag it so it appears above the whole note.

Placing the Tempo Alteration on All Staves Using a New Staff List

Finale places the expression above the top staff only because the Tempo Alterations category includes a Staff List definition. **Staff Lists** allow you to assign tempo and rehearsal marks to multiple staves. Finale does a pretty good job setting those up for you, so you shouldn't have to worry about them much. But, in this case, the poor basses need to look across quite a bit of space to notice that tempo alteration way up there. It should really appear on all the staves. To do this, edit the Tempo Alteration Staff List:

1.   Double-click the senza rit. marking. The Expression Selection dialog box appears. The Tempo Alterations category should be selected.

2.   Click Edit Categories. The Category Designer dialog box appears.

3.   From the Staff List drop-down menu, choose Staff List 2.

4.   Click the Edit button to the right. The Staff List dialog box appears. Staff List 2 should be selected in the list to the left.

5.   Under the Score column check Check All Staves and uncheck the Top Staff check box.

6.   Click OK. You return to the Category Designer.

7.   Click OK. You return to the score.

You have just defined the second of four possible Staff Lists. In expressions assigned to Staff Lists, the top occurrence is called the **Master Expression**. Click and drag the top senza rit. marking to move all subsequent markings uniformly. Click and drag the other occurrences to move them independently, until each is placed appropriately above its staff.

Copying to the Alto Staff

The soprano and alto parts are identical until measure 16, where the alto part drops an octave and goes off into its own direction. Let's copy the music, transpose it, and tweak the pitches accordingly.

1.   Press Esc to choose the Selection Tool.

2.   Click measure 15 in the Soprano staff to highlight it.

3.   Shift+click the last measure in the Soprano staff. Measures 15–19 should be selected in the Soprano staff. (We needed to move the dotted half note in measure 15 down as well because the last system will begin on measure 15 when we adjust the measure layout later.)

4.   Click the highlighted region, drag down to the Alto staff until measures 15–19 are surrounded with a black border, then release the mouse button.

5.   Select measures 16–19 of the Alto staff and press the 8 key. Finale transposes the last three measures of the Alto staff down an octave.

Now let's use the Simple Entry Tool to change the pitches of the notes in measures 17 through 19.

1.   Choose the Simple Entry Tool .

2.   Hold down Ctrl (Option), then click the C and drag it up to the second-space A.

3.   Do the same for the D in the last measure.

4.   Add the secondary notes in Layer 2; see Figure 10.11.

Figure 10.11   Remember to use hidden rests in Layer 2 to begin entering at a beat other than beat 1.

Double Stems

Often you can add Layers 1 and 2 on top of one another to get the double-stem effect. We have already done this if you take a look at, for example, measure 9 in the bass part. This doesn't work as well for dotted notes, as Finale tends to place two augmentation dots instead of just the one required (since their positioning differs depending on the stem direction). To add double stems on dotted notes, such as the last note in the Soprano staff, use the Double/Split Stem Tool:

Note: In this score, the following steps are adequate (and often useful). But, if overlapping notes with augmentation dots are common, consider going to Document > Document Options > Augmentation Dots and unchecking Adjust Dot for Multiple Voices so they overlap automatically.

---

1.   Windows users, from the Window menu, choose Advanced Tools Palette.

2.   Choose the Special Tools Tool 🔧.

3.   Choose the Double/Split Stem Tool 🎵.

4.   Choose Layer 1 from the layer-selection buttons (pop-up menu) in the lower-left corner of the document window.

5.   Click the dotted half note in measure 19 of the Soprano staff to bring up handles above and below the staff.

6.   Click the handle above the staff to enter the double stem. It will play back automatically.

Setting Words to Music (Adding Lyrics)

In Chapter 8 you read how to type lyrics directly into the score, which is great for lead sheets. But when the same text is used multiple times (on different staves and/or different measures, for instance), you might tire of typing the same thing over and over again. Because redundancy is the root of all forces opposing creative activity, let's see what we can do to avoid it.

Finale allows you to enter lyrics once and then enter them into the score as many times as you want by clicking with the mouse. Let's add our lyrics using this method, called Click Assignment.

1.   Click the Lyrics Tool 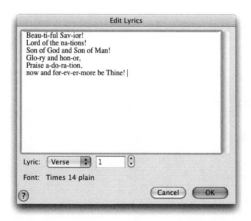.

2.   From the Lyrics menu, choose Edit Lyrics.

3.   Type the lyrics into the Edit Lyrics dialog box. See Figure 10.12. It's verse 4 of the hymn translated by Joseph A. Seiss. Be sure to mind the hyphenation.

Figure 10.12   Type lyrics into the Edit Lyrics dialog box if you intend to enter the same set of lyrics multiple times. Note that carriage returns do not apply to the score.

4.   When you have entered the lyrics, click OK.

5.   From the Lyrics menu, choose Click Assignment. The Click Assignment dialog box appears. Now you simply click a note to add the left-most lyric.

6.   Be sure you are in Layer 1. Use the layer-selection buttons in the lower left of the document window.

7.   In the Soprano staff, click the first four notes, skip the second beat of measure 2, then click the half note on beat 3 of measure 2. Finale places the lyrics and hyphenates automatically. Finale will also add word extensions automatically. See Figure 10.13.

Figure 10.13   Click to easily add lyric syllables with Click Assignment.

8.   Continue entering lyrics, clicking each note that requires a syllable. Press Ctrl+Z (Command+Z) if you make a mistake to undo, then use the arrows on the scroll bar to navigate to the appropriate syllable. See Figure 10.14.

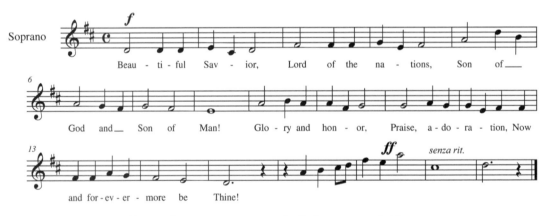

Figure 10.14   Finale adds word extensions automatically between syllables.

9.   When you reach measure 15, you will notice you are out of syllables. The Click Assignment dialog box is empty. But, you still need to enter the last phrase again. No problem, just click the left arrow several times until "Now" appears on the left edge (see Figure 10.15).

10.   Click the remaining lyrics into the Soprano staff; see Figure 10.16.

11.   From the Lyrics menu, choose Clone Lyric.

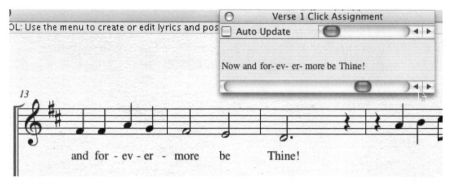

Figure 10.15 Use the arrows in the Click Assignment dialog box to navigate back and forth through the verse.

Figure 10.16 The same source is used for both copies of the same phrase.

12. Click to highlight measure 15 in the Soprano staff; then Shift+click measure 1 in the Soprano staff. Measures 1–15 will be highlighted.

13. Click and drag the highlighted region down to the Tenor staff. When measures 1–15 are highlighted, release the mouse button. See Figure 10.17.

Figure 10.17 Use Clone Lyrics to quickly copy verses to different staves.

Note: After you clone lyrics, the word extensions and hyphens do not always update immediately. When you apply Music Spacing, they will fall in line accordingly. Or, choose Utilities > Update Smart Word Extensions and Hyphens.

---

14. Use Click Assignment to finish entering the lyrics. You need to add "Glo-ry and ho-nor" beneath measures 8–10 of the Bass staff and "Now and for-ev-er-more be Thine!" beneath measures 15–19 of the Tenor staff. Use Figure 10.18 as a reference. Finale will add an extra-long word extension after your last note in the Bass staff (measure 10). Shorten this in the next step.

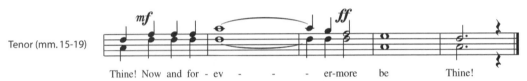

Figure 10.18 Use Click Assignment to add the remaining lyrics.

15. From the Lyrics menu, choose Edit Word Extensions. Click the handle and press Delete to remove it.

Lyrics are one of those things that always seem to flow easily in theory, but can quickly become a nightmare if you aren't careful. As you enter lyrics, remember that when you copy music with the Selection Tool, the lyrics come along for the ride unless you use the filter to exclude them (via the Edit Filter dialog box). Copying music with lyrics causes source text duplication, and you can end up with a big mess in the Edit Lyrics dialog box.

Adjusting the Vertical Lyric Positioning

Notice the extra space above the lyrics. For example, you can move the lyrics beneath the top staff in all four systems upwards slightly. To get the tightest spacing possible, you will need to reposition these lyrics. This will become especially important later when you are adjusting the vertical staff spacing to fit more music on the page.

1. Click the Lyrics Tool.

2. From the Lyrics menu, choose Type Into Score. Now when you click a staff, you will see four positioning triangles appear to the left.

3. Click the top staff of the top system. (If you moved to Scroll View, press Ctrl+E [Command+E] to return to Page View.)

4. Drag the third positioning triangle up slightly. The lyrics in that staff and in that system reposition accordingly. You need to use the third triangle to specify the top staff in the

top system only, for example. Remember, the first triangle repositions all lyrics (all staves) and the second repositions all lyrics in that particular staff throughout the score.

5. Repeat steps 3 and 4 for any other staff whose lyrics you can move up. Every little bit of extra space helps.

Adding the Slurs (Melismas)

Whenever multiple notes are sung on the same syllable, the notes are generally slurred. These figures are called **melismas**. Finale comes equipped with a very nice tool that makes it easy to add melisma slurs.

1. Press Esc to choose the Selection Tool.

2. Press Ctrl+A (Command+A) to select all.

3. From the Plug-ins 🎵 menu, choose Lyrics > Auto Slur Melismas.

4. Move to measure 10, click the absurdly huge slur, and press Delete to remove it.

Finale identifies all the melismatic passages and adds slurs accordingly. Unfortunately, it only recognizes the lyric's layer (in this case, Layer 1), so you will need to manually add the slurs on Layer 2 using the Smart Shape Tool.

Removing Extra Hyphens

By default, Finale adds more hyphens than necessary. To fix that, do the following:

1. From the Document menu, choose Document Options and select Lyrics.

2. For Maximum Space Between Hyphens, enter 2.

3. Click OK. The extra hyphens in measures 9–10 of the Bass staff and measures 16–17 in the Tenor staff disappear.

Adjusting the Measure, Staff, and System Layout

Now that you have entered the music it is time to deal with the measure, system, and page layout. The energy you have been using to compose must now be diverted to the completely different, practical aspects of making the score legible for your vocalists. We want to fit the score into four systems on one page, remove the Alto staff in the first three systems (as it doubles the Soprano staff), and leave enough space so it doesn't look too cluttered. See Figure 10.19.

Remember, we are not shooting for publisher-quality layout here. That would take too much time and years of engraving experience. You need to give your vocalists a reasonably legible score without spending too much of your life agonizing over Finale's quirks.

Figure 10.19   Use Fit Measures, the Selection Tool, the Page Layout Tool, and the Resize Tool to adjust the layout.

Here is one way to shape up your score. I am leaving the page size 8.5×11 because that is the size of most printer paper, and we might as well use the real estate we have. If you intend to print to Octavo, the steps in this section will be a bit different, but the general procedure will still work. Before we move into the layout, we need to move the text blocks around a bit:

1. From the Edit menu, choose Measurement Units and ensure Inches is checked (Finale 2009 > Preferences > Measurement Units > Inches).

2. Click the Text Tool **A**.

3. Click the [Subtitle] text block and press Delete to remove it.

4. Right-click (Ctrl+click) the handle on the title and choose Frame Attributes. The Frame Attributes dialog box appears.

5. Under Alignment and Positioning, for Vertical (Top) (Header), enter .3 and click OK.

6. The same way, set the Lyrics By and Music By text blocks to −.15, then set Arranged By to −.35.

Now we have enough space to start thinking about fitting all of our systems on the page.

Fitting Measures

First, let's confirm the number of measures per system. Your systems may already be five measures long, or your last system may be only two measures long. (To be honest, I still haven't figured out all the variables regarding Finale's default measure layout, so let's just run Fit Measures to make sure we're on the same page.)

1. From the Utilities menu, choose Fit Measures. The Fit Measures dialog box appears.

2. Enter 5 for Lock Layout With and click OK.

3. Press Esc to choose the Selection Tool.

4. Click to select measure 15 and press the down arrow key. Finale moves measure 15 to the last system. There should now be five measures on the first, second, and fourth system, and four measures on the third.

Optimizing

Optimization (a.k.a. "French scoring") removes empty staves from systems to free up space for staves that contain music (thus "optimizing" the space on the page). The piece we are working with is an excellent example of the merits of optimization because the Alto staff is unnecessary in the first three systems, and we definitely need that space to fit these four systems on one page. By optimizing we can eliminate those empty staves and allow individual vertical staff positioning within each system.

1.   Choose the Page Layout Tool .

2.   From the Page Layout menu, choose Optimize Staff Systems. The Staff System Optimization dialog box appears.

3.   Leave the default settings as shown in Figure 10.20. These settings will apply optimization to all systems in the score.

Figure 10.20 Optimizing can remove empty staves from Page View and/or make staves in specified systems independently adjustable. This "post-optimization" adjusting is done with the Staff Tool.

4.   Click OK. Finale removes the Alto staff for the first three systems; see Figure 10.21.

At this point the score is probably acceptable if you simply need a legible score, even though the second page only contains one system. An engraver would either put two systems on each page, or squeeze that fourth system onto the first page. For our purposes, assume we absolutely need to squeeze that fourth system onto the first page. After all, two pages are twice as many that can fall down between the risers.

Changing the Staff Name

The top staff doesn't just belong to the sopranos. They need to share with the altos for the first 14 measures. Let's change the staff name to indicate that.

1.   Choose the Staff Tool .

2.   Right-click (Ctrl+click) the handle on the Soprano staff name and choose Edit Full Staff Name.

Figure 10.21   Optimized systems are marked with an optimization icon to the right of each system.

3.   Below Soprano, enter Alto and click OK to return to the score.

4.   Click the updated staff name and press the up arrow to center it with the staff.

If you want to add an A beneath the S on the subsequent two systems, use a Staff Style; see Figure 10.22.

Figure 10.22   Use a Staff Style to change the abbreviated staff name for the second two systems.

1.   Choose the Staff Tool ▦.

2.   From the Staff menu, choose Define Staff Styles. Click New and type Soprano-Alto Staff Name.

3. Click Edit next to Abbreviated Staff Name. The Edit Text dialog appears.

4. Type S, Return, A. Click OK twice.

5. Highlight measures 6–14 in the Soprano staff, right-click (Ctrl+click), and choose Soprano-Alto Staff Name (the Staff Style you just defined). The abbreviated staff name changes to SA.

6. Click the updated abbreviated staff name and press the up arrow to center it with the staff.

Resizing the Systems

If we are going to fit this piece onto a single page we need to get aggressive, and that means resizing all the music. We could resize the whole page, but that would include the title and composer, which we do not want to change. Let's resize the systems:

1. Choose the Resize Tool ⅋.

2. Right-click (Ctrl+click) a system and choose Resize System to open the Resize Staff System dialog box.

3. Enter 80 for And Resize System.

4. Click OK.

Finale reduces the size of all the music and all the markings attached to the music and staves. The title and composer are unchanged.

Adjusting the Staff Positioning

We are closer to fitting all four systems of the page, but we still need more room. And, we don't want to make the music any smaller than it already is. So, let's squeeze the staves together as much as we can. Remember, all of our systems are already optimized, so each staff is independently adjustable.

1. Choose the Staff Tool 𝄞. Two handles appear on the left edge of each staff on every system.

2. Drag up the lower handle on all the staves as much as you can before colliding with the lyrics above. See Figure 10.23.

Adjusting the System Positioning

Now that all of our systems are as short as possible, let's see if we can get that fourth one on the first page. When you increase the amount of space at the bottom of page 1 enough, the fourth system will snap back to fill that space automatically.

Figure 10.23 Use the lower staff handle to adjust the staff positioning individually in each system.

1. Choose the Page Layout Tool ▢. The system and page margins appear. First, there is some room between the top system and the composer/title text, so let's move it up a bit. As you do, all other systems on the page will follow suit.

2. Click the upper-left handle on the top system and drag it just below the Lyrics By text.

3. Click the middle of the first system and drag it up as high as it will go. See Figure 10.24.

4. Click the middle of the second system and drag it all the way up against the first.

5. Click the middle of the third system and drag it up against the second.

6. Click the fourth system on the next page and drag it all the way to the top. If your music is spaced tightly enough, it snaps back to the first page. If not, check for any remaining extra space and crunch the music further using the Staff Tool, Lyrics Tool, and Page Layout Tool.

Resizing the Lyrics

The lyrics are a bit small at a system reduction of 80%. To increase the lyric size, do the following:

1. Click the Lyrics Tool ▢.

2. From the Lyrics menu, choose Edit Lyrics.

3. Press Ctrl+A (Command+A) to select all.

4. From the Text menu, choose Size > 14, then click OK.

Adjusting the Page Margins

Finally, let's increase the left and right page margins a bit:

1. Choose the Page Layout Tool ▢.

Figure 10.24 Drag the upper-left handle of the top system down, and then click the middle of the system to drag it, and subsequent systems, toward the top of the page.

2. From the Page Layout menu, choose Page Margins > Edit Page Margins. The Edit Page Margins dialog box appears.

3. In the Left and Right text boxes, enter 1, as shown in Figure 10.25. This will give us a little more breathing room on either side of the page.

4. Click Apply and then close out of the dialog box to return to the score.

Figure 10.25   Use the Edit Page Margins dialog box to review and change the page margins.

Voilà! You've just notated a reasonably involved piece of music and seen some of the common obstacles that plague choral composers (and engravers) everywhere. It isn't a classic work of (visual) art, but it will get the job done. This one took a little longer than expected (and I sort of feared the wrath of God if I got anything wrong). I'll try to be nicer next chapter.

11 Guitar Scores

Writing for guitar is no different from writing for any other instrument, except most guitarists can't read music very well. So, we have this elaborate fingering-chart-notation hybrid called **tablature**. In reality, the physical appearance of fretted instruments happens to resemble staff lines, so adding a logical fingering guide beneath the staff makes a lot of sense, especially considering things like bends, hammer-ons, and so on. Anything to make your music more accessible to a larger group of performers is a good thing, right? (Even if their lifestyles do frighten and confuse you.)

Although guitar scores are unique in many ways, tablature is an alternative notation style entirely, and a distinguishing element of guitar music (and one that Finale supports rather well). Tab is therefore the focus of this chapter. Each line of a tablature staff represents a physical string on the instrument and the fret numbers placed on the lines represent the fret in which the string should be depressed. The curvy lines and other zaniness indicate the various ways you can manipulate the strings/pickups, and the golden splattering is from when Darth's duck walk met a high-hat stand shooting streams of beer across the stage.

Here's a summary of what you will learn in this chapter:

- Starting a new guitar score
- Notating a guitar piece with tablature
- Adding guitar markings

Starting a New Guitar Score

We will notate a piece I wrote in the Blue Ridge Mountains of North Carolina. This one includes regular notation, accompanying tablature, chord symbols with fretboards, "let ring" indications, hammer-ons, pull-offs, and slides...a good start. See Figure 11.1.

Finale comes with a few nice guitar templates, so let's begin with one. From the File menu, choose New > Document from Template and open Finale 2009/Templates/Guitar Templates/House Style 3. I'll let you finish the setup procedure. Note the following:

- The title is "Blue Mountain Étude."

Blue Mountain Étude *Mark Johnson*

Figure 11.1 We will notate "Blue Mountain Étude" with tab using Simple Entry.

- The composer is Mark Johnson. (That's me!)

- It is in 4/4 time.

- It is in A major (three sharps).

- The tempo is ♩ = 120.

Remember, to add the É, you can use your operating system's Character Map (Character Palette). You can specify everything else after completing the Setup Wizard. When you complete the Setup Wizard, your score should look like Figure 11.2.

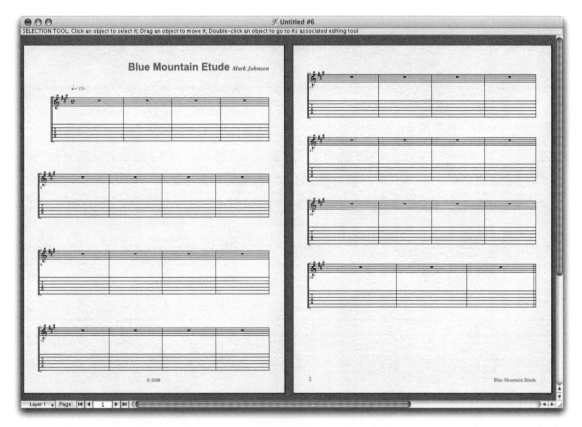

Figure 11.2 Isn't this a nice template? I really think this is a nice template.

You can also create a guitar score with tablature from the Setup Wizard. While adding instruments, simply add Guitar and Guitar [TAB] from the Fretted Instruments category. The Setup Wizard includes a variety of different types of fretted instruments including banjo, lute, mandolin, and dulcimer, among others.

Notating a Guitar Piece with Tablature

The first thing to recognize about writing guitar parts with Finale is that standard notation and guitar tablature are completely interchangeable. You can copy music from a standard staff into a tablature staff (or vice versa), and Finale does the translation automatically. Therefore, the method you use for composing guitar music depends heavily on your proficiency with standard notation versus tablature. If you are composing at the piano and are more familiar with standard notation, you will enter into the standard staff. If you are composing with a guitar, you will likely want to enter your composition directly into the tablature staff. I will cover both methods.

For this example, we will assume you are composing for a standard guitar-string tuning (E, A, D, G, B, E).

Note: You can use any string-tuning or fretboard configuration you like by editing the Fretboard Instrument Definition dialog box. Finale's tablature *is* compatible with your experimental homemade mountain dulcimer.

Converting Standard Notation to Tablature

To demonstrate Finale's prowess with automatic tablature generation, let's notate the first four measures in the standard staff and copy it down:

1.   Choose the Simple Entry Tool 🎵.

2.   Enter the first four measures as shown in Figure 11.3.

     For more details regarding Simple Entry, see Chapter 8, "Lead Sheets," in this book, or see the "Simple Entry" section in the Finale user manual. You can actually use any entry method you like to enter this.

Figure 11.3   Enter this excerpt into measures 1–4 using Simple Entry (or the entry method of your choice).

3.   Press Esc to choose the Selection Tool.

4.   Click and drag over measures 1–4 to select them.

5. Click the highlighted region and drag down to measures 1–4 of the tablature staff. Then, release the mouse button. The Lowest Fret dialog box appears. The ability to designate a lowest fret is nice if you are using a capo or want to specify that the piece should be performed higher on the fretboard.

6. Click OK to translate the regular notation to fret numbers automatically. See Figure 11.4.

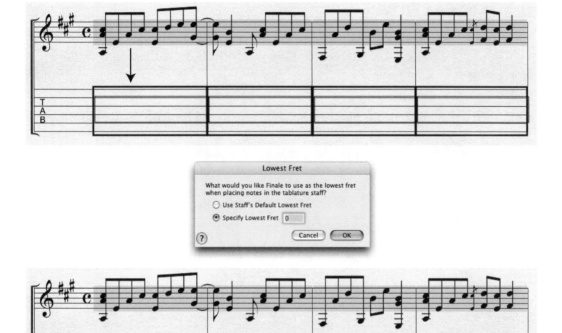

Figure 11.4 Create fret numbers automatically by simply copying standard notation into a tablature staff.

If you need to change the regular notation, you can simply repeat the same procedure to overwrite existing tablature.

Entering Directly into a Tablature Staff

And now for a completely different way to enter music—place fret numbers directly onto strings of a tablature staff.

1. Choose the Simple Entry Tool . We will enter the next four measures of "Blue Mountain Étude" directly into the tablature staff.

2.   Select the duration (in this case, an eighth note).

3.   Press the 4 key on the numpad (or click the Eighth Note Tool in the Simple Entry Palette).

4.   Click the B string (second from the top). Finale places a 0 on the B string.

5.   Type 2 on the numpad (laptop users, press Ctrl+Shift+2 [Option+Shift+2]). Finale changes the fret number to 2.

Tip: To reference all Simple Entry tablature keyboard shortcuts, from the Simple menu, choose TAB Specific Commands.

---

6.   Click each string and type the number the same way to enter the remainder of measure 5 and the first note of measure 6, as shown in Figure 11.5. Now let's add the tie between the last beat of measure 5 and the first beat of measure 6.

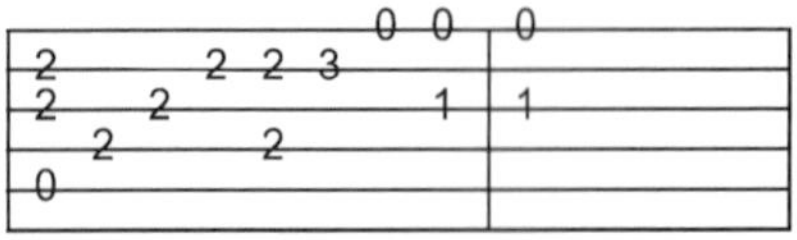

Figure 11.5 Click and type the fret number to quickly enter notes of the same duration.

7.   Hold down Ctrl+Shift (Option+Shift) and click both fret numbers on the last beat of measure 5 so they are selected.

8.   Press T to automatically hide the first fret numbers in measure 6. When you drag this music up to the regular staff, Finale will know there is a tie here and include it accordingly. Now, let's change durations to a quarter note.

9.   Press Ctrl+Alt+numpad 5 (Command+Option+numpad 5) to change the cursor to a quarter note.

10.   Click the B string and then (directly below) the D string and type numpad 2. Now, we need to switch back to entering eighth notes.

11.   Press Ctrl+Alt+numpad 4 (Command+Option+numpad 4) to change the cursor back to an eighth note.

12.   Use these techniques to complete measures 5–8, as shown in Figure 11.6. (The tie in measure 7 is to another, invisible, eighth note.)

In the preceding steps you essentially learned how to convert the physical fingerings on your guitar fretboard to notes on a treble-clef staff. Western music notation has now been opened

Figure 11.6 Using duration, tie, and fret-number keystrokes, you can quickly click in tablature.

up to your neighborhood's high-school garage band. Welcome to the future! Note that Finale automatically transposes down an octave, which is standard guitar tuning.

> **Note:** You can enter directly into a tab staff or a regular staff using a MIDI guitar. See "Entry Using a MIDI Guitar" in Chapter 7 of the *Finale Installation and Tutorials Guide*.

Converting Tablature to Standard Notation

Transferring tablature to a standard staff is as easy as dragging and copying it.

1.   Press Esc to choose the Selection Tool.

2.   Click and drag over measures 5–8 in the tablature staff to highlight them.

3.   Click the highlighted region and drag up until measures 5–8 of the standard staff are surrounded with a black border. Then, release the mouse button. Finale translates the tablature to standard notation. See Figure 11.7.

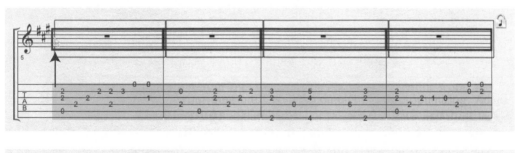

Figure 11.7 Simply drag+copy to a standard staff to convert tablature to regular notation.

Now use one of the methods to complete the last eight measures of the piece; see Figure 11.8. Keep these pointers in mind:

- Finale only hides fret numbers when the tie extends to and from all notes on the beat. If you are entering the fret numbers, enter ties between measures 9 and 10, 11 and 12, and 13 and 14.

- Use Ctrl+F (Command+F) to flip ties.

- If you are copying to the tablature staff, leave the Lowest Fret setting at 0. (When the Lowest Fret dialog box appears, just click OK.)

Figure 11.8 Today's tablature in Finale kicks gluteus maximus (compared to the old days).

Note: You can add stems and beams to your tablature in the Staff Stem Settings dialog box. Double-click the tablature staff with the Staff Tool and click Stem Settings.

Adding the Chords and Fretboard Diagrams

These chord symbols are pretty basic. You can find all the suffixes in the default chord suffix library. Use the same instructions to add these chord suffixes as you would for lead sheets. (See "Adding the Chord Symbols" in Chapter 8.)

The only difference is the use of fretboard diagrams. To add fretboard diagrams, choose Show Fretboards from the Chord menu. Finale displays the fretboards automatically. Here are some important notes regarding Finale's fretboard diagrams:

- If you need to reposition the fretboards vertically, choose Position Fretboards from the Chord menu. Then use the positioning triangles to adjust the fretboard baselines.

- Chords and fretboards automatically transpose when you transpose the music.

- You can display an alternate fingering, or create new fingerings, in the Fretboard Editor dialog box. To get there, in the Fretboard section of the Chord Definition dialog box, click Edit. (To get to the Chord Definition dialog box, click a note with Manual Input selected under the Chord menu.)

Guitar Markings

What fun would guitar notation be without a mess of special markings designed specifically for all the crazy things guitarists have figured out how to do: bends, tremolos, slides, harmonics, and all that jazz. One could hardly imagine the boredom. You will be relieved to hear the many doodads are pretty much always just a few clicks away. The following sections detail how to add them.

Hammer-Ons and Pull-Offs

Hammer-ons are just a way of telling your guitarist to temporarily leave the string depressed at a lower fret while pressing it down on a higher fret. **Pull-offs** indicate removing the finger from the higher fret. It's basically a helpful (sometimes necessary) performance suggestion.

Measure 8 in our example has a pull-off between the G sharp and G natural. To add hammer-ons and pull-offs, you need to first add the letter (H or P) using a Smart Line, and then add a regular slur beneath it.

1. Choose the Smart Shape Tool ▚.

2. Ctrl+click (Option+click) the Custom Line Tool 🛠 to open the Smart Line Selection dialog box.

3. Scroll down and choose the P (pull-off) smart line. See Figure 11.9.

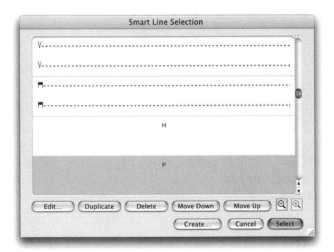

Figure 11.9   Choose the H or P custom Smart Line to add a hammer-on or pull-off.

4. Click OK.

5. Click the 1 fret number (on the "and of 2") and drag to the next fret number 0. When you release the mouse button, Finale adds a P above and between the fret numbers. See Figure 11.10.

Figure 11.10 The vertical position depends on where you click, so take care to click so that the P appears between the staff lines.

6. Click the Slur Tool in the Smart Shape Palette.

7. Double-click the 1 fret number to extend the slur between the two fret numbers. See Figure 11.11.

Figure 11.11 Use the Slur Tool to extend a slur between the fret numbers.

Enter hammer-ons the same way, using the H option in the Smart Line Selection dialog box.

Slides

Slides are glisses for guitar, and are probably called slides because you need to physically slide your finger against the fretboard to create the effect of a seamless pitch change. This technique marking/musical symbol is placed in both the tablature and the standard notation.

1. Choose the Smart Shape Tool.

2. Choose the Tab Slide Tool in the Smart Shape Palette.

3.   Double-click the second space A on beat 2 of measure 8. Finale adds a tab slide.

4.   Double-click the 2 on beat 2 of measure 8 in the tablature staff. Finale adds a tab slide. See Figure 11.12.

Figure 11.12   Finale automatically positions the tab slide appropriately when you click a regular note versus a fret number.

You can repeat the same process to add tab slides to all other required notes and fret numbers (measures 9, 12, and 13), as shown in Figure 11.1.

Let-Ring and Other Extensions

This piece contains some **let-ring** performance markings to tell the guitarist to allow the string to vibrate until a certain point in the music. When you add this marking as a custom Smart Line, you can click and drag it to whatever length you need, even over a system break. Note that these are added the same way as the following markings:

- Palm mute (P.M.) P.M.---------------------
- Artificial harmonic (A.H.) A.H.---------------------
- Natural harmonic (N.H.) N.H.---------------------
- Pinch harmonic (P.H.) P.H.---------------------
- Hold bend hold bend -----------------
- Down pick ⊓---------------------
- Up pick V---------------------
- Tremolo ∿∿∿∿∿∿∿∿∿∿

To add a let-ring marking:

1.   Choose the Smart Shape Tool ▱.

2.   Ctrl+click (Option+click) the Custom Line Tool ? to open the Smart Line Selection dialog box.

3.   Scroll down and choose the let-ring custom line.

4.   Click OK.

5.   Double-click above the second note of the first measure (standard staff), and drag to the second-to-last note (top space), as shown in Figure 11.13.

Figure 11.13   Use a Smart Line to create let-ring extensions.

If you need to drag an extension across systems, simply move the mouse cursor down over the next system; Finale will continue the Smart Line accordingly.

More Guitar Markings

By this point we have pretty much notated this whole piece and run out of markings. Before we add the chords and fretboards, let's discuss some other common guitar figures. To test these, start a new House Style 3 guitar tablature template or use the piece we have been notating as a guinea pig (perhaps by adding a few measures).

Bends

Graphic guitar bends are a special tablature feature of Finale, which even has its very own tool (the Guitar Bend Tool). **Guitar bends** are basically arrows that represent the pitch change applied by bending the string. When you apply a guitar bend to your tablature, Finale can automatically hide unnecessary fret numbers and understand the music well enough to add the correct arrow direction.

For example, if you want to indicate a bend of a whole step, notate the music as you would normally—Finale's Guitar Bend will accommodate the need to hide the fret number. Also, when you click a subsequent note, Finale can indicate the release amount; see Figure 11.14.

Here's how to add the guitar bend:

1.   Choose the Smart Shape Tool [icon].

2.   Choose the Guitar Bend Tool [icon] in the Smart Shape Palette.

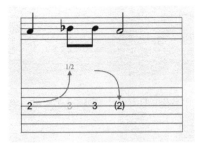

Figure 11.14   Finale automatically hides the 0 fret number and adds the full (or 1/2) text based on the interval. The release is also accompanied with the appropriate interval.

3. Double-click the fret number that begins the bend. Finale adds the first bend figure and adds 1/2 or full accordingly (hiding the now-superfluous fret number).

4. Double-click the fret number that begins the release. Finale adds the second arrow and, if necessary, the number of half steps in parentheses. See Figure 11.14.

Picking Figures

Picking figures indicate the direction the pick should strike the string: V for up, and ⊓ for down. Add these as articulations (metatools D and U). You can also add them as Smart Shapes by selecting them from the Smart Line Selection dialog box.

Fingerings

Guitar music includes two types of **fingering** indications.

Left (fretboard) hand fingerings appear, for the most part, as numbers:

- Index (1)
- Middle (2)
- Ring (3)
- Pinky (4)
- Thumb (T)

Picking hand fingerings appear as letters:

- Index (i)
- Middle (m)
- Ring (a)

- Pinky (c)

- Thumb (p)

Add these fingerings as articulations.

If you did not begin with one of Finale's guitar templates, these articulations may not appear in your articulation library. If this is the case, follow these steps:

1.   From the File menu, choose Load Library.

2.   Open the Tablature Libraries folder.

3.   Double-click the Guitar Articulations file.

Now these characters will be available in the Articulation Selection dialog box.

12 Percussion

Thinking about percussion notation in Finale evokes the sense of being thrust into battle to the thundering of giant war drums. That probably comes from the hours of tech support calls devoted to fixing users' documents whose percussion staves had been mangled beyond recognition. Now my battle cadence is pounded to advance the cause of keeping you out of trouble in the first place, which is a whole lot easier (for both me and you).

Like tablature, non-pitched percussion notation is an entirely different animal than standard notation. In a percussion staff, the lines and spaces represent different instruments. Rather than a range of several octaves, each instrument can be performed with a few different methods, which are represented with different noteheads and/or articulations. The interface Finale uses to prepare these things can be your gauntlet or your secret weapon. In any case, I will try to keep you as far away from the front lines as possible. And, if there are any stampeding war elephants, I'd like to be sure you are holding the reigns.

In this chapter I will demonstrate a few short percussion examples and describe a method for notating them. You can use the Selection Tool to copy them to your heart's content (or, use Staff Styles to indicate one- and two-bar repeats). Then you will learn how to change other aspects of percussion notation, like the number of staff lines, rolls, and special noteheads for things like rimshots.

Here's a summary of what you will learn in this chapter:

- Starting a new percussion part

- Notating percussion

- Percussive pleasantries

Starting a New Percussion Part

Whether you are starting a new marching percussion score or adding a percussion part to your existing score, you should always use the Setup Wizard.

- If you are starting a new score, choose File > New > Document with Setup Wizard. Click Next to move to the second screen.

- If you are adding a percussion part, choose the Staff Tool. Choose Staff > New Staves (with Setup Wizard).

In either case, choose the Percussion, Drums, or Marching Percussion instrument category and select the desired instruments from the list on the right.

If you are writing for drumline, Finale also includes a selection of Tapspace drumline instruments. To see the Tapspace instruments, from the Instrument Set drop-down menu, choose Tapspace Instruments for Finale 2009.

To demonstrate how percussion works in Finale, let's begin a new percussion part using the Setup Wizard:

1.   Choose File > New > Document with Setup Wizard.

2.   Click Next to move to the second screen.

3.   From the left list, choose Drums.

4.   Double-click Drum Set in the middle list to add it to the list of score instruments on the right.

5.   Click Next > Next > Finish to open the new document.

Finale begins a new document with a Drum Set staff with a percussion clef. Now all we need is to discover how to add the appropriate note durations on the proper staff lines with the desired noteheads and playback instrument. It sounds kind of complicated but, like a difficult rhythm, once you learn how to do it right once, you can do it hundreds of thousands of times with much less effort.

Note: Finale sets Percussion staves to channel 10, the General MIDI percussion channel, automatically when you begin with the Setup Wizard.

Notating Percussion

When you begin a percussion part with the Setup Wizard, Finale assigns a percussion map to the staff. The percussion map is simply the way Finale connects MIDI notes, staff positions, note-heads, and instrument sounds. To get right to the core, let's take a look at our document's percussion map:

1.   Choose the Staff Tool ▤.

2.   Double-click the staff to open the Staff Attributes dialog box.

3.   Next to Notation Style, to the right of the Percussion drop-down menu, click Select. The Percussion Map Selection dialog box appears. Drum Set should be selected.

4.   Click Edit. Voilà! The Percussion Map Designer dialog box appears. This is your key to percussion entry. See Figure 12.1.

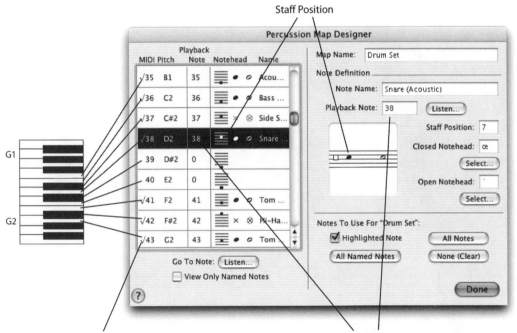

Active ("Highlighted") notes are indicated by check marks or an * (asterisk)   Playback Note

Figure 12.1   The Percussion Map Designer is kind of like the Rosetta Stone, unlocking the secrets behind percussion staves.

Here are a few tips regarding Percussion Map Designer:

- To use a percussion map slot, it must be **highlighted**, meaning marked with an asterisk in Windows (and checked in a Mac). To highlight a slot, select it and check Highlighted Note.

- The MIDI Pitch column represents the pitch you need to play on a MIDI keyboard to enter the note.

- The Playback Note column represents the MIDI note performed during Finale playback.

- The Noteheads column represents the note's placement on the staff and the notehead character (for both open and closed).

- The Name column lists the name of the instrument, in this case, the General MIDI instrument.

Tip: To view a diagram of a keyboard with its MIDI pitch and note-number equivalents, search the Finale user manual's index for "MIDI Note to Pitch Table." For a quick reference, remember that middle C = 60.

---

5.   Click Done > Select > OK to return to the score.

Note that you can change the resulting playback note to whatever you want. For now, we'll use the default arrangement, where the playback note is the same as the MIDI note. In the future, you may want to edit this setting to allow for easier recording from your MIDI keyboard.

Now let's enter a basic percussion part.

Percussion Entry with a MIDI Keyboard

I always recommend entering percussion using a MIDI keyboard if it is an option. For this excerpt we will enter a basic drum set part with bass drum, snare, and a high hat using Simple Entry with MIDI. (If you do not have a MIDI keyboard, skip to the next section.)

There are several reasons to use step-time Simple Entry to notate percussion, which I will illustrate in these steps. Use the numeric keypad for all numbers:

1.   Click the Simple Entry Tool ♪. The Simple Entry Caret appears at the beginning of the first measure.

2.   Press 4. The caret should look like an eighth note and appear at the beginning of measure 1. You generally enter the snare and cymbal of a drum set part at the same time, and in Layer 1. Enter the following, specifying the pitches using your MIDI keyboard. Use the notation shown in Figure 12.2 as a guide. (Snare is D2 and Hi-Hat is F#2.)

Figure 12.2   Finale automatically enters appropriate noteheads and staff positions when entering from a MIDI keyboard.

Tip: Open the EntryExercises.mus file in the Finale 2009/Tutorials folder for an excellent Simple Entry tutorial.

---

3. From the layer-selection buttons (pop-up menu) in the lower-left corner of the document window, choose Layer 2. We're going to enter the bass drum. We want quarter notes with stems down.

4. Ctrl+click (Option+click) measure 1 to display the caret.

5. Press 5 to select a quarter note.

6. Enter the bass-drum notes as shown in Figure 12.3.

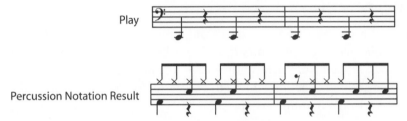

Figure 12.3   Finale flips the stems appropriately when you add the Layer 2 bass drum notes.

7. From the layer-selection buttons (pop-up menu) in the lower-left corner of the document window, choose Layer 1.

8. Let's say we want a cymbal in place of the eighth rest. Ctrl+click (Option+click) to select the eighth rest.

9. Play an F sharp (F#2) like we did earlier to add an X notehead above the top line. By selecting a note and playing, you can change any note easily.

10. Now, let's add a snare to beat 4 of the second measure. Ctrl+click (Option+click) the X on beat 4 of measure 2.

11. Play both the D2 and F#2 on your MIDI keyboard simultaneously. Finale replaces the existing note with the notes you play (see Figure 12.4)

Figure 12.4   You can edit percussion notes easily by selecting them with Simple Entry and specifying the new notes with your MIDI keyboard.

If you find specifying the duration a drag, you can speed up the process by recording percussion in real time with HyperScribe. (See Chapter 10, "Choral Scores," for more information regarding setting up and recording with HyperScribe.)

Tip: Remember, you can change all aspects of any percussion instrument notation style (staff position, notehead, and so on) in the Percussion Map Designer dialog box. If you are using something other than a General MIDI playback device, you may need to edit these settings to acquire the proper playback sound.

Percussion Entry Without a MIDI Keyboard

If you do not have a MIDI keyboard, you can still enter percussion and, yes, you can still make it sound right. It will just take a little finagling.

Multiple instruments can share the same staff line or space, and even the same notehead. Sans MIDI keyboard, this factor complicates percussion entry because clicking or pressing a keyboard shortcut does not tell Finale which instrument/notehead to add. Also, once a note is in the score, there isn't always a definitive indication of the instrument the note represents, which can make assigning playback a bit more work. It's nothing we can't handle.

Let's begin a new percussion staff, then add percussion in Simple Entry without a MIDI keyboard:

1. Choose the Staff Tool 🎼.

2. From the Staff menu, choose New Staves (with Setup Wizard).

3. From the drop-down list at the top, choose SmartMusic SoftSynth. This is Finale's General MIDI sound bank.

4. Choose Percussion in the left list.

5. Double-click Percussion in the middle list to add it.

6. Click Finish to add the Percussion staff to your document.

This staff is assigned to a different percussion map than our Drum Set staff. In this one, each MIDI pitch is highlighted from #35 (B1) all the way up to #81 (A5). Several instruments in this map are assigned to almost every staff position, which is perfect for demonstrating how to select a specific one for entry.

1. Double-click the Percussion staff. The Staff Attributes dialog box appears.

2. Choose Select from the Percussion drop-down menu. The Percussion Map Selection dialog box appears. General MIDI Entry & Playback should be selected.

3. Click Edit. The Percussion Map Designer dialog box appears. Notice #37 (Side Stick), #38 (Snare [Acoustic]), and #40 (Snare [Electric]), are all assigned to the third space. See Figure 12.5.

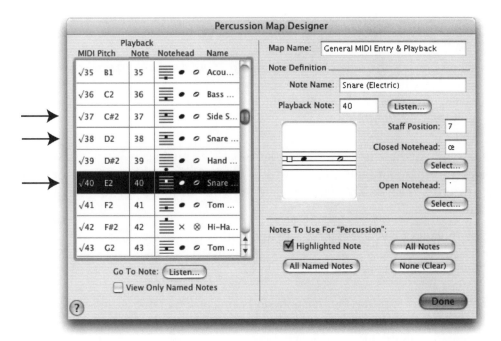

Figure 12.5   When you click percussion notes into a staff, Finale adds the lowest MIDI note assigned to the clicked staff position. You can press + (plus) to move to the next slot or – (minus) to move to the previous.

4. Click Done > Select > OK to return to the score.

5. Choose the Simple Entry Tool ♪. You need to listen to identify the proper instrument, so be sure your speakers or headphones are on.

6. From the Simple menu, choose Simple Entry Options.

7. Make sure Playback Notes on Entry is checked; click OK.

8. Press 5 (or click the Quarter Note Tool in the Simple Entry Palette) and click the third space in the first measure of our percussion map. You should hear a side stick. But, say we don't want a side stick. We want an electric snare.

Tip: If you do not hear anything, choose MIDI/Audio > Device Setup > MIDI Setup (MIDI/Internal Speaker Setup). Windows users, make sure a SmartMusic SoftSynth is selected for MIDI Out. (Macintosh users, set Playback to SmartMusic SoftSynth.) Then click OK. For more details, see the installation and MIDI setup chapters of the *Finale Installation and Tutorials Manual.*

---

9.   Press + (plus) in the numpad. Finale plays an acoustic snare sound. You have just changed the note to slot #38, as shown in Figure 12.5.

10. Press + again. Finale plays an electric snare sound. You have just changed the note to slot #40 (the next MIDI pitch set to the third space). You can continue pressing + (or −) to cycle through the three percussion-map slots assigned to the third space. (This percussion map has only three.)

Yes, all this just to show you how to add a single note without a MIDI keyboard, and change it to the correct percussion-map slot/sound. This is why folks are confused about percussion entry without a MIDI keyboard in Finale, so I figure why beat around the bush? The rest is much like entering into a regular staff.

Say you also want to enter a ride cymbal on this staff with an X notehead. You refer to the Percussion Map Designer to discover that MIDI Note 59 (B3) is assigned to Ride 2 and the staff position is the fourth line. Let's add it:

1.   Click the fourth line to add a quarter note on beat 2 of the first measure. Finale adds a Tom 3 Low, because it is also assigned to the fourth staff line. Tom 3 Low is set to MIDI Note 45 (A2) in the Percussion Map Designer.

2.   Press +. Finale plays a ride cymbal sound and changes the notehead to an X; see Figure 12.6. Now, let's say the ride cymbal is the only instrument you care to enter on the fourth space, and don't want to press the + key every time. No problem.

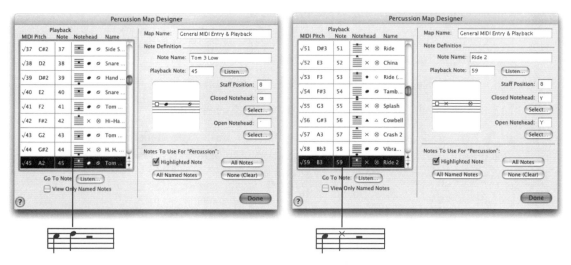

Figure 12.6   Noteheads also respect the percussion-map settings when you change a note's instrument with the + and − keys.

3.   Click to deselect the Tom 3 Low note. Click the Staff Tool ▦.

4.   Open the Percussion Map Designer for the staff.

5.   Double-click the Percussion staff.

6.   Click Select > Edit from the Percussion drop-down menu.

7.   Scroll down to MIDI Note 45 Tom 3 Low and click the slot to highlight it.

8.   Uncheck Highlighted Note in the lower right of this dialog box.

9.   Click Done > Select > OK to return to the score.

10.   Select the Simple Entry Tool. Click the fourth line. Ride 2 is the lowest/only MIDI note assigned to the fourth space, so Finale adds it the first time you click.

You can use these procedures along with the other Simple Entry methods to efficiently enter the percussion notes. But, percussion notation includes many other unique and interesting figures. Let's escape the notes themselves and take a look into the many other factors you need to consider as you nurse your rhythmic rhizome.

Percussive Pleasantries

Properly propagating your percussive prowess is probably more pertinent than plain pleasantry. Pardon my pedagogy, it prevents persistent pedantic pros.

Changing the Number of Staff Lines

Percussionists have no problem reading a snare drum part on a single staff line. If it isn't helping in sheet music, it's just getting in the way, so let's eliminate those extra staff lines:

1.   Choose the Staff Tool 📊.

2.   Double-click the Percussion staff. The Staff Attributes dialog box appears.

3.   Click the Staff drop-down menu and choose the desired number of staff lines. Figure 12.7 shows an example, 1-line with Short Barline. Choosing Other opens the Staff Setup dialog box, which allows you to set any number of staff lines.

4.   Click OK to return to the score.

Tip: You can set measure regions within a staff to use a different number of staff lines using Staff Styles.

Rolls

Choose the Articulation Tool 🎵 and do the following to add a roll quickly using metatools:

■   Press 6+click a note to add an eighth note roll ♪.

■   Press 7+click a note to add a sixteenth note roll ♪.

■   Press 8+click a note to add an open roll ♪.

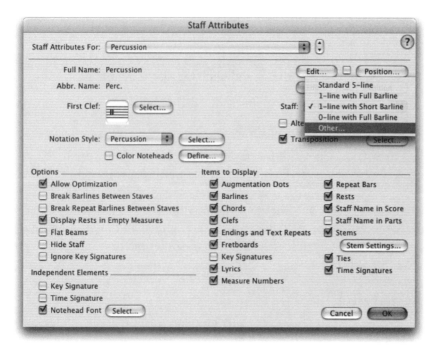

Figure 12.7 Change the number of staff lines in the Staff Attributes dialog box.

That is all. Human Playback will interpret these for you during playback.

Flams, Drags, and Ruffs

Flams, **drags**, and **ruffs** are figures that tell the percussionist to strike slightly ahead of the main note. You can specify these by adding grace notes in Simple Entry (using the Grace Note Tool ) or in Speedy Entry. Then, add slurs using the Slur Tool in the Smart Shape Palette . See Figure 12.8.

Figure 12.8 Use the Simple Entry and Smart Shape Tools to add flams, drags, and ruffs.

Tip: In Simple Entry, press Alt+G (Option+G) to change a selected note to a grace note or toggle between a regular grace note and a slashed grace note.

Sticking Indications and Other Markings

Add sticking indications as articulations. You can add many other markings, such as stops, open/closed symbols, and center/edge indications, as articulations. Finale doesn't include R, L, or many other possible markings, so you will need to add them to the library yourself.

1. Choose the Articulation Tool ![articulation tool icon].

2. Click a note to open the Articulation Selection dialog box.

3. Click Create to open the Articulation Designer dialog box.

4. Skip to step 6 if the symbol you need to add is in the default music font. Otherwise, go to step 5.

5. Click the Set Font button, choose the desired font and size, and click OK. For this example, we will choose Arial 12 plain for L and R markings.

6. Click the Main button to open the Symbol Selection dialog box.

7. Double-click the desired symbol. This figure will appear on the main side of the staff (above/below), which is a consideration when adding articulations that must be displayed upside down when they appear over, rather than under, the staff (or vice versa). In this case, for L and R symbols we need only specify a main symbol. See Figure 12.9.

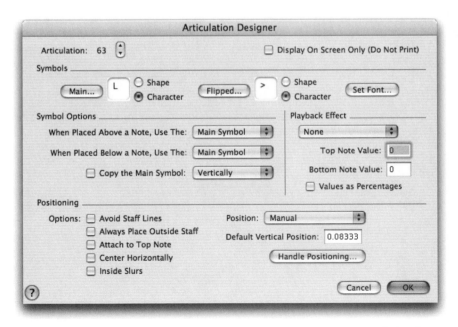

Figure 12.9   Define new articulations in the Articulation Designer dialog box.

8. Under Positioning, check Always Place Outside Staff and Center Horizontally.

9. Click the Position drop-down list and choose Above Note.

10. Click OK. Follow the same steps to add an R articulation.

Tip: You can also duplicate the L articulation (in the Articulation Selection dialog box) to preserve the font and positioning settings, then change the L to an R.

---

11. Add the articulations like you would normally.

13 Instrumental Ensembles

It seems like most folks, including myself, spend the balance of their worldly effort struggling to make things easy: work overtime, receive extra coin, hire dude to clean out the gutters so you don't have to. Composers have it completely backward: leave work early, place hands on keyboard, brazenly write yourself into completely unknown territory and then agonize over every note, navigating your ill-prepared butt out. Only we can know the true limits of our potential, which we blithely overestimate, but with luck emerge from the chaos stronger. The trade-off seems to be wisdom as we desperately seek that next self-inflicted torture device. Masochism— it's the innovator's favorite dish.

And throughout this process we find little pathways we've encountered before. They are like little nitrous charges that propel us through the straightaways and into the next difficult curve. Did we really want to get there so fast? I suspect so. Ideally the road is all curves, each unique and each handled with a bit more grace and aplomb than the previous. Each is unique because we have the smarts to figure out why Jim Bob spun out, and the courage to take our own shot anyway.

In this chapter we will confront an excerpt from the timeless "Air on the G String" by J.S. Bach with the audacity to venture one possibility regarding its conception. I can't really make any assumptions regarding the mind of a genius, but I can't imagine he'd mind my feeble conjecture. I wonder if someone will take a look at my work 400 years from now. By then the now-experimental "Mind Entry" method will no doubt be perfected and make most of these steps obsolete. Still, I suppose it behooves me to consider the possibility and return the favor in advance the best way I can, just in case. Besides, risking such possibilities allows us to take some of those curves before anyone else can imagine they existed in the first place.

Here's a summary of what you will learn in this chapter:

- Starting an instrumental ensemble
- Notating an instrumental ensemble

Starting an Instrumental Ensemble

If a template exists that includes your ensemble, I encourage you to use it. The templates were scrutinized by an able engraver for Finale 2009, so they represent a higher standard than in previous versions. To start using a template, choose File > New > Document with Template and choose from the Templates folder.

Finale doesn't always include a template that matches your needs. Even when it does, you can use the Setup Wizard to design new, custom documents or add instruments to existing ones:

- If you are starting a new score, choose File > New > Document with Setup Wizard. Click Next to move to the second screen.

- If you are adding an instrumental part, choose the Staff Tool. Choose Staff > New Staves (with Setup Wizard).

If you use the Document Setup Wizard, notice the ensembles on the left of the first screen. I recommend using one of these if you find one that resembles the ensemble you are starting. You can edit the included instruments and the order on the next screen.

Tip: If you choose one of the Garritan ensembles, you can always tell Finale to play through MIDI (MIDI/Audio menu) to improve performance during editing and then turn on VST/AU when you are ready to audition playback or create an audio file.

Let's begin a new string quartet using the Setup Wizard (File > New > Document with Setup Wizard). Here is what you need to know as you go through the wizard:

- You are writing for string quartet, so on the first screen, select the Garritan String Quartet ensemble if the Garritan Instruments for Finale are installed and you want to (eventually) use the nifty string sound samples. If you do not have Garritan installed, choose String Quartet.

- The title is, at this point, unknown.

- The composer is J.S. Bach. Although we are pretending to compose this, we should be sure he is listed in the upper right in case we get carried away.

- We aren't sure what the time signature will be, so choose the default 4/4 time.

- Let's say the key is unknown right now, so leave it at C.

Finale begins a new document with four staves. All of the clefs, staff names, and other score information is already set up.

Notating an Instrumental Ensemble

In this tutorial I am going to take off the training wheels and allow you to enter the notation using whatever method you prefer. In this chapter we will focus on the evolution of a composition, exploring the several ways a piece might change as it comes into its own. During this process, try to ignore the obvious mistakes Bach would have probably been incapable of making. You are here to learn Finale, so bear with me.

Hanging On to the Music

Capturing an idea is just as important as imagining it in the first place. Have you ever woken up to experience the fading vibes of a spectacular dream drift away into nothingness? Maybe you know what it's like to have an excellent musical idea, only to discover it has vanished by the time you launch Finale or find some staff paper. Our goal here is to place the music on the page before it gets tossed on the huge pile of Wonderful Ideas Never Realized. This means ignoring some notation aspects in favor of documenting a sketch.

1. The first vague ideas emerge from the cerebrum, and you struggle to extract them, plugging in the violin part as shown in Figure 13.1.

Figure 13.1 You kind of know what key you're in, but don't need to worry because you can always move the key later to match your music.

2. The general bass line that accompanies the melody has taken shape, and you enter it without embellishment, as shown in Figure 13.2.

Figure 13.2 You recognize that all these notes might be half the required duration at a faster tempo, but that concern is secondary.

3. Press Ctrl+spacebar (Option+spacebar) and drag over the score.

   You use audio spot-check to listen to the sonorities.

4. Enter quarter = 40 in the Playback Controls (click the expand arrow and type quarter = 40 in the Tempo text box) and listen to the first four measures in time. Hey, sounds pretty nice, but it needs some inner voices.

5. Enter the second violin and viola voices as shown in Figure 13.3.

Figure 13.3 To audio spot-check a single staff, press Shift+Ctrl+spacebar (Shift+Option+spacebar). This is helpful while entering inner voices.

Now that you're comfortable with the first few measures, you can perhaps sit back for a moment and think more closely about the tempo and the desired durations.

Doubling the Duration and Setting the Tempo

The actual durations for this piece depend on the version, but for this demonstration we assume you want to stretch the notes and increase the tempo accordingly (as we discussed in Chapter 7, "The Composer's Wild Kingdom"). I'd rather read eighth notes than sixteenths, so we'll double the durations and set the tempo to lento with a quarter note at 60 beats a minute:

1.   Press Esc to choose the Selection Tool.

2.   Highlight the first four measures, all staves.

3.   Choose Utilities > Change > Note Durations to open the Change Note Durations dialog box.

4.   Choose 200% for Change All Note Durations By, as shown in Figure 13.4.

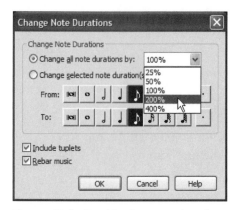

Figure 13.4 Double the note durations using the Change Note Durations dialog box.

5.   Make sure the Rebar Music check box is checked.

6.   Click OK. Finale distributes your music over the first eight staves.

7.   Press Ctrl+A (Command+A) and then press 4 to apply note spacing.

By now we've decided on a starting tempo. When this is the case, it's time to add a tempo marking:

1.   Choose the Expression Tool 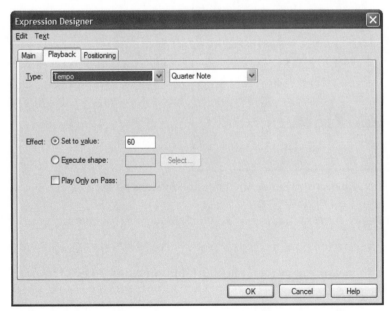.

2.   Double-click the first measure to open the Expression Selection dialog box.

3.   Choose the Tempo Marks category.

4.   Click Create Tempo Mark to open the Expression Designer dialog box.

5.   Type Lento and click the Playback tab.

6.   Choose Tempo for Type. Quarter Note should appear in the drop-down list to the right.

7.   Enter 60 for Set to Value, as shown in Figure 13.5.

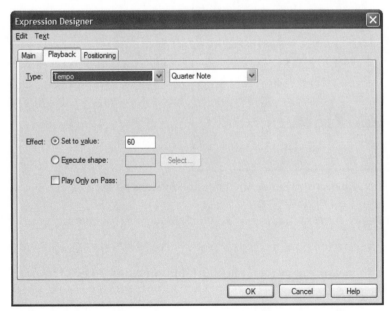

Figure 13.5   Use the Expression Designer's Playback tab to set the playback tempo.

8.   Click OK, then Select to add the expression to the score.

This is starting to look better, but that bass line is pretty boring right now. Something needs to be done about that.

Embellishing the Bass Line

Instead of half notes, you think quarter notes with octave jumps capture the feel and suggestion of steady movement you are looking for.

1. Press Esc to choose the Selection Tool.

2. Click to the left of the Cello staff to select the entire staff.

3. From the Plug-ins menu 🎵, choose Note, Beam and Rest Editing > Rhythmic Subdivisions.

4. Under Change, choose All Selected Entries.

5. Under Subdivide Entries Into, choose Rhythmic Duration, and select the quarter-note icon. 1024 EDUs should appear in the box to the right, as shown in Figure 13.6.

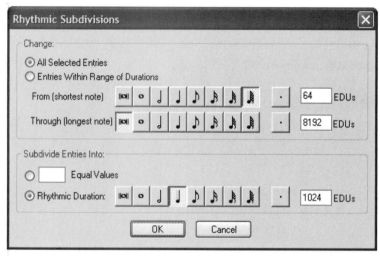

Figure 13.6   Chop notes into smaller durations with the Rhythmic Subdivisions plug-in.

6. Click OK. All the half notes are now quarters. Now let's add those octave leaps.

7. Press Esc to choose the Selection Tool.

8. Highlight beats 2 and 3 of measure 1 in the Cello staff and press the 9 key. The notes move up an octave; see Figure 13.7.

9. Use the transposition metatools to transpose notes in the remaining measures of the cello line; see Figure 13.8. Use the 9 key to transpose up and the 8 key to transpose down.

Now we have an acceptable bass line, but the key signature isn't right. We should change that before we go any further.

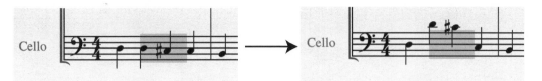

Figure 13.7   Those Selection Tool transposition metatools come in awful handy.

Figure 13.8   Again, those Selection Tool transposition metatools come in awful handy.

Changing the Key Signature Without Changing the Notes

Since we are definitely within the realm of tonality, we owe it to our instrumentalists to adorn this number with the appropriate key signature. The notes are already in the right spot. All we need to do is shift the key behind them and eliminate those extra accidentals. This technique is also mentioned in Chapter 7.

1.   Choose the Key Signature Tool 🎼.

2.   Double-click the first measure. The Key Signature dialog box appears.

3.   Next to the key-signature display, click the top arrow on the scroll bar twice to change the key to D major.

4.   Under Transposition Options, choose Hold Notes to Original Pitches Enharmonically. (If Enharmonically isn't already selected, choose it from the drop-down menu.)

5.   Click OK. The key signature changes and the notes stay put.

Adding a Slashed Grace Note

There is a slashed grace note in measure 3 of the Violin staff leading to beat 3. Let's add that now:

1.   Click the Simple Entry Tool 🎵.

2.   Choose the Eighth Note Tool and the Grace Note Tool in the Simple Entry Palette.

3. Double-click between beats 2 and 3 of measure 3 in the Violin staff, as shown in Figure 13.9.

Figure 13.9 Add slashed grace notes with Simple Entry.

The first click adds the grace note, the second adds the slash.

Adding a Trill

This is really easy, but I suppose it can have its own section:

1. Click the Articulation Tool ⬛.

2. Hold down the T key while clicking the half note at the beginning of measure 4 in the Violin 1 staff.

Adding the Dynamics and Slurs

Breaking from what might be considered Baroque tradition, let's add some dynamic markings to ensure all four performers benefit from a common interpretation of the first few bars. It's also important to remember the slurs...

1. Choose the Expression Tool ⬛. Now let's say we want to mark all four voices pianissimo at the first measure. Piece of cake.

2. Hold down the 7 key while click+dragging over measure 1, all staves. Finale adds the markings beneath each staff in the first measure. This technique is called **drag-apply**, and is new to expressions in Finale 2009. See Figure 13.10.

3. Hold down 6 while click+dragging over all staves in measure 6. Finale adds a mezzo forte marking beneath each staff.

4. Choose the Smart Shape Tool ⬛.

5. Choose the Crescendo Tool ⬛ in the Smart Shape Palette.

6. Double-click and drag from the pianissimo marking to the mezzo forte in each staff, as shown in Figure 13.11.

Figure 13.10   Use drag-apply to add expressions to multiple staves. This works with or without a metatool.

Tip: Select multiple hairpins, right-click (Ctrl+click) one of them, and choose Align Horizontally to set all hairpins to the same distance below/above the staff.

---

7.   Click the Slur Tool ▨ in the Smart Shape Palette.

8.   Add slurs as shown in Figure 13.11. Remember, double-click to extend a slur to an adjacent note.

Tip: Press Play in the Playback Controls. Garritan instruments and Human Playback do a pretty good job with this one. To choose the Baroque Human Playback Style, from the MIDI/Audio menu, choose Human Playback > Baroque.

Adding the Title and Subtitle

A title is seldom chosen prior to the first notes being entered. For me, it's usually the last thing pondered, and often a decision made with great difficulty. So, here's how to quickly and easily

Figure 13.11 After adding the slurs, the first eight measures are pretty much done short of any tweaking.

exchange that ominous "Title" that has been haunting the top of the first page into something a bit more descriptive.

1. Choose File > File Info. The File Info dialog box appears.

2. Enter Air in the Title field.

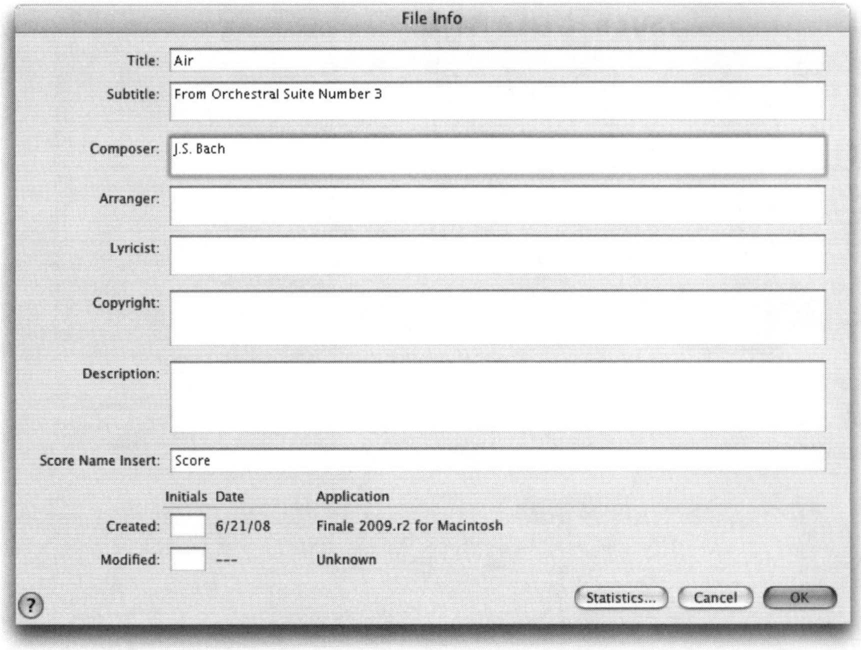

Figure 13.12 Use the File Info dialog box to enter the title, composer, lyricist, and other score information.

3. Enter From Orchestral Suite Number 3 in the Subtitle field, as shown in Figure 13.12.

4. Click OK. The text blocks appear at the top of the page accordingly.

Finishing Up

This is too beautiful a piece to leave you hanging after the first eight measures, so let's use the remaining music as entry practice. Once you are finished entering, Bach's masterful loveliness will be your reward. As you notate, keep in mind the following:

- In Simple Entry, press the P key to cycle between courtesy accidental, parenthesized courtesy accidental, and no accidental.

- Use the Repeat Tool ▤ context menu to add the repeats. Highlight measures 11–12, right-click (Ctrl+click), and choose Create First and Second Ending. Use Create Forward Repeat Bar for measure 15 and Create Backward Repeat Bar for the last measure. Playback will honor these repeats properly.

- You can remove repeat endings from all but the Violin 1 staff using a repeat staff list. Right-click (Ctrl+click) a repeat ending handle and choose Edit Ending > Staff List > Edit to define the staff list. Specify Top Staff for both the Score and Part and click OK to return to the score.

Figure 13.13 Bach is the best musician who ever lived.

Figure 13.13   Continued

Figure 13.13   Continued

- Select All and use Fit Measures under the Utilities menu to set four measures per system.

- Select the last two measures and press the up arrow key to move them to the previous system.

- To tighten up the vertical staff spacing, choose the Staff Tool ![icon]. From the Staff menu, choose Respace Staves. Under Distance Between Systems, enter 85% for Scale To, and click OK.

- After your staves are respaced to 85%, choose the Page Layout Tool ![icon]. Click in the middle of each system and drag up as far as it goes to place three systems on the second two pages (as shown in Figure 13.13). Once all systems are on the page, you can use Space Systems Evenly under the Page Layout menu to have Finale space systems for you automatically.

- You can optimize the first two systems to space out the staves a bit manually, since you probably don't have room to fit three systems on the first page. To optimize, choose the Page Layout Tool ![icon], right-click (Ctrl+click) the system, and choose Allow Individual Staff Spacing. Then click the Staff Tool ![icon] and drag the lower handle on the staves to position them. See Chapter 15, "Wrapping Up," for more info regarding optimization.

14 Jazz Band

T his book wouldn't be complete without a word on arranging for jazz band. After all, these organizations are one of the world's great music manufacturing plants. In the Twin Cities area, the Nova Big Band is an inspiration. After taking in a number that swings harder than a populist, a player will rise for a second and wave casually as if to say, "It was nothing, these guys did all the work." By the end of the night your humble observer has heard a slice of original compositional brilliance from each and every player, written, improvised, and otherwise. What a treat.

Several volumes could be dedicated to the creation of jazz-band charts in Finale, and many jazz-band arrangers are far more qualified in the practice than I. In this chapter my goal is to help open a few doors. With some luck you cats will get something out of it.

Here's a summary of what you will learn in this chapter:

- Starting a new jazz-band score

- Composing for jazz band

Starting a New Jazz-Band Score

In this chapter, we'll arrange a few measures of our "Autumn Leaves" score from Chapter 8, "Lead Sheets," for jazz band. Rather than add staves to that document, it's easier to begin a new score with the Setup Wizard, copy the music over, and edit from there.

Begin a new jazz-band score using the Setup Wizard (File > New > Document with Setup Wizard). Here is what you need to know as you go through the wizard:

- Select the Jazz Band ensemble and the Handwritten Style (Jazz Font) Document Style on the first screen. (In the future, this is where you would indicate landscape orientation, which is common for jazz-band charts.)

- The title is Autumn Leaves.

- The composer is Joseph Kosma.

- It is in common time.

271

- The key is G (one sharp).

- There is a three-beat (equivalent to a dotted half note) pickup.

- After you are finished, press Esc to choose the Selection Tool. Then click the Subtitle and Arranged By text inserts and press Delete. You should end up with something that looks like Figure 14.1.

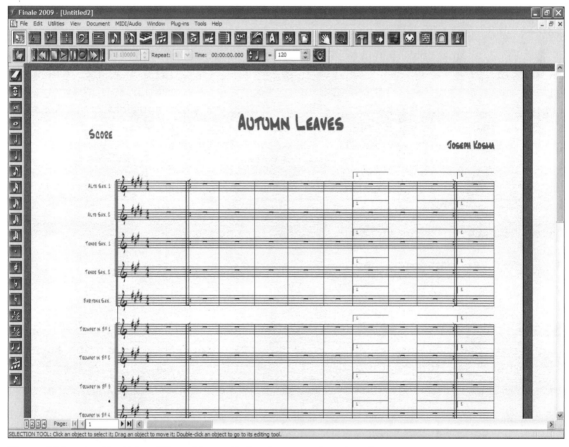

Figure 14.1 Use the Setup Wizard to easily begin a new jazz-band score.

Note: When you use the Handwritten Style Document Style, Finale includes a different set of libraries tailored for jazz music. By choosing this style, you are doing quite a bit more than just selecting the jazz font.

Composing for Jazz Band

Once you have a melody and chord symbols to work with (refer to Chapter 8), the possibilities are endless. Finale can suggest harmonies, orchestrate automatically, and even add a rhythm section for you. We will take the first few measures of "Autumn Leaves" and use them to demonstrate some of Finale's key tricks. If you saved the "Autumn Leaves" example and it is available, do the following. If not, skip these steps:

1. Open the "Autumn Leaves" lead sheet you created in Chapter 8. We will copy this music to our jazz-band score. We don't need lyrics, so specify that we want those to slip through our filter.

2. Choose Edit > Edit Filter. Click All, uncheck Lyrics, and click OK.

3. Press Esc to choose the Selection Tool.

4. Press Ctrl+A (Command+A) to select all.

5. Press Ctrl+C (Command+C).

6. Press Ctrl+Tab (Command+´ [accent mark]) until you are viewing the new jazz-band score. Or, choose the jazz-band score (listed as Untitled) from the bottom of the Window menu.

7. Press Ctrl+A (Command+A) to select all.

8. Press Ctrl+V (Command+V). Finale pastes the music into place.

9. Choose Document > Pickup Measure.

10. Choose the dotted half note icon and click OK. (I'm not sure why the pickup needs to be applied again, but it does.)

11. Press 4 to apply the Note Spacing function. Now you can skip to Auto Harmonizing.

Tip: If the chords collide with the repeat brackets, select the Chord Tool ⟦CM7⟧ and use the left-most baseline positioning triangle to drag the chord symbols up a bit.

If you do not have the "Autumn Leaves" example, notate the music shown in Figure 14.2 into measures 1–9.

Figure 14.2   If you need help notating this, consult Chapter 8.

Auto Harmonizing

Let's kick it off with a nice, rich sax sound. We'll use Finale's Band-in-a-Box Auto-Harmonizing plug-in for some inspiration:

1.   Press Esc to choose the Selection Tool.

2.   Click to the left of the top (Alto Sax 1) staff to select it.

3.   From the Plug-ins 🔌 menu, choose Scoring and Arranging > Band-in-a-Box Auto-Harmonizing. The Band-in-a-Box Auto-Harmonizing dialog box appears.

4.   Choose Five Part for Number of Voices. Then choose Drop Two (SuperSax). Now, let's tell Finale to distribute the notes into the four subsequent sax staves.

5.   Under Place New Voices Into, choose Four Existing Staves Starting With Staff.

6.   From the drop-down menu, choose Alto Sax. 2, as shown in Figure 14.3.

Figure 14.3 Yes, you can use widgets in the Auto-Harmonizing plug-in and keep it real at the same time.

7.   Click OK. Finale distributes the notes into each staff of the sax section, as shown in Figure 14.4.

8.   Before you play back, click the Chord Tool [CM7].

9.   From the Chord menu, uncheck Enable Chord Playback (to focus on the notes).

10. Click the Play button in the Playback Controls to listen. You can't hear the change at measure 4. The plug-in didn't add an A there, so we'll edit that ourselves.

11. Choose the Simple Entry Tool [♪].

12. Ctrl+click (Option+click) the half note on the second beat of measure 3 in the Baritone Sax staff and press T to remove the tie.

Figure 14.4 The Auto-Harmonizing plug-in can also distribute (explode) music into staves for you automatically.

13.   Press the right arrow key to select the quarter note. Then press the up arrow to move it up a step to A.

14.   Now play it back. Ah, much better.

Tip: You can distribute stacked chords from one staff into many using Explode Music or consolidate notes from several staves into one using Implode Music (both under the Utilities menu).

Adding a Rhythm Section

I'm not going to lie to you. If you are using Finale for Windows, creating a rhythm section with piano, walking bass, and drums automatically is way easier. But if you are using a Mac, Finale can still help you out quite a bit.

Tip: If you want to eliminate extra staves from view, now is an appropriate time to switch to Scroll View and create a Staff Set. (See Chapter 2, "Getting the Best Angle.") If you do this, display all staves except the Trumpet and Trombone staves; we will be using the others.

Using the MiBAC Jazz Rhythm Section Generator (Windows Only)

Yes, Finale can add piano comping, a walking bass line, and a drum-set part for you automatically based on the chord symbols and a few other settings. Here's how...

1.   Press Esc to choose the Selection Tool.

2.   Click measure 1 of the top staff (Alto Sax 1) to select it.

3. Press Shift while clicking measure 9. (We'll just apply this to a few measures to get the idea.)

4. From the Plug-ins 🖋 menu, choose Scoring and Arranging > MiBAC Jazz Rhythm Section Generator. The MiBAC Jazz Rhythm Section Generator dialog box appears.

5. Under Place Music Into, choose Existing Staves as Specified.

6. For Piano, choose [Staff 15] (or the top Piano staff).

7. For Bass, choose Bass; for Drum Set, choose Drum Set, as shown in Figure 14.5.

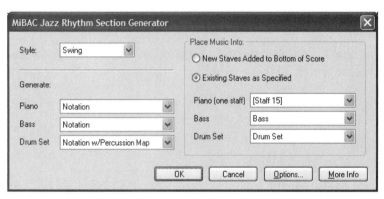

Figure 14.5 This is cool.

8. Click OK. Scroll down to the bottom of your score. Finale has added the piano, bass, and drums for you, as shown in Figure 14.6.

Figure 14.6 There you have it. Now you know, so don't let it go to your head.

Don't let a computer's ability to automatically generate music frighten you. Before long we might consider the possibility that most art will be composed by software, remembering that software is a sort of art itself, meticulously programmed by a human. But this does beg the question: Where does art stop and science begin, and what exactly is the difference? (A topic that perhaps breaches the scope of this book . . . .)

Adding a Drum-Set Part with Drum Groove

Windows and Mac users can both benefit from this one. Let's see what kind of set Finale's Drum Groove plug-in offers:

1. Press Esc to choose the Selection Tool.

2. Click to the left of the top (Alto Sax 1) staff to select it.

3. From the Plug-ins 🎤 menu, choose Scoring and Arranging > Drum Groove. The Drum Groove dialog box appears.

4. Under Style, choose StraightSwing.

5. Under Place Music Into, choose Existing Staff. Then click the drop-down arrow and choose Drum Set, as shown in Figure 14.7.

Figure 14.7 Drum Groove has a bunch of nice beats to choose from.

6. Click OK. Finale adds the drum-set part.

You might want to experiment with the many different options until you find the one you like best. Also note that Finale includes a Latin Percussion plug-in, which allows you to automatically apply Latin percussion rhythms and instruments. See Chapter 12, "Percussion," for more info.

Slash Notation (Comping)

Being the collaborative effort it is, jazz composers get a lot of help, and are not afraid to accept it. For example, you wouldn't bother to write out that rhythmic piano part (as Windows users did earlier with the Rhythm Section Generator). Your pianist is down, and needs nothing more than comping slashes and chord symbols—not to mention your star saxophonist, who will need plenty of heat to bring it down right.

Adding slashes with chords to indicate improvisation is easy in Finale once you get the hang of it. Just use the Slash Notation Staff Style:

1. If you already applied the Jazz Rhythm Section Generator, and your Piano staff includes that notation, move to the next step. If not, add quarter-note rests in the top staff of the piano for the first six measures. (These are placeholders that can be used as attachment points for chord symbols.) Now, we will copy the chords down from the top staff.

2. Choose Edit > Edit Filter.

3. Click None, check Chords and Fretboards, and click OK.

4. Press Esc to choose the Selection Tool.

5. Click to the left of the top Alto Sax 1 staff to select it and press Ctrl+C (Command+C).

6. Click to the left of the top Piano staff to select it and press Ctrl+V (Command+V). Finale pastes the chord symbols. You can use the Chord Tool to adjust them vertically.

7. Choose the Staff Tool ![staff tool icon].

8. Shift+click to the left of both the left and right hand of the Piano staff.

9. Right-click (Ctrl+click) the highlighted area and choose Slash Notation, as shown in Figure 14.8. Staff Styles are indicated with a horizontal blue line.

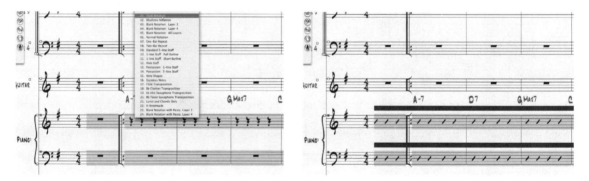

Figure 14.8   Use a Staff Style to apply slash notation.

Rhythmic Notation

When you need to offer your guitarist a bit of rhythmic genius, or keep a few of your players on the same page, you might use rhythmic notation. You can add rhythmic notation as a Staff Style like slash notation. Let's add some rhythmic notation to our guitar part:

1. Enter the rhythm as regular notation. These placeholder notes dictate the rhythm. For now, enter some eighth and quarter notes into the first few measures like those shown in Figure 14.9.

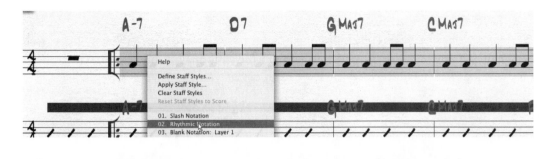

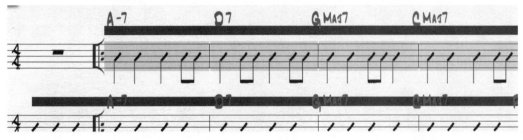

Figure 14.9   Use a Staff Style to apply rhythmic notation.

2.   Copy the chords down from the top staff.

Tip: If you do not want your rhythmic notation placeholder notes to play back, you can mute the staff (or a layer in the staff) using the Instrument List.

---

3.   Choose Edit > Edit Filter.

4.   Click None, check Chords and Fretboards, and click OK.

5.   Press Esc to choose the Selection Tool.

6.   Click to the left of the Alto Sax 1 staff to select it and press Ctrl+C (Command+C).

7.   Click to the left of the Guitar staff to select it and press Ctrl+V (Command+V). Finale pastes the chord symbols. You can use the Chord Tool to adjust them vertically.

8.   Choose the Staff Tool .

9.   Right-click (Ctrl+click) the highlighted area and choose Rhythmic Notation, as shown in Figure 14.9. Staff Styles are indicated with a horizontal blue line.

One- and Two-Bar Repeats

Although it's just as easy to make 100 copies of a one- or two-measure phrase, you might as well let your performer know she doesn't need to stay on the lookout for subtle differences. Staff Styles come to the rescue again to offer easy creation of one- and two-bar repeats.

1. Choose the Staff Tool 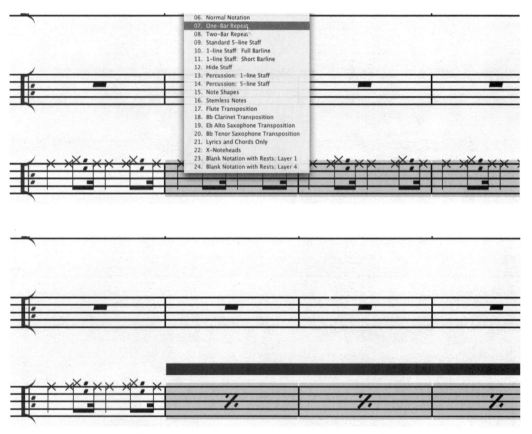.

2. Highlight the measures you want converted to one- or two-bar repeats.

3. Right-click (Ctrl+click) the highlighted area and choose One-Bar Repeat or Two-Bar Repeat; see Figure 14.10.

Figure 14.10   Use a Staff Style to easily create one- and two-bar repeats.

Tip: You can use metatools to quickly assign Staff Styles. Press S for slash, R for rhythmic, O for one-bar repeat, and T for two-bar repeat.

---

15 Wrapping Up

Composing is basically all about communication, and now that you've learned how to extract the music from your brain and transfer it to Finale, it's time to polish the appearance so your performers can read and conceive it. That may mean adding cue notes, adjusting the layout to accommodate realistic page turns, or moving overlapping notes and markings. Yes, any number of factors can prevent your performers from seeing what you mean, and it's time to eliminate as many of those factors as possible.

Here's a summary of what you will learn in this chapter:

- Music spacing
- Layout
- Finishing touches

Music Spacing

Finale's automatic music spacing is often adequate. I'm going to describe the most important things you need to know about music spacing when it is not adequate, and then send you to the user manual (which explains the nuts and bolts all too well).

- **Apply Note Spacing manually.** Highlight a region of measures (full measures, all staves) with the Selection Tool and press 4 to apply Finale's Note Spacing feature. Finale uses the Fibonacci music-spacing library to calculate the spacing.

Tip: If you don't like the Fibonacci spacing settings, you can load a different music-spacing library (Loose, Medium, or Tight). From the File menu, choose Load Library. You will find these libraries in the Music Spacing folder. After loading the library, apply Note Spacing to review the results.

- **Adjust the measure width manually.** To expand or contract a measure and reposition its notes proportionally, use the Measure Tool ▤. Simply click and drag the top barline handle. See Figure 15.1.

Figure 15.1 Use the Measure Tool to adjust the measure width.

- **Edit the beat positioning.** To vertically adjust beat positioning (all notes on a beat vertically), use the beat chart shown in Figure 15.2. Select the Measure Tool  and click the lower handle on the barline to display the beat-chart spacing handles above the measure.

- **Lock systems.** To prevent Finale from automatically shifting measures from one system to the next (or previous) one, lock the system. To lock a system, highlight a portion of the system and press Ctrl+L (Command+L). Lock systems when the spacing is adequate, starting from the first system. Locked systems are marked with a padlock icon like the one shown in Figure 15.2.

Note: When you manually shift measures from one system to another (using the up/down arrow keys), Finale locks the systems automatically.

- **When all else fails, use the Note Position Tool .** You will find the Note Position Tool in the Special Tools Palette (click the Special Tools Tool). You can use it to drag or nudge notes individually.

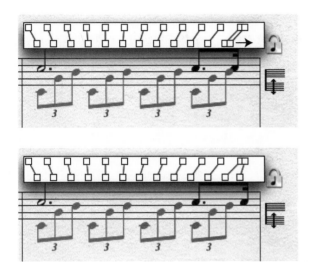

Figure 15.2   Use the beat chart to move beats (a vertical slice) horizontally.

Layout

For most of this book, you could have been working in Scroll View without giving the slightest thought to the appearance of the printed page. In fact (as already mentioned), I recommend doing so, and it suits most composers just fine. We dabbled in page layout a bit in Chapters 10, "Choral Scores," and 13, "Instrumental Ensembles," but your score might require a completely different series of procedures depending on many factors. I will offer a general formula that should accommodate most projects.

I have used different combinations of these methods earlier in this book, but I'd like to list some important considerations in the order I suggest you consider them.

Measure Layout

Measure layout (the number of measures on each system) is integral to both the music spacing and page/system layout, so if it seems I have dwelled on this topic, I probably have. The thing is, once you decide to change the measure layout manually, the system(s) become locked, and that prevents Finale from moving measures from system to system according to its music-spacing inclinations. This is fine, as long as you know what is happening and why Finale makes some of your systems look pretty while leaving others unchanged. With that, a reminder on how to edit the measure layout:

■ **Use Fit Measures.** From the Utilities menu, choose Fit Measures. The Fit Measures dialog box lets you specify a certain number of measures per system. If you select a region beforehand, the Fit Music On settings are already filled to match your selection.

- **Move measures up/down systems.** Highlight a measure and press the up arrow key to move it to the previous system (or press the down arrow key to move it to the next). This is worth repeating; I didn't know about it for the first few months learning Finale.

Note: Locked systems are marked with a padlock icon. To ensure these icons are visible, choose View > Show and be sure Page Layout Icons is checked.

Resizing

You can change the overall size of just about anything on the page, but adjusting the system size is perhaps the most useful way to resize your music. When you do this, Finale resizes all of the music without changing any other text blocks, including the title, composer, or page numbers. Resizing systems is important if you are trying to, for example, fit an extra system on each page or increase the size of existing systems to use all the available page space.

Resize systems like so:

1. Choose the Resize Tool .

2. Right-click (Ctrl+click) a system and choose Resize System. The Resize Staff System dialog box appears, as shown in Figure 15.3.

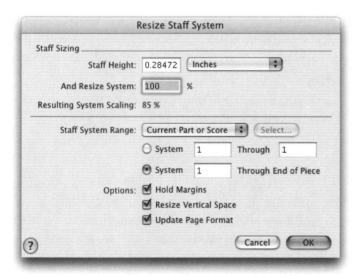

Figure 15.3 Use the Resize Staff System dialog box to change the size of the music without resizing other items.

3. Type the desired percentage for And Resize System.

4. Be sure the desired systems are chosen and other settings in this dialog box meet your requirements. (Click the Help button for a full description.)

5. Click OK to resize the systems (all the music) based on your settings.

Note: To change the size of the staves without adjusting the space between them, edit the Staff Height value in the Resize Staff System dialog box.

Overall Staff Spacing

The space between your staves is adjusted on a system-by-system basis later, but first you might want to ballpark it by setting a reasonable staff spacing for all systems in your score. To do so, use the Respace Staves dialog box:

1. Choose the Staff Tool 🎼.

2. Choose Staff > Respace Staves. The Respace Staves dialog box appears, as shown in Figure 15.4.

3. For Distance Between Staves, either enter a negative Set To value or choose Scale To and enter a percentage. I prefer to use a percentage; see Figure 15.4.

4. Click OK to resize the space between all staves in all systems.

Optimization

Now it is time to **optimize** the available page space by eliminating empty staves. This elimination, also called **French scoring**, is particularly helpful when composing for large ensembles. In addition to removing empty staves, once you optimize a system you can reposition each staff vertically within the system without affecting other systems.

Caution: Always be sure your measure layout is complete before optimizing. Adjusting measures between systems after optimization can result in missing measures in scores and parts.

To optimize your score:

1. Choose the Page Layout Tool 🗋.

2. Choose Page Layout > Optimize Staff Systems. The Staff System Optimization dialog box appears.

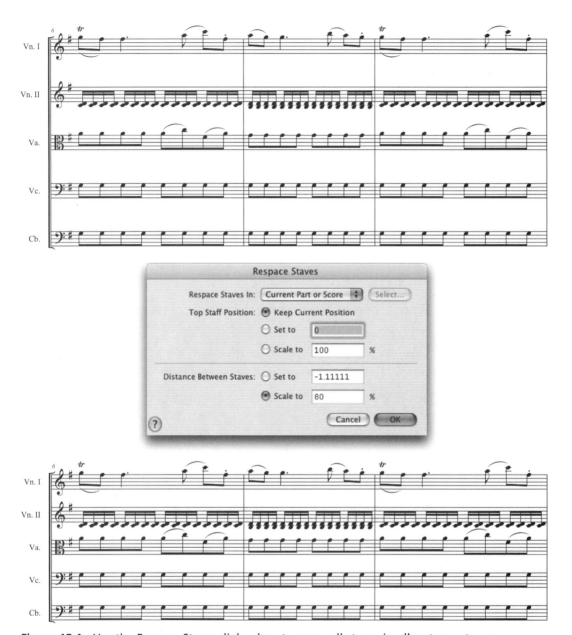

Figure 15.4   Use the Respace Staves dialog box to space all staves in all systems at once.

3.   Click Optimize Staff Systems and check both these options: Remove Empty Staves and Keep at Least One Staff. For this example, we'll optimize all systems, so choose All Systems of Current Part/Score. See Figure 15.5.

4.   Click OK to remove empty staves throughout your score. An optimization icon appears next to every optimized system, as shown in Figure 15.6.

Figure 15.5   Notice the empty Trumpet 2 staff is removed after optimization. In larger scores with many extra staves, the benefits of optimization are more dramatic.

Figure 15.6 Optimized staves are marked with this optimization icon.

Individual Staff Spacing

Now that your systems are optimized, each system's staff spacing can be adjusted independently.

1.   Choose the Staff Tool ![icon]. Two handles appear on the left edge of every staff, one on the top line and one on the bottom.

2.   Click+drag (or select and nudge) the bottom staff handle to adjust its vertical position independently; see Figure 15.7.

Figure 15.7 Use the bottom staff handle to change the vertical position of a single staff.

Note: Shift+click and drag to enclose the bottom handles of multiple staves in a system to reposition them simultaneously.

System Spacing

Now that your staves are all tightly wrapped in neat packages (read: systems), it's time to squeeze as many of those systems on a page as possible. Remember, it's always important that the score is *legible* first; then think about crunching systems together.

When you select the Page Layout Tool, dotted lines surround each system. These lines are the **system margins**. We would like to be able to move these systems into place without adjusting the margins themselves. The system height is basically an accumulation of staff height and staff spacing within the system, so if there is extra space on the page, you can go back and increase the staff size or spacing a bit. If you think reducing the staves and staff spacing will allow additional staves to snap to the page, you might go back and reduce them a bit.

Here's the way moving systems works: When you click and drag a system up, all subsequent systems move up uniformly (unless stuck at the top of the page). When there is enough room at the bottom of a page, the next system automatically snaps back to fill the space. You can manually reposition systems and/or use Finale's Space Systems Evenly options to finalize the system spacing.

Here is one effective method for dealing with systems:

1. Choose the Page Layout Tool [icon]. The system and page margins appear.

2. Choose Page Layout > Space Systems Evenly. The Space Systems Evenly dialog box appears. You can use these commands to space systems evenly on the page and specify how many systems you want to fit on a page. Use this dialog box at any point while dealing with the system spacing.

3. Click OK to evenly space your systems. However, there may be too much space between them. You might need to move the first system on the next page to the bottom of the current page.

4. Click+drag systems toward the top of the page until the correct number of systems appears on each page. Drag a system down to push the lowest system to the next page. See Figure 15.8.

Here are some more tips regarding positioning systems:

- **Ctrl+click+drag (Option+click+drag)** to move a system without affecting any other system.

- **Apply Space Systems Evenly (Page Layout menu)** whenever the correct number of systems is on a page. You can also use this dialog box to specify a specific number of systems on a page (which is particularly useful when you want to spread systems out over multiple pages rather than consolidate them).

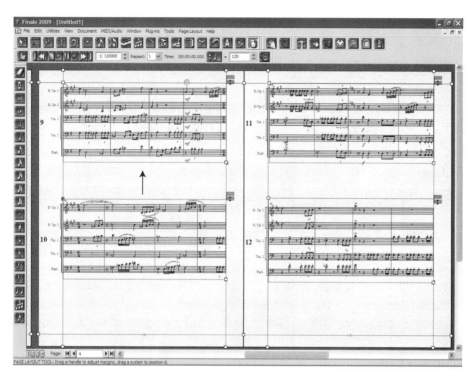

Figure 15.8 Finale places the maximum number of systems that will fit on a page. Edit staves within systems, then drag the systems until they are positioned appropriately on the page.

- **Use the Edit System Margins and Edit Page Margins dialog boxes** to precisely change margins as well as the space between systems. These dialog boxes are under the Page Layout menu.

Tip: Finale's Vertical Collision Remover plug-in allows you to automatically check for collisions between systems and staves. From the Plug-ins 🎼 menu, choose Scoring and Arranging > Vertical Collision Remover.

Finishing Touches

Consider just a few more things before unleashing your creation.

Parts

Finale's linked parts allow you to work on your score and parts simultaneously. Finale generally takes care of things for you, but you need to check over each part carefully before printing. Here is some advice:

- **Navigation.** Press Ctrl+Alt+> (Command+Option+>) to move forward a part. Press Ctrl+Alt+< (Command+Option+<) to move back a part.

- **Old Finale files.** If you are editing a score created in an earlier Finale version, it might not include parts yet. Choose Document > Manage Parts > Generate Parts to create them.

- **Multiple-part staves.** If a staff includes multiple parts (flutes 1 and 2, for instance), enter each part into a separate layer. Use the Voicing for Staff in Part dialog box (Click Edit Voicing in the Manage Parts dialog box) to specify which layer to display. If your multi-part staff is a bit more complicated, consider extracting the part and using the TGTools Smart Explosion plug-in (www.tgtools.de) to separate two voices from one staff into two separate staves.

- **Rich scores.** If you are notating your magnum opus and find yourself spending as much time maintaining the score/part relationship as you are composing, consider tearing off a separate document. Use one for the full score and one for all the parts. You do have to make each edit twice, but this is much better than using a separate file for every single part. In other words, one document can be used for the score output (disregarding parts' appearance), and the other can be used exclusively for parts output (disregarding the score's appearance)

Page Turns

As an unfortunate side effect of the fact your parts will be read from a piece of pulverized wood, you will need to allow your performers enough time to flip the page every so often. Is anyone else bemused by this? Shouldn't we have goggles with a continuous scrolling display projected against our retinas by now? Anyway, apart from using the up and down arrow keys to move measures between systems, Finale offers a nifty plug-in to identify proper page-turn locations automatically.

Note: Finale does not allow you to apply any plug-ins to linked parts, so applying plug-ins must be the very last step of part editing (and applied to each part's autonomous document separately) if your part requires a plug-in. See "Extracting Parts" in the user manual for details.

Here's how to use the Smart Page Turns plug-in on your parts:

1. Extract the part into its own document.

2. From the Plug-ins 🖉 menu, choose Scoring and Arranging > Smart Page Turns. The Smart Page Turns dialog box appears, as shown in Figure 15.9.

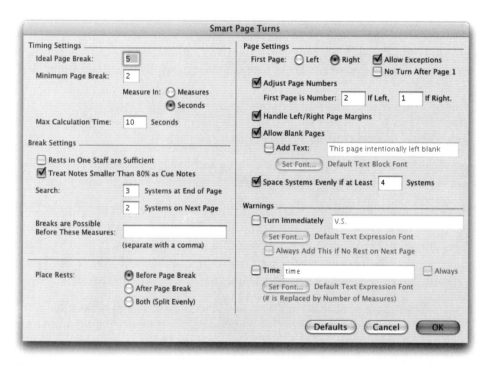

Figure 15.9 Use the Smart Page Turn plug-in to find appropriate spots for page turns.

3. Look at all the choices!

4. Click OK. The plug-in scans your file and suggests appropriate page turns.

Whether you find the Smart Page Turns plug-in helpful or not, you must consider page turns before distributing parts (unless you enjoy the sound of stands falling over and the subsequent mayhem that ensues).

Cue Notes

Being nice to your performers means more than keeping stands off their heads; it means present-
ing them with a cautionary hint, before their next entrance, in the form of **cue notes**. If they have
nodded off, or are vocalists at heart, these little signals allow them to jump back in with hardly
any counting ability whatsoever.

Finale includes a few ways to enter cue notes; the Smart Cue Notes plug-in is the latest and
greatest. This plug-in finds suitable locations for cue notes and adds them for you automatically.

1.   Open your full score.

2.   From the Plug-ins 🖉 menu, choose Scoring and Arranging > Smart Cue Notes.
      The Smart Cue Notes dialog box appears.

3.   Click Start Search. The plug-in scans the score for places that might be suitable for cue
      notes. Of course, you can adjust this dialog box to specify what exactly the plug-in
      should be looking for. When it has found a region that pleads for cue notes, the plug-in
      displays the staff and measure as shown in Figure 15.10.

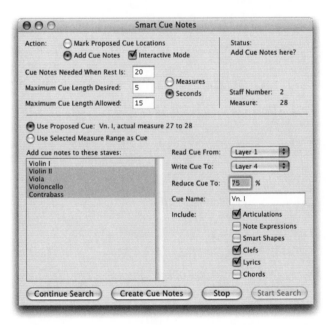

Figure 15.10   Use the Smart Cue Notes plug-in to easily add cue notes where appropriate.

4.   Click Create Cue Notes to add the proposed cue notes in the layer specified (Layer 4
      by default).

5.   Click Start Search to continue looking for the next proposed cue note location.

Beautify Your Beams

I mentioned this earlier, but it's worth repeating. This can makes your entire score look more professional and it only takes a couple seconds:

1. Choose Document > Document Options > Beams.

2. Check Allow Primary Beam Within a Space.

3. Be sure Extend Beams Over Edge Rests is checked and Max Slope is a multiple of 6 EVPUs.

4. Click OK.

5. From the Plug-ins 🎵 menu, choose Note, Beam, and Rest Editing > Patterson Plug-Ins Lite > Patterson Beams. The Patterson Beams dialog box appears. The default settings work alright. If you want to learn more, search for "Patterson Beams" in the user manual.

6. Click OK and then OK again. Congratulations, your score has just been beautified.

16 Unleashing Your Masterpiece

Well, I'm certainly prepared to write this chapter; I've been working on the Finale for over 10 years (rim shot).

Once you've packaged the goods, it's time to distribute them. Your creation wants to frolic across cities, nations, and oceans. Or, maybe it just wants to be printed and handed to the members of your brass quintet, who have been waiting patiently for you to finish the last couple bars.

Whether you need to generate a PDF, save an audio file, or distribute your Finale file online, getting in the right format should never be the roadblock. In other words, whatever comes between your finished creation and its anxious beneficiaries must be dissolved, and thankfully, Finale and the Internet provide many ways to do just that.

Here's a summary of what you will learn in this chapter:

- Printing

- Creating PDFs

- Exporting audio files

- Sharing with others online

Printing

Press Ctrl+P (Command+P) and press Enter. Voilà! You've printed your document! If it were always that easy there wouldn't be much reason for this section. What if you need to print batches or in booklet format? Finale actually makes these things easy if you know where to look.

Batch Printing

Batch printing just means printing a whole bunch of documents (for instance, extracted parts) at once instead of opening each one and printing them separately. To batch print, use FinaleScript:

1. Put in the same folder all the files you want to print.

2. From the Plug-ins 🎯 menu, choose Finale Script > FinaleScript Palette.

3.   Open the Batch Process folder, shown in Figure 16.1.

Figure 16.1   Use FinaleScript to print a bunch of files at once.

4.   Click Batch Printing and click the Play button. A message appears: The Batch Process Folder is not Specified! Would you like to choose it now?

5.   Click Yes.

6.   Navigate to the folder containing the files you want to print and click OK (Choose). FinaleScript opens and prints all documents in the folder.

Booklets

Finale already includes a description for booklet printing in its user manual. Simply search for "Booklets." Windows users can also use a third-party plug-in to quickly and easy print to booklet format.

1.   Visit http://www.jwmusic.nu/freeplugins/index.html.

2.   Download the JW Booklet plug-in (by Jari Williamsson). The Finale 2000–2005 version does work with Finale 2009.

3.   Place the jwbooklet2000 file in the Finale 2009/Plug-ins folder. The plug-in appears under the Plug-ins menu the next time you launch Finale.

Other Printing Techniques

Here are a few more ways to help make printing as pain free as possible:

■   To print two Finale pages on the same printed piece of paper (side by side), set the orientation to Landscape and select the 2-Up option in the Print dialog box's Layout section.

- To automatically resize the page to whatever size medium you are printing to, choose 1-Up in the Layout section of the Print dialog box and check Fit to Page.

- To tile pages (print 11×17, but on two 8.5×11 inch sheets of paper), see "Tiling Pages for Printing" in the Finale user manual.

Creating PDFs

If you want to send parts to someone via e-mail or need to electronically transfer a score or parts as sheet music, save the file as a PDF. PDF stands for Portable Document Format, and was created by Adobe Systems for electronic document exchange. By taking advantage of PostScript, press-quality PDFs can be created from Finale. However, PDF is the recommended format for any Finale document transfer when playback is not required.

To open a PDF, use Adobe's free Acrobat Reader available at www.adobe.com. Macintosh users can also open PDFs using Preview, which is part of the OS X operating system.

Saving as a PDF on Windows

Sorry Windows users: PDF generation is not included with your operating system. To save a PDF, you must purchase some sort of PDF-generation tool like Adobe Distiller (at www.adobe.com) or the less costly PDF995 (at www.pdf995.com).

Once you have, use the following steps to create a PDF:

1. Set up Adobe Distiller/Adobe PDF/PDF995 as a printer. This may occur automatically when you install these products. See your Adobe Acrobat instruction manual for instructions.

2. Choose File > Print.

3. In the Print dialog box, click the Setup button.

4. Click the Printer/Name menu and choose Adobe PDF or PDF995.

5. Click OK to return to the Print dialog box.

6. Click OK to open the Save As dialog box.

7. Name the file, choose a destination, and click Save.

Saving as a PDF on Macintosh

Complete the following steps to create a PDF on Macintosh:

1. Choose File > Print.

2. If the Page Setup dialog box appears, set up the page size and layout as you would normally. Click OK.

3. Click PDF > Save as PDF in the Print dialog box.

4. Enter a name, specify a location, and click OK.

Sharing with Others Online

If you would like to share more than just a PDF of your creation, you can easily present your full Finale document to anyone who cares to listen. Post the file on your Web site or attach it to an e-mail and have the recipient open it using Finale NotePad.

Finale NotePad is baby notation software that offers minimal editing capability and basic (SmartMusic SoftSynth) playback sounds. It makes up for these deficiencies by being inexpensive and capable of opening any Finale file. That's right—anyone with an Internet connection can download Finale NotePad for a small fee and listen to even your most bloviated concerto. You can download Finale NotePad at www.finalemusic.com/notepad. And, if you want to share your lovely audio handiwork complete with Garritan (or other VTSi/AU) sounds, you can always include an MP3.

Tip: Feel free to list your composition on Finale's Web site for your waiting fans: http://www.finalemusic.com/showcase.

Exporting Audio Files

Think your creation sounds pretty good directly from Finale? Need to send a demo to Hollywood to begin your long overdue career as a film composer? Why not save an audio file?

1. Set up your score so it plays back like you want it to. The resulting audio file will sound just like Finale playback. (Choppy playback that plagued Finale for Windows has been fixed in 2009. Woo hoo!)

2. Choose File > Export to Audio File. The Save as Audio File dialog box appears.

3. Choose Standard Audio File to save in WAV (AIFF) format. Choose Compressed mp3 file to save in MP3 format (for a smaller file).

4. Choose a location and click Save.

Finale

Oh, the times have I written that word. Alas, it never comes. But, as the quest for Finale fluency continues, this book must now come to an end...a small skirmish in a lengthy conquest. Many things can be said with music; how to learn a software program is simply not one of them. Even so, I hope you enjoyed reading this book as much as I enjoyed composing it.

Go out there and create something great! Take the limits of your mind, your soul, and your completely unique perspective and bring them to life in a way only you can. Imagine the possibilities, select your battles, and then face them earnestly using your talent, experience, skills, and sweat. There is plenty of work to be done, so do it!

Music making, after all, is a perpetual work in progress, and one that grows richer and more interesting with every new creation. From each work sprouts a dozen more. Before long we are overwhelmed with such beauty, wonder, and downright fantasticalness that inspiration itself is impossible to crush. In so much we can certainly hope that the actual finale will never come.

Index